ONLINE SOCIAL RESEARCH

Steve Jones
General Editor

Vol. 7

PETER LANG
New York • Washington, D.C./Baltimore • Bern
Frankfurt am Main • Berlin • Brussels • Vienna • Oxford

ONLINE SOCIAL RESEARCH

METHODS, ISSUES, & ETHICS

EDITED BY

MARK D. JOHNS,
SHING-LING SARINA CHEN,
& G. JON HALL

PETER LANG
New York • Washington, D.C./Baltimore • Bern
Frankfurt am Main • Berlin • Brussels • Vienna • Oxford

Library of Congress Cataloging-in-Publication Data

Online social research: methods, issues, and ethics / edited by
Mark D. Johns, Shing-Ling Sarina Chen, G. Jon Hall.
p. cm. — (Digital formations; v. 7)
Includes bibliographical references and index.
1. Sociology—Research—Methodology. 2. Sociology—Research—
Computer network resources. 3. Social sciences—Research—Methodology.
4. Social sciences—Research—Computer network resources.
5. Research—Moral and ethical aspects. I. Chen,
Shing-Ling. II. Hall, G. Jon. III. Series.
HM571.O55   301'.0285678—dc21   2002025388
ISBN 0-8204-6101-6
ISSN 1526-3169

Bibliographic information published by **Die Deutsche Bibliothek**.
Die Deutsche Bibliothek lists this publication in the "Deutsche
Nationalbibliografie"; detailed bibliographic data is available
on the Internet at http://dnb.ddb.de/.

Cover design by Sophie Boorsch Appel

The paper in this book meets the guidelines for permanence and durability
of the Committee on Production Guidelines for Book Longevity
of the Council of Library Resources.

© 2004 Peter Lang Publishing, Inc., New York
275 Seventh Avenue, 28th Floor, New York, NY 10001
www.peterlangusa.com

Printed in the United States of America

Contents

Part I—Methods of Online Social Research

Part II—Issues of Online Social Research

Part III—Ethics of Online Social Research

Acknowledgments

THE "BORNING CRY" FOR THIS BOOK was "Sarah's" cry for help in an Internet support group (see the chapter, "'NEED HELP ASAP!!!': A Feminist Communitarian Approach to Online Research Ethics" in Part III). "Sarah" was a student in Shing-Ling Sarina Chen's research methods class, and this encounter of the classroom with real-world research ethics launched the larger inquiry. As teachers we all learn from our students, and first and foremost we thank "Sarah" and all those in our classrooms who question us, push the edges of our knowledge, and drive us to research.

The inspiration and driving force for this book, however, has been Shing-Ling Sarina Chen herself. It was Sarina who hatched the idea with Jon Hall and brought him on board as able co-editor. It was Sarina who contacted series editor, Steven Jones, and secured the support with which he has been so generous, and it was Sarina who recruited all the rest of us who contributed our work as chapter authors.

Only after misfortune struck was Sarina forced to back away from this project. When Sarina and her husband, James Hu, learned that their young son, John, had become the victim of acute leukemia, her time and energy were redirected toward that much higher priority. As I took over editorial duties midstream, Sarina remained this book's primary cheerleader, and as her family has enjoyed occasional brief respites from John's ongoing battle, the book has benefited from her editorial insights as well.

There are many others to thank for their roles in bringing the present volume to its final completion. Thanks to co-editor, Jon Hall, for his quiet steadiness that kept us on an even keel throughout the project, for his deft handling of administrative details, and for his keen eye for detail in the editing of copy. Many thanks to Chris Myers and the staff at Peter Lang Publishing for their extraordinary patience and understanding as we missed one deadline after another. And a big thank you to the Graduate College of the University of Northern Iowa for funding our two very able student editorial assistants, Tai Mengtsung and Paulina Andrade, and staff associate, Jenni Colsch.

Certainly, no book of this sort would be possible without its contributing authors. The contributors to this volume have not only demonstrated their expertise in their writing, but have also proved flexible in accepting editorial feedback, prompt in meeting deadlines, and endlessly cooperative in every respect. The editors are grateful to all of them. Several took on the additional burden of writing introductions and conclusions that serve as reflections on the work of others. To Norman Denzin for his comprehensive introduction, to Clifford Christians and Amy Bruckman for their unique insights, to Steve Jones for tackling this task in addition to his ongoing encouragement as series editor, and to Charles Ess for his forward-looking conclusion, our abundant thanks.

Yet, despite all of the wonderful work by all of these wonderful people, surely none has been challenged as greatly nor worked so hard as little John Hu-Chen in his struggle with leukemia. We pray that he continues to win the fight, and dedicate this book to him.

Mark D. Johns
Cedar Falls, Iowa
January 2003

Prologue: Online Environments and Interpretive Social Research

୬৹৹৻

Norman K. Denzin

QUALITATIVE INQUIRY is a name for a "reformist movement that began in the early 1970s in the academy" (Schwandt, 2000, 189; Denzin and Lincoln, 2000a, x). The interpretive and critical paradigms, in their several forms, are central to this movement, as are complex epistemological and ethical criticisms of traditional social science research. Qualitative online, Internet research is a movement within this larger movement. Online research uses the methods, technologies, and languages of the Internet and its complex cultures. Online research molds traditional qualitative research methods to the Internet environment. This environment encompasses a variety of venues and spaces, including e-mail, chatrooms, web pages, listservs, various forms of "instant messaging," MUDs and MOOs, USENET newsgroups, audio, and audio and video exchanges.

Internet research represents a key transformation within this broader social movement. It folds virtual and real-world inquiry into the same set of interpretive practices. Together, these two fields now have their own journals, scientific associations, conferences, and faculty positions. Participants in the two movements have made significant in-roads into many social science disciplines, including communications research.

The transformations in online and real-world qualitative inquiry that gained momentum in the late 1990s continue into the new century. If today few look back with skepticism on the narrative turn in the social sciences, fewer still question the pervasive presence and relevance of online environments for qualitative inquiry.

The appeal of a critical qualitative inquiry model across the social sciences and the humanities increases. Some term this the seventh moment of inquiry (Denzin and Lincoln, 2000b, 2, 12).[1] This is a period of ferment and explosion. It is defined by breaks from the past, a focus on previously silenced voices, a turn to performance texts, and a concern with moral discourse, with critical conversations about democracy, race, gender, class, nation, freedom, and community (Lincoln and Denzin, 2000, 1048).

In the seventh moment, at the beginning of the 21st century, there is a pressing demand to show how the practices of online critical, interpretive qualitative research can help change the world in positive ways. It is necessary to examine new ways of making the practices of online critical qualitative inquiry central to the workings of a free democratic society. Furthermore, there is a need to bring these practices more centrally into the field of communications research. This is my agenda in this short introduction, to show how the discourses of traditional and online qualitative inquiry can be put to critical advantage by communications researchers.

Online Inquiry in the Seventh Moment

The chapters in this volume attest to the vitality of this new form and field of inquiry. Two main themes (to be elaborated below) organize this collection. The first theme concerns the ways in which traditional qualitative research methods have failed to keep pace with technological advancements in online environments. Clearly, computer-mediated interactions call for a different methodological orientation on the part of the researcher. A number of the chapters outline what this different orientation looks like. A second major theme takes up the myriad of problems not usually addressed by existing texts, including issues of visibility, representing the virtual Other, intimacy, research ethics, eavesdropping, and institutional review boards. Thus, the three parts of this collection interrogate the methods of online social research, identify key issues of online inquiry, and examine the ethical issues involved in this research. In what follows, I locate these themes and essays within a larger interpretive framework.

Bricoleurs and Hybridity

As online inquiry gains momentum, it does so against the backdrop of larger movements within qualitative research more generally.[2] Indeed, hybridity is the operative term, movement back and forth between real and virtual sites, research about the Internet as well as Internet research. There also is movement back and forth between online environments, traditional social research methods, and research sites. Internet research is "not only concerned with the study of online behavior...it is also concerned with using computer-based tools and computer-accessible populations to study human behavior in general" (Mann and Stewart, 2000, 5).

As bricoleurs, online researchers are continually inventing or piecing together new research tools, fitting old methods to new problems (Mann and Stewart, 2000, 5). Online bricoleurs fit their methods to concrete problems, and the questions they are asking. The choices of which interpretive practices to apply cannot be set in advance. As a methodological bricoleur, the online researcher becomes adept at performing a wide range of tasks, from online interviewing, to conducting virtual focus groups, to lurking, to doing discourse analysis of conversational threads. The online bricoleur is theoretically sophisticated, able to move back and forth through multiple theoretical spaces, from feminism, to critical and queer theory, to Marxism and cultural studies. The researcher-as-bricoleur theorist works between and within competing and overlapping perspectives and paradigms.

The interpretive bricoleur understands that online research is an interactive process shaped by personal history, biography, gender, social class, race and ethnicity, and that of the people in the setting. The political bricoleur knows that science is power, for all research findings have political implications. There is no value-free science. A civic social science based on a politics of hope is sought. The gendered, narrative bricoleur also knows that researchers tell stories about the worlds they have studied. Thus, the narratives, or stories, scientists tell are accounts couched and framed within specific storytelling traditions, often defined as paradigms (e.g., positivism, postpositivism, constructivism).

The result of the interpretive bricoleur's labor is a complex, quilt-like bricolage, a hypertext, a reflexive, collage or montage; a set of fluid, interconnected images and representations. This interpretive structure is like a montage, a performance text, a sequence of representations connecting the parts to the whole.

Online Qualitative Research as a Site of Multiple Interpretive Practices

Online qualitative research, as a set of interpretive activities, privileges no single methodological practice over another. As a site of discussion, or discourse, qualitative research is difficult to define clearly. It has no theory or paradigm that is distinctly its own. Multiple theoretical paradigms claim use of online qualitative research methods and strategies, from constructivist, to cultural studies, feminism, Marxism, and ethnic models of study. Online qualitative research is used in many separate disciplines, as I discuss below. It does not belong to a single discipline.

Nor does online qualitative research have a distinct set of methods or practices that are entirely its own. Online qualitative researchers use semiotics, narrative, content, discourse, archival and phonemic analysis, even statistics, tables, graphs, and numbers. They also draw on and utilize the approaches, methods, and techniques of ethnomethodology, phenomenology, hermeneutics, feminism, rhizomatics, deconstructionism, ethnographies, interviews, psychoanalysis, cultural studies, survey research, and participant observation, among others.[3] No specific method or practice can be privileged over another.

The many histories that surround each online method or online research strategy reveal how multiple uses and meanings are brought to each practice. Online textual analyses in literary studies, for example, often treat texts as self-contained systems. By contrast, a cultural studies or feminist perspective reads a text in terms of its location within a historical moment marked by a particular gender, race, or class ideology. A cultural studies use of online ethnography would bring a set of understandings from feminism, postmodernism, and poststructuralism to the project. These understandings would not be shared by mainstream postpositivist sociologists. Similarly, postpositivist and poststructural historians bring different understandings and uses to the methods and findings of online historical research. Many of these tensions and contradictions are all evident in the chapters in this volume.

These separate and multiple uses and meanings of the methods of online qualitative research make it difficult to agree on any essential definition of the field, for it is never just one thing.[4] Still, a definition must be made. Modifying Denzin and Lincoln (2000b, 7): Online qualitative research is an interdisciplinary, transdisciplinary, and sometimes counterdisciplinary field. It cross-cuts the humanities, the social sciences, and the physical sciences. Online qualitative research is many things at the same time. It is multiparadigmatic in focus. Its practitioners are sensitive to the value of the multimethod approach. They are committed to the naturalistic perspective, and to the interpretive understanding of human experience. At the same time, the field is inherently political and shaped by multiple ethical and political positions.

Online qualitative research embraces two tensions at the same time. On the one hand, it is drawn to a broad, interpretive, postexperimental, postmodern, feminist, and critical sensibility. On the other hand, it is drawn to more narrowly defined positivist, postpositivist, humanistic, and naturalistic conceptions of human experience and its analysis. Furthermore, these tensions can be combined in the same project, bringing both postmodern and naturalistic, or critical and humanistic perspectives.

This rather awkward statement means that online qualitative research, as a set of practices, embraces within its own multiple disciplinary histories, constant tensions and contradictions over the project itself, including its methods, and the forms its findings and interpretations take. The field sprawls between and cross-cuts all of the human disciplines, even including, in some cases, the physical sciences. Its practitioners are variously committed to modern postmodern, postexperimental sensibilities and the approaches to social research that these sensibilities imply.

So today, online researchers, like old-fashioned ethnographers, are telling their tales from the field. And as these researchers write their stories, they understand that writing is not an innocent practice. Men and women write culture differently, including those who write culture on the Internet.

Sociologists, anthropologists, and communications scholars continue to explore new ways of composing ethnography, including texts based on online inquiry. More than a few are writing fiction, drama, performance tests, and ethnographic poetry. It is common today to read e-mail postings in ethnographic texts, as writers move between virtual and real environments. Social science journals are holding fiction contests. Online ethnographers are experimenting with various forms of critical ethnography.

The Historically Situated Online Researcher

The online qualitative researcher is not an objective, politically neutral observer who stands outside and above the study of these media processes and the circuits of culture. Rather, the online researcher is historically and locally situated within the very processes being studied. A gendered, historical self is brought to this process. This self, as a set of shifting identities, has its own history with the situated practices that define and shape the consumption of cultural goods and commodities.

In the social sciences today there is no longer a God's-eye view that guarantees absolute methodological certainty. All inquiry reflects the standpoint of the inquirer. All observation is theory-laden. There is no possibility of theory- or value-free knowledge. The days of naive realism and naive positivism are over. In their place stand critical and historical realism, and various versions of relativism. The criteria for evaluating online research are now relative. This is the nonfoundational position.[5]

An antifoundational, critical social science seeks its external grounding not in science, in any of its revisionist, postpositivist forms but, rather, in a commitment to a post-Marxism and communitarian feminism with hope but no guarantees. It seeks to understand how power and ideology operate through and across systems of discourse, cultural commodities, and cultural texts. It asks how words and texts and their meanings play a pivotal part in the cultures "decisive performances of race, class [and] gender" (Downing, 1987, 80).

Interpretive Criteria in the Seventh Moment

In the seventh moment, the criteria for evaluating critical online qualitative work are moral and ethical. The following understandings structure this process. First, this is a political, ethical, and aesthetic position. It blends aesthetics, ethics, and epistemologies.[6] It understands that nothing is value-free, that knowledge is power. Furthermore, those who have power determine what is aesthetically pleasing, and ethically acceptable. Thus, this position erases any distinction among epistemology, aesthetics, and ethics.

Second, in a feminist, communitarian sense, this aesthetic contends that ways of knowing (epistemology) are moral and ethical (Christians, 2000). These ways of knowing involve conceptions of who the human being is (ontology), including how matters of difference are socially organized. The ways in which these relationships of difference are textually represented answer to a political and epistemological aesthetic that defines what is good, true, and beautiful.

All aesthetics and standards of judgment are based on particular moral standpoints. There is no objective, morally neutral standpoint. Hence, for example, an Afrocentric feminist aesthetic (and epistemology), stresses the importance of truth, knowledge, and beauty ("Black Is Beautiful"). Such claims are based on a concept of storytelling, and a notion of wisdom that is experiential and shared. Wisdom so conceived is derived from local, lived experience, and expresses lore, folktale, and myth (Collins, 1991).

Third, this is a dialogical epistemology and aesthetic. It involves a give and take and ongoing moral dialogue between persons. It enacts an ethic of care, and an ethic of personal and communal responsibility (Collins, 1991, 214). Politically, this aesthetic imagines how a truly democratic society might look, including one free of race prejudice and oppression. This aesthetic values beauty and artistry, movement, rhythm, color, and texture in everyday life. It celebrates difference and the sounds of many different voices. It expresses an ethic of empowerment.

Fourth, this ethic presumes a moral community that is ontologically prior to the person. This community has shared moral values, including the concepts of shared governance, neighborliness, love, kindness, and the moral good (Christians, 2000, 144–149). This ethic embodies a sacred, existential epistemology that locates persons in a noncompetitive, nonhierarchical relationship to the larger moral universe. This ethic declares that all persons deserve dignity and a sacred status in the world. It stresses the value of human life, truth-telling, and nonviolence (Christians, 2000, 147).

Fifth, this aesthetic enables social criticism, and engenders resistance. It helps persons imagine how things could be different. It imagines new forms of human transformation and emancipation. It enacts these transformations through dialogue. If necessary, it sanctions nonviolent forms of civil disobediance (Christians, 2000, 148).

Sixth, this aesthetic understands that moral criteria are always fitted to the contingencies of concrete circumstances, assessed in terms of those local understandings that flow from a feminist, communitarian moral (Christians, 2000). This ethic calls for dialogical research rooted in the concepts of care and shared governance. How this ethic works in any specific situation cannot be given in advance.

Seventh, properly conceptualized, online research becomes a civic, participatory, collaborative project, a project that joins the researcher with the researched in an ongoing moral dialogue. This is a form of participatory action research. It has roots in liberation theology, neo-Marxist approaches to community development, and human rights activism in Asia and elsewhere (Kemmis and McTaggart, 2000, 568). Such work is characterized by shared ownership of the research project, community-based analyses, an emancipatory, dialectical, and transformative commitment to community action (Kemmis and McTaggart, 2000, 568, 598). This form of consumer research "aims to help people recover, and release themselves, from the constraints embedded in the social media" (Kemmis and McTaggart, 2000, 598). This means that the researcher learns to take on the identities of consumer advocate and cultural critic.

Accordingly, eighth, this ethic asks that online interpretive work provide the foundations for social criticism and social action. These texts represent calls to action. As a cultural critic, the researcher speaks from an informed moral and ethical position. He or she is anchored in a specific community of moral discourse. The moral ethnographer takes sides.

Taking sides is a complex process (Becker, 1967), involving several steps. First, researchers must make their own value positions clear, including the so-called objective facts and ideological assumptions that they attach to these positions. Second, they identify and analyze the values and claims to objective knowledge that organize positions that are contrary to their own. Third, they show how these appeals to ideology and objective knowledge reflect a particular moral and historical standpoint. Fourth, they show how this standpoint disadvantages and disempowers members of a specific group.

Fifth, they next make an appeal to a participatory, feminist, communitarian ethic. This ethic may represent new conceptions of care, love, beauty, and empowerment. Sixth, they apply this ethic to the specifics of a concrete case, showing how it would and could produce social betterment.

Seventh, in a call to action, online researchers engage in concrete steps that will change situations in the future. They may teach consumers how to

bring new value to commodities and texts that are marginalized and stigmatized by the larger culture. They will demonstrate how particular commodities or cultural objects negatively affect the lives of specific people. They
indicate how particular texts directly and indirectly misrepresent persons
and reproduce prejudice and stereotypes.

Eighth, in advancing this utopian project, the critical online researcher
seeks new standards and new tools of evaluation, including, for example,
those feminist criteria outlined above.

Problems and Practices in Online Inquiry

The foregoing offers a framework for reading the problems and practices of
online inquiry, as discussed by the contributors to this volume. In Part I, in
their overview of issues in online research, Christians and Chen compare
the history of technological development with the evolution of research
methods. They show how the Internet allows for expedient data collection
from large, previously hard to reach samples. The Internet offers 24-hour
accessibility and instantaneous communication.

Williams and Robson discuss the issues involved in fitting the focus
group methodology to asynchronous and synchronous online environments. Sharon Kleinman used a multiple-method approach in her implementation of a four-year intrinsic case study of a computer-mediated group.
She discusses a wide range of problems, including obtaining a sample, developing valid content analysis categories, and addressing copyright and fair use
issues regarding e-mail messages posted on a public listserv. Kathleen
LeBesco takes up the dilemmas she faced in mediating virtual and real interactional space, as she moved from online, text-only interactions, to group
and individual interviews. Mary Walstom contrasts two interpretive online
positions, and their ethical implications: discourse analysis versus support
group participant. She takes up the ethical dilemma that arises when
researchers do not participate in the online groups they study.

Amy Bruckman introduces the papers in Part II, which examine issues
of online research. She raises several key ethical issues involved in the study
of computer-mediated communication, including when consent is required,
when privacy must be maintained, and so forth. Johns, Hall, and Crowell
provide a valuable review of existing institutional guidelines regarding
online research practices. Attempts are under way to address the special features of online inquiry, as the older criteria of respect, beneficence, and justice are maintained. Recommendations are provided to assist online
researchers who must secure permission from review boards. Lori Kendall
reflects on what it means to do participant observation ethnography online.

Annette Markham uses narrative to discuss three online ethnographic issues, including the restriction of certain senses; the impossibility of ever really knowing who the participant is; and how you represent the voice of the Other. Chen, Hall, and Johns report on a study of mailing list owners and newsgroup moderators. This project is important because it reveals how list owners and newsgroup members regard the presence of researchers in their group. The responses ranged from animosity, to conditional acceptance, but only with assurances of confidentiality and privacy. Respondents felt that researchers should disclose their identities, and also secure informed consent. Respondents differed in how they defined the online environment; for some, it was a private space, for others, a public space. Those who see it as a private site tend to hold to a participant-oriented, feminist ethic, rather than researcher, utilitarian-oriented ethic. Chen, Hall, and Johns discuss the value of feminist, communitarian ethics for online community life, for research that makes a difference in the lives of real people in the virtual world.

Steve Jones introduces the five papers in Part III, which are on the ethics of online social research. Jones outlines the complex discourses in this field, noting how Institutional Review Boards (IRBs) are now attempting to regulate research in cyberspace, often with little concern over whether or not there are Internet-specific ethical concerns that are distinct from legal issues. Of course, anonymity, consent, privacy, and confidentiality are always issues, but are there others? Chen, Hall, and Johns think there are. I agree.

Jim Thomas contends that we need to reexamine the ethics of Internet research, contrasting the "pseudo ethics" of IRBs, to genuine ethical imperatives, and ethical understandings that would shape conduct on the Net. Thomas is convinced that there are few if any new ethical issues raised by the new computer technologies; on this, he is clear: "It is better to do good than ill." Susan Barnes discusses the public versus private nature of computer-mediated communication, and the ethical issues involved therein. If online communication is public, then the real names of people should be printed. In contrast, if this communication is private, then the privacy and confidentiality rights of persons should be maintained. To date, she argues, there are no established Internet research guidelines on these issues. Katherine Clegg Smith takes up electronic eavesdropping, and also confronts the ethical problem of when is Internet conduct private and when is it public.

Hall, Frederick, and Johns discuss teaching students how to do online research, including instructions in netiquette, and the relevance of communitarian ethics for such inquiry. When applying the feminist communitarian approach to online research, five ethical directives emerged as central:

(1) online community is prior to online research; (2) online researchers should be neighborly and seek to establish a relationship of trust and respect with those they are working with; (3) online research is participant not researcher driven; (4) online researchers adhere to the norms of interpretive sufficiency, genuine care, and shared emotionality; (5) online research should enact a form of cooperative mutuality between the researcher and researched. Charles Ess brings this discussion full circle, noting that there is an emerging consensus in this field, an agreement that a code of ethics has to be solidified, and it has to be sensitive to the nuances of online inquiry.

Conclusion

Online research in the seventh moment is moving in several directions at the same time, as is the larger movement of qualitative inquiry. As the chapters in this volume reveal, researchers are concerned about moral, ethical, and political issues. As bricoleurs, researchers in virtual and real worlds are fitting traditional research methods, and theories to new problems, new research questions, and new technologies.

And scholars struggle with how to write themselves into their texts. That is, the Internet is a site in which selves and identities are created, lived, performed. Each performance of the self is unique. This is a semiotic self; its presence is established in and through language, the printed word on the computer screen. This self exceeds language; its meanings overflow, and spill off of the computer screen. The self in its plenitude can never be reduced to the traces on this screen. The self and its meanings are always in motion.

The method of instances structures this interpretive process (Denzin, 1999). The analyst's task is to understand how an event, a spoken conversation, a performance of the self that is an instance and its intersections with other instances, works. The analyst shows which rules of interpretation are operating, the rules that map and illuminate the structure of the interpretive event itself. Of course, every interpretive event online is unique, and contextual; it has never happened before.

Borrowing from Sterne, "It is never possible to specify in advance the effects of whatever is being studied (1999, 263). Such effects are always local, contingent, and contextual. The objects of inquiry that online researchers take up, including the self and its twitches and gestures, are always constituted through the act of research. How these things are connected and given meaning can usually only be understood after the fact. These connections are always political; hence, online researchers must always be sensitive to the political and economic dimensions of their work.

The Internet is a commodity and a communication technology, suggesting that as a commodity it is bound up in issues of gender, race, class, and power (Sterne, 1999, 279).

The problems of social science inquiry have always been moral and political and ethical. These are the issues that trouble the authors in this collection, and this places their work on the cutting-edge. It is especially refreshing to see so much interest in feminist, communitarian models of inquiry and practice. Such concern suggests that online researchers may well be the leaders in this new discourse, and it will be to them that the broader field looks when new ethical codes of conduct are formulated. We thank them and their coeditors for this.

Notes

1 Denzin and Lincoln (2000b, 2) define the seven moments of inquiry, all of which operate in the present, as: the traditional (1900–1950), the modernist (1950–1970), blurred genres (1970–1986), the crisis of representation (1986–1990) postmodern, or experimental (1990–1995), postexperimental (1995–2000), and the future (2000–).

2 The following section draws from and reworks Denzin and Lincoln (2000b, 4–7).

3 Here it is relevant to make a distinction between techniques that are used across disciplines, with methods that are used within disciplines. Ethnomethodologists, for example, employ their approach as a method, while others selectively borrow that method-as-technique for their own applications. Harry Wolcott (in conversation) suggests this distinction. It is also relevant to make a distinction between topic, method, and resource. Methods can be studied as topics of inquiry; that is, how a case study gets done. In this ironic, ethnomethodological sense, method is both a resource and a topic of inquiry.

4 Indeed, any attempt to give an essential definition of qualitative research requires a qualitative analysis of the circumstances that produce such a definition.

5 There are three basic positions on the issue of evaluative criteria: foundational, quasi-foundational, and nonfoundational. Foundationalists apply the same positivistic criteria to qualitative research as are employed in quantitative inquiry, contending that there is nothing special about qualitative research that demands a special set of evaluative criteria. Quasi-foundationalists contend that a set of criteria unique to qualitative research must be developed (see Smith and Deemer, 2000). Nonfoundationalists reject in advance all epistemological criteria.

6 Definitions—Aesthetics: Theories of beauty; Ethics: Theories of ought, of right; Epistemology: Theories of knowing.

References

Becker, H. S. "Whose Side Are We On?" *Social Problems 14* (1967): 239–247.

Christians, C. "Ethics and Politics in Qualitative Research," in *Handbook of Qualitative Research, 2/e.* Ed. Norman K. Denzin and Yvonna S. Lincoln, 133–155. Thousand Oaks, CA: Sage, 2000.

Collins, P. H. *Black Feminist Thought.* New York: Routledge, 1991.

Denzin, N. K. "Cybertalk and the Method of Instances," in *Doing Internet Research.* Ed. Steve Jones, 107–126. Thousand Oaks, CA: Sage, 1999.

Denzin, N. K. and Y. S. Lincoln. "Preface," in *Handbook of Qualitative Research, 2/e.* Ed. Norman K. Denzin and Yvonna S. Lincoln, ix–xx. Thousand Oaks, CA: Sage, 2000a.

———. "Introduction: The Discipline and Practice of Qualitative Research," in *Handbook of Qualitative Research, 2/e.* Ed. Norman K. Denzin and Yvonna S. Lincoln, 1–29. Thousand Oaks, CA: Sage, 2000b.

Downing, D. B. "Deconstruction's Scruples: The Politics of Enlightened Critique," *Diacritcs 17* (1987): 66–8l.

Kemmis, S. and R. McTaggart. "Participatory Action Research," in *Handbook of Qualitative Research, 2/e.* Ed. Norman K. Denzin and Yvonna S. Lincoln, 567–606. Thousand Oaks, CA: Sage, 2000.

Lincoln, Y. S. and N. K. Denzin. "The Seventh Moment: Out of the Past," in *Handbook of Qualitative Research, 2/e.* Ed. Norman K. Denzin and Yvonna S. Lincoln, 1047–1065. Thousand Oaks, CA: Sage, 2000.

Mann, C. and F. Stewart. *Internet Communication and Qualitative Research: A Handbook for Researching Online.* London: Sage, 2000.

Schwandt, T. A. "Three Epistemological Stances for Qualitative Inquiry," in *Handbook of Qualitative Research, 2/e.* Ed. Norman K. Denzin and Yvonna S. Lincoln, 189–213. Thousand Oaks, CA: Sage, 2000.

Smith, J. K. and D. K. Deemer. "The Problem of Criteria in the Age of Relativism," in *Handbook of Qualitative Research, 2/e.* Ed. Norman K. Denzin and Yvonna S. Lincoln, 877–896. Thousand Oaks, CA: Sage, 2000.

Sterne, J. "Thinking the Internet: Cultural Studies Versus the Millennium," in *Doing Internet Research.* Ed. Steve Jones, 257–288. Thousand Oaks, CA: Sage, 1999.

Part I

Methods of Online Social Research

Introduction: Technological Environments and the Evolution of Social Research Methods

ॐ☙

Clifford G. Christians
Shing-Ling Sarina Chen

TECHNOLOGIES are not neutral, but value-laden throughout. Valuing penetrates all technological activity, from our selecting which technological problems need to be addressed, through the processes of design and fabrication, to the use of tools and products. Certain resources are consumed and not others. The problems of one group are addressed and the necessities of others ignored. Technological objects are unique, not universal. Jacques Ellul calls our communications media "the innermost, and most elusive, manifestation" of human technological activity (Ellul, 1978, 207ff). All artifacts communicate meaning in an important sense, but media instruments carry that role exclusively. Information technologies incarnate the properties of technology while serving as the agent for interpreting the very phenomenon they embody. The media do not transmit neutral messages, but subtly weave users and society into the warp-and-woof of an efficiency-dominated culture (Ellul, 1965).

Print

Thus, in historical terms, print technology, the growth of science, and experimental research methodologies were implicated in one another as the age of modernity took shape. The standardization and indexing fostered by print technology enabled the growth of scientific research. The ability to reference identical pieces of information, as well as to organize empirical observations, and to incorporate new findings in manageable and systematic fashion was impossible in oral societies. The use of print expanded researchers' capacities to ask new questions, tackle a broader range of issues, gather novel data, and analyze them. The form of research activity is shaped by the available tools from the larger technological environment. Technological development and the evolution of research methods have an ecological correlation. The characteristics of research methods bear the imprints of the type of technology used.

Elizabeth Eisenstein (1979) provides a detailed and systematic historical analysis of the development and consequences of the printing press in early Western Europe. The print medium as a new technology was so powerful in her view that it established the Renaissance and made the Reformation possible. The ninth-century Carolingian and twelfth-century Gothic renascences were limited and transitory. The preservative power of Gutenberg's invention in 1453 made the stirrings of this new age decisive and total. The printing press reformatted human communication at a historical watershed, standardizing written forms of language, insisting on such typographic conventions as paragraphing and headings, and fostering prescriptive truth. Print helped to decentralize papal authority by empowering the home and countryside with vernacular Bibles and Luther's pamphlets. Secular issues began dominating the center stage of intellectual inquiry rather than the concerns of tradition and religious belief.

As a central figure in the transition from medieval thought to modern science, Galileo Galilei (1564–1642) mapped reality in a new way: "This great book, the Universe....is written in the language of mathematics, and its characters are triangles, circles, and geometric figures" (Galileo, 1957, 238f). Matter alone mattered to him; all nonmaterial was considered immaterial. He separated the qualitative as incapable of quantitative certainty. Within a century, the Englishman Isaac Newton could describe the world in his *Principia Mathematica* (1687) as a lifeless machine composed of mathematical laws and built on uniform natural causes in a closed system. All phenomena could be explained as the outcome of an order extending to every detail. Arbitrary mystery was defined away. All but quantity or number were called sophistry and illusion. And, within that pattern from Galileo to the all-pervasive scheme of Newton, stands René Descartes (1596–1650) who cut the mathematical truths of science into human being itself. Mechanistic rationality is the same for all thinking subjects, all nations, all epochs and cultures. Descartes insisted on the noncontingency of starting points, unconditioned by circumstance. He presumed clear and distinct ideas, objective and neutral, apart from anything subjective. Two plus two equals four was lucid and testable, and all genuine knowledge in Descartes's view should be as cognitively clean as arithmetic (Descartes, 1964). Science and calculation were accepted as the ideology by which humans ought to live, even as print forms of communication began monopolizing Western language. Print was a stunning achievement. Within 60 years, it had swept across Europe from Germany to Hungary, and within a century the known handwritten materials were available in printed form. As genuine knowledge was built up in linear fashion, the technology of print helped imagine and foster it.

In the social sciences, the establishment of mathematical formulas and controlled laboratory settings fostered the development of quantitative research methods. Preoccupied by numerical and laboratory techniques, social scientists utilized survey and experimental research methods to study social phenomena. They took a one-point-in-time approach, either trying to describe an existent situation, or trying to identify the causal relationship between two variables. Early social research in the fields of psychology, sociology, and communication were marked by such kinds of research efforts. The predictive, deterministic, and linear features of mathematics and the laboratory came to be reflected in survey and experimental designs. The founder of sociology, August Comte, for example, asserted that human thought moves through the stages of religious speculation, to metaphysical abstractions, and finally to scientific reasoning (Comte, 1910). In his view, instead of the primitive tools of theology and philosophy, social studies, to become scientific, should be ordered on statistical precision; that is, on sophisticated procedures of induction and logic. Communications research reflected this positivist temper as well. Surveys, lab experiments, and content analyses became preoccupied with operational precision, internal and external validity, independent and dependent variables in experimental design, and statistical inferences. The groundbreaking work in information signaling by Claude Shannon and Warren Weaver (1949) explicitly adopted this scientific rationality in its title, *The Mathematical Theory of Communication*.

Audio and Video

The advent of audio- and video-recording technologies and playback systems opened new opportunities for social researchers. Early in the 20th century, photographs and moving image cameras were used for ethnographic research, but not until Margaret Mead and Gregory Bateson's 16mm filming and 35mm photography in Bali in 1936–1939 did visual media yield significant scholarship (Bateson and Mead, 1942). With the growth in image-making technologies since World War II, knowledge of visual discourse and visual competence have emerged as important aspects of qualitative methodology. Visual anthropology, in fact, has become a subdiscipline, especially through documentaries and ethnographic filmmaking (Banks, 1998). Visual sociology is now a useful framework for recording technologically the aural and visual aspects of social reality.[1]

One notable example of image-based research is that of Carl Couch and associates, who utilized audio- and video-recording equipment for data collection in a laboratory setting, and playback systems for data analysis.

They created the New Iowa School of Symbolic Interaction, an innovative research method as well as a unique epistemological approach for studying social processes and relationships (Couch, 1989). Essentially, Couch and associates situated human subjects in the laboratory to study the process of developing social relationships. Participants were assigned identities similar to their real-life personae, informed by the researchers about the context of interaction, and given a social objective to accomplish within a designated period of time. Participants assumed the identity assigned and the context given as real; they interacted with each other to achieve the assigned objective, and their interaction was videotaped.[2]

New technologies provide new opportunities for research by relieving researchers from the constraints of the old tools. Audio- and video-recording systems allow researchers to collect processual data with high fidelity. The recording of such data allows researchers to examine the development of relationships over time, releasing them from the one-point-in-time constraint imposed by quantitative research methods. The high fidelity of the audio and video recordings allows researchers to have a complete set of data, a relief from the constraint of incomplete notes experienced by field researchers. In addition, the playback systems permit researchers to review the data over and over again. More important, the technologies enable researchers to specify the sequence of interaction with great precision, an achievement that is unattainable using traditional field observation.

New technologies not only offer fresh opportunities for research but also impose new limitations. The New Iowa School researchers had several obstacles to resolve, such as the participants' hesitancies about recording machines, and the authoritarian nature of the laboratory setting. To overcome resistance to being videotaped, Couch and associates built into their research design a demanding task for participants in the laboratory. Their research showed that once participants had an interesting and challenging task to perform in the laboratory, they would quickly forget about being videotaped (Couch, 1989). To address the authoritarian nature of the laboratory, Couch treated participants as intelligent beings, allowing them to anticipate and interact naturally in the laboratory. He argued that the artificial and authoritarian dimension of the laboratory was lessened as the participants were asked to interact, and not simply to react or respond. The opportunities and limitations of the New Iowa School approach reflect the technological features of audio- and video-recording/playback systems and the laboratory structure.

Internet

The maturation of Internet technology marks another era of rapid growth in social research. Mass media technologies are converging into digital formats. The World Wide Web, e-mail, chatrooms, MUDs (multiuser domains), web-based publication, and the ability to hyperlink bring new forms of interaction and structure. The 3-D virtual world is the innovative edge of these online technologies also called CMCS (Computer-Mediated Communication Systems). Interactive Internet technology gives people a voice and connects users directly without professionals or gatekeepers in between. Internet technologies are democratic tools in principle that serve people's everyday needs, rather than those of special interest groups or the market's.

Digital technology presents social researchers with new opportunities that ease many constraints previously experienced using traditional research methods. For example, the Internet, with its 24-hour accessibility and instantaneous communication, provides expedient data collection, a feature that was available previously only to telephone surveys and group administration. The Internet, with its worldwide connections, allows the access of a massive sample, a feature previously available only to mail survey. Newsgroups and mailing lists provide identifiable topic-based interest groups, and allow easy access to hard-to-reach populations, a feature that was available previously only to field research. Other great features of the Internet for social research include its low cost, the readily available logs of conversation, the freedom from transcribing interview data, the automatic categorization of survey data, and so forth.

These promising attributes of the Internet led many social researchers to an optimistic view that the Internet presents an ideal environment for research. Many have rushed to conduct research online. Not knowing what an effective method would be for online research, researchers typically have applied offline methods to online environments. But direct application of traditional research methods to cyberspace often generates difficulties in execution or unsuccessful results. The Internet presents a new technology for research, and the formal features of the Internet need to be taken into consideration when implementing it as a research strategy.

In this methods section, several veteran online social researchers describe how they modified traditional research methods for their online research endeavors, in light of the characteristics of online environments. They share with readers how they utilized the opportunities offered by Internet technologies, and how they handled the challenges presented by the online environments as well. Matthew Williams and Kate Robson detail how to handle asynchronous and synchronous focus groups online. Sharon

Kleinman adapts the traditional case study method for online research. Kathleen LeBesco discusses the epistemological and methodological issues of conducting critical ethnography online. Mary Walstrom applies the interpretive interactionist method to study an online support group. These discussions demonstrate how the authors utilize the capacities and manage the limitations of their respective research method when applying these techniques in online environments. Reading these analyses, readers will gain a good understanding of key issues involved in using these methods in online environments, as well as successful strategies for handling the methodological challenges.

Concern for Technology

The detailed work of these authors on using Internet technologies for research is interwoven with the concerns of technology as a whole. Three long-term issues are introduced on a short-term basis in the following chapters.

The Bias of Technology

Harold Innis, the founder of Canadian Communication Theory, argued that social change results from media transformations, and changes in symbolic forms alter the structure of consciousness. He studied the introduction of papyrus, the printing press, radio, and the telegraph, and documented a bias—a tendency or propensity—regarding space and time (Innis, 1951). Oral communication systems, he argued, are biased toward time, rendering time continuous while making space discontinuous. Print systems by contrast are biased toward space, making geography continuous and breaking time into distinct units. Thus, from the introduction of cuneiform writing to today's World Wide Web, scholars in the Innis tradition examine all significant shifts in technological form, identifying from them subsequent alternations in culture and in perception. Within this paradigm of bias in communication systems, the intellectual challenge is to identify the distinguishing properties of particular media technologies such as books, cinema, satellites, and the Internet. Regarding television or radio or fiber optics, communications scholars must work deeply into their fundamental properties in order to know them distinctly as their own.

The overall task while using Internet technologies in research is to discover their optimum qualities. What are their peculiar properties that give them particular possibilities as a medium, while making them less advantageous than other media?

The Technological Imperative

Innis argued that one form of communication tends to monopolize our knowledge and render other forms residual (Innis, 1952). The various media do not exist innocently alongside one another. Oral culture continued to exist after print became the dominant medium, but the oral-aural mode was no longer the standard of truth nor the centerpiece of education and power politics. In contemporary affairs, electronic systems monopolize our way of thinking and social structures, leaving print and oral modes of secondary importance. Given the explosive growth of Internet technology and the rhapsodies accompanying it, cyberspace tends to monopolize electronics now.

In its extreme forms, the technological imperative sweeps aside other alternatives. The operational dictates of a technology become the primary rationale for action and policy. In the case at hand, the character and validity of social science research are determined by the skillful or novel use of Internet technology. In Ellul's terms, technology itself can be beneficent—the danger is technicism, our sacralizing it as the technological fix.

Even in its moderate form, the monopoly of computer-mediated knowledge is an ongoing challenge for research. As James Carey puts it, "For all the vaunted capacity of the computer to store, process, and make available information in densities and quantities heretofore unknown, the pervasive tendency to monopolize knowledge in the professions and data banks continues unabated" (Carey, 1997, 57). Or, as he describes the thinking of Innis's successor at Toronto, Marshall McLuhan: "Media of communication are vast social metaphors that not only transmit information but determine what is knowledge, that not only orient us to the world but tell us what kind of world exists" (Carey, 1967, 18). With electronic media understood in McLuhan's terms as an extension of the human nervous system, the dominant forms establish authority for their own representational capacity. In that sense, instrumental views of truth dominate, with a photograph or Internet conversation seen as direct encoding of reality rather than a partial representation of it.

Organic Communities

If oral cultures make time stand still and print technologies foster empire and objectivism, the current shift to electronic culture dislocates us from both space and history. It ruptures historical consciousness and disconnects us from our geographical home in mediating structures. Without specific anchors in time and space, primary groups—family, school, church, neighborhoods, and voluntary associations—lose their resonance. Irretrievably and congenitally, symbols are embedded in sound. Walter Ong reminds us that the oral-aural center of human life is irrevocable (Ong, 1967).[3] Oral life is our common property, all humans learning to speak and hear at roughly the same age in languages of equal complexity. Acoustical symbols draw persons and experiences into dialogic relations; spoken words create life in the present. In terms of media bias and monopolies of knowledge, oral culture has permanent relevance.

Communities are organic, and from this perspective Internet research of even the most sophisticated kind should never cut itself loose from everyday experience. The anonymity of online relations, and the disconnections from time and space among digital entities, cannot be subsumed into a world of its own making. In the legacy of Harold Innis, the offline world establishes the context, issues, hypotheses, and research framework.

Because technologies are value-laden, underlying values are the final arbiter of quality in Internet research. Certainly ideas and the material are interactive, but the former are *primus inter pares*. Constant repetition of a technology leads to research that is conceptually thin. "Recall that Bateson and Mead both spent several years in the field, and had completed ethnographic studies before they then turned to the subject with their cameras. The theories they explored with photographs were grounded in anthropological knowledge" (Harper, 1998, 29). Even as the authors in the following chapters demonstrate how digital tools can be used effectively in interpretive research, they remind us that creative imagination, theoretical substance, and broad learning are indispensable.

Notes

1 For a state-of-the-art treatment of visual techniques in social research, see Jon Prosser (1998). See also Douglas Harper's overview chapters in *Handbook of Qualitative Research*, 1st and 2nd editions, 1994 and 2000.

2 For elaboration in the context of media technologies generally, see Carl Couch (1996).

3 See also Walter Ong (2002).

References

Banks, M. "Visual Anthropology: Image, Object and Interpretation." In *Image-based Research: A Sourcebook for Qualitative Researchers.* Ed. Jon Prosser. London: Falmer Press, 1998.

Bateson, G., and M. Mead. *Balinese Character: A Photographic Analysis.* New York: New York Academy of Sciences, 1942.

Carey, J. W. "Harold Adams Innis and Marshall McLuhan." *The Antioch Review 21* (Spring 1967), 5–39.

———. "The Roots of Modern Media Analysis: Lewis Mumford and Marshall McLuhan." In *James Carey: A Critical Reader.* Ed. Eve S. Munson and Catherine A. Warren. Minneapolis: University of Minnesota Press, 1997.

Comte, A. *A General View of Positivism.* Translated by J. H. Bridges. London: Routledge, 1910. Original work published 1848.

Couch, C. J. *Researching Social Processes in the Laboratory.* New York: Aldine De Gruyter, 1989.

———. *Information Technologies and Social Orders.* Ed. David R. Maines and Shing-Ling Chen. New York: Aldine De Gruyter, 1996.

Descartes, R. "Rules for the Direction of the Mind." Translated by L. J. Lafleur. In his *Philosophical Papers*, 147–236. Indianapolis, IN: Bobbs-Merrill, 1964.

———. *Discourse on Method*, 1637.

Eisenstein, E. *The Printing Press as an Agent of Change: Communications and Structural Transformations in Early-Modern Europe* (vols. 1–2). New York: Cambridge University Press, 1979.

Ellul, J. *Propaganda: The Formation of Men's Attitudes.* Translated by K. Keller. New York: Alfred A. Knopf, 1965.

———. "Symbolic Function, Technology and Society." *Journal of Social and Biological Structure* (October 1978): 207–218.

Galileo G. *Discoveries and Opinions of Galileo.* Translated by S. Drake. Garden City, NY: Doubleday, 1957.

Harper, D. "On the Authority of the Image: Visual Methods at the Crossroads." In *Handbook of Qualitative Research. 1st ed.* Ed. Norman K. Denzin and Yvonna S. Lincoln. Thousand Oaks, CA: Sage, 1994.

———. "An Argument for Visual Sociology." In *Image-based Research: A Sourcebook for Qualitative Researchers.* Ed. Jon Prosser. London: Falmer Press, 1998.

———. "Reimagining Visual Methods: Galileo to Neuromancer." In *Handbook of Qualitative Research. 2nd ed.* Ed. Norman K. Denzin and Yvonna S. Lincoln. Thousand Oaks, CA: Sage, 2000.

Innis, H. *The Bias of Communication.* Toronto: University of Toronto Press, 1951.

———. *Empire and Communication.* Toronto: University of Toronto Press, 1952.

Ong, W. J. *The Presence of the Word: Some Prolegomena for Cultural and Religious History.* New Haven, CT: Yale University Press, 1967.

———. *Orality and Literacy.* Florence, KY: Taylor and Francis Books, 2002.

Prosser, J., ed. *Image-based Research: A Sourcebook for Qualitative Researchers.* London: Falmer Press, 1998.

Shannon, C., and W. Weaver. *The Mathematical Theory of Communication.* Urbana: University of Illinois Press, 1949.

Reengineering Focus Group Methodology for the Online Environment

❧❦

Matthew Williams
Kate Robson

A S ONLINE ENVIRONMENTS have been established as cultural contexts in their own right, there has been both a degree of anxiety and innovation surrounding the application of methods that have, until recently, been reserved for the study of offline or "real-life" settings (Hine, 2000). Both quantitative and qualitative approaches are being subjected to rigorous methodological, philosophical, and epistemological evaluation via their application to a myriad of online populations. The "traditional" field methods of participant/nonparticipant observation, interviewing, focus groups, and survey research have been employed to gather data from these new social groups with varying degrees of success (see Baym, 1995a, 1995b; Correll, 1995; Markham, 1998; Witmer, Colman, and Katzman, 1999). Qualifying the "success" of a method may seem at first problematic, but essentially the survivability of "traditional" methods within a computer-mediated setting is dependent on their ability to utilize and adapt to the technology that mediates human interaction online. The manifestation of these technologies of mediation varies, yet each one presents opportunities for the evolution of "traditional" methods of social investigation. This chapter takes the established focus group method and evaluates its success in online settings, drawing practical examples from two distinct pieces of research. Robson's (1999) research into the employment experiences of inflammatory bowel disease sufferers exemplifies the use of asynchronous online focus groups, identifying key practical issues such as online moderation and the analysis of digital data. In contrast, Williams's study into deviance within online groups (2003) provides examples of how synchronous forms of online focus groups, held within 3-D graphical environments, creates further challenges for the researcher, highlighting unique ethical considerations of conducting fieldwork in cyberspace. The chapter draws together the author's experiences of applying the method to offer insights into the viability and practicability of online focus groups.

Defining the Focus Group

The focus group method of social inquiry originated at Columbia University in the 1940s. They were first employed in commercial market research to gather information on consumer opinion. Following the publication of Merton and Kendall's (1946) paper "The Focused Interview" in the *American Journal of Sociology*, the method became established outside of commercial uses, being employed to gather data on more salient social issues.

The main premise of the focus group, and what distinguishes it from other forms of qualitative interviewing, is its ability to tap into the meanings, processes, and normative understandings behind a group's assessments and collective judgments. Therefore, the method can be employed to gather data from most social groups in which there is a general understanding of a certain social issue or phenomenon that is under investigation. For example, focus groups might be used by those wishing to uncover the processes though which a group evaluates a certain product, or the social researcher who attempts to discover the meanings and processes of political affiliation.

Networked computer technologies hold further potentials for the focus group method. Although the use and outcomes of online focus groups remain the same as offline focus groups, the ways in which they are conducted and mediated have to be reengineered in light of both the constraints and advantages of new communication technologies. The remainder of this chapter examines these constraints and advantages in detail, while documenting recent trends in focus group research, both on- and offline.

Recent Uses of Online Focus Groups in the Social Sciences

"Online focus group" is both a familiar term and method in market research, but its use in academic research has so far been limited, with computer-administered questionnaires, and covert observation of online interactions being far more popular developments. Administering questionnaires by computer-mediated communications has become fairly commonplace (Witmer, Colman, and Katzman, 1999). However, many that have embraced this innovation are unaware that a suspicion of online survey research among many online participants, because of its quantitative nature, feeds a reluctance to participate in such studies by many users. At the other end of the spectrum, covert observation and collection of naturally occurring online discussions and communities has been a common approach among researchers of cyber phenomena. While similar to online focus groups, such research falls outside of our definition of online focus group in exactly the same way that a covertly observed real-life discussion does not constitute an "offline" focus group. "Harvesting" (the term for the collection of material from computer-mediated interactions without prior consent) is viable and legal, and may be attractive as a speedy way of collecting rich data (Sharf, 1999). However, like online surveys, it flouts the conventions of the medium's users, and thus presents ethical problems in its employment in social research. Harvesting online conversations also limits the amount of background information the researcher is privy to prior to investing their time and resources in collecting the data. As these two extremes of online research methods that have courted popularity are inherently problematic in their suitability for the populations they target, the slow development of online focus groups in academic research has been a surprising missed opportunity.

One of the first documented uses of online focus groups in academic social research was Murray's (1997) study of health professionals with an expertise in computer-mediated communication. The combination of geographic dispersal and familiarity with computerized communications made the use of an online focus group singularly appropriate in the research. Like traditional focus groups, Murray's online groups consisted of six to eight members, although it was acknowledged that larger groups might be appropriate to achieve the level and style of discussion sought by the researcher. In Murray's smaller groups, simultaneous conversational threads did not develop. "Threading" is characteristic of naturally occurring online discussions, and refers to the simultaneous conduct of multiple topics of conversation. To an observer, threading may make the discussion appear chaotic, but participants are usually adept at maintaining distinctions between the different threads of a discussion. Similarly, in the online setting the mediator is more able to identify and control threats, an advantage not afforded to the moderator of offline focus groups. Using an asynchronous discussion form (mailing list) precluded the mirroring of the length of discussion from traditional focus groups. Murray's groups ran for approximately four weeks, which allowed time for the discussion to develop, but encouraged active discussion by signaling the finite nature of the list. Murray found that too high a level of questioning from the researcher resulted in contributions consisting of serial direct answering by the participants to the researcher, rather than stimulating discussion among the participants.

Robson's (1999) use of online focus groups was part of a project on employment experiences of inflammatory bowel disease sufferers. Having conducted face-to-face research with members of a "real-life" patient support group, participants in online patient support networks were recruited for an online focus group. Like Murray, a closed subscription private distribution list was used, but larger numbers were recruited, with 57 participants subscribed. The larger group size allowed the threading of discussions, with multiple topics simultaneously discussed, while the group nonetheless remained open, responsive, and familiar with each other. The discussion ran for two months, with minimal guidance or questioning from the researcher, beyond defining the general area of discussion and providing opening questions at the outset.

Unlike Murray's and Robson's focus groups, Stewart, Eckermann, and Zhou (1998) conducted a synchronous online focus group discussion. Their pilot study of young women's health risk perceptions was conducted primarily to investigate the usefulness of the Internet as a qualitative public health research tool. Participants were located in four sites in China and Australia, with the chat software configured for private access by participants only. The discussions took place in a parent conference area that had four sub-conference areas, with one online facilitator who entered and exited the different chatrooms during the discussions. The primary role of the facilitator was to ensure that all the discussion topics were covered, and they made minimal contributions to the discussions. The discussions lasted for nearly twice the expected one-hour duration, and were described by the researchers as serious and entertaining exchanges.

Facilitating the discussions was described as being more problematic than is usually the case in traditional focus groups, or as would be the case in other asynchronous forms of online focus group, because of the speed and frequency with which topics changed. Thus, it was harder to ensure that all the planned topics for discussion were covered by participants, and also harder to probe issues. However, Stewart, Eckermann, and Zhou (1998) concluded that the study demonstrated a viable methodological approach in cross-cultural research, highlighting a similarity in public discourse about health risk issues in a way that traditional face-to-face forms of research could not.

Population Dynamics and Access

Identifying and gaining access to populations for research purposes is very often the first milestone to overcome. Researching Internet populations is no exception. Indeed, there are some similarities, such as ascertaining what kind of population is required for the research, and what criteria the population must adhere to. Although focus groups have been employed both in market research and the social sciences, in neither case has there been the goal to generalize the findings to a particular population. The aim of the focus group is to yield data on the meanings, processes, and normative understandings that lie behind group assessments that are unlikely to be statistically applied to a general population (Bloor et al., 2000). On this basis, adhering to the principles of systematic random sampling to obtain recruits for an online focus group are less important. Typical methods of recruitment in offline settings have therefore relied more on tapping into preexisting social groups or samples, individual canvassing, and snowball sampling (using contacts of respondents as a sample). However, the applicability of these recruiting conventions to online settings has been met with varying degrees of success.

Taking advantage of existing social groups online is by far the most common and successful method of recruiting participants (Murray, 1997). Notably, medical sociology and health research has taken advantage of the "captive populations" online, characterized by health and illness support networks, in conducting a few online focus groups (Murray, 1997; Stewart, Eckermann, and Zhou, 1998). However, the same has not been done for more exploratory ethnographic research that is devoid of such a rigid and defined population. Williams (2003), in conducting research into deviance within online graphical communities, was not fortunate enough to identify a cohesive preexisting sample or group with which to recruit from. While Williams's population was definable by membership to an online community, its membership and social bonds were far more fluid and turbulent than those found in online health support networks.

The individuals who frequented the online community did so for varying reasons and motives; there was no overarching reason for these individuals to take up membership. This makes recruiting a population for more exploratory ethnographic research online problematic. To overcome this stumbling block, sampling conventions from online survey research were adopted. Taking a similar approach to Witmer, Colman, and Katzman (1999), a suitable population base had to be identified, guided by the research aims. It was found that newsgroups presented the researcher with a large and varied database of potential focus group participants. The newsgroup identified adhered to the research criteria in being both a technical and social support network for the members of the online community being studied. Essentially this method allowed for the canvassing of a very large general Internet population with e-mails inviting individuals to take part in the research.

In evaluating this approach to recruitment, Witmer, Colman, and Katzman (1999) discovered newsgroups to be useful in attaining a population sample for two reasons: (1) they represented a broad demographic range of end users, and (2) they were easily accessible and allowed a publicly posted e-mail address to be drawn for a sample. While at first glance these two points support the use of newsgroups for research canvassing, there still remains an important ethical issue. While it remains an established understanding that newsgroups are a public medium intended for public consumption, the emerging recognition that these spaces are being used for private discourse calls into question the usability and accessibility of this medium for research purposes.

Research has highlighted the disinhibiting effect of computer-mediated communication, meaning members of online communities while acknowledging the environment as a "public" space very often use it to engage in what would be considered "private talk."[1] The ephemeral nature of Internet interactions, including anonymity, a reduction in social cues, and the realization of time-space distanciation, leads individuals to reveal more about themselves within online environments than would be done in offline equivalents. Indeed, Witmer, Colman, and Katzman (1999) found a hostile response from several of those canvassed. Many of those contacted objected to receiving "junk mail," while in Williams's study (2003) several respondents were concerned with the infringement of privacy resulting in many of the responses demanding to know how the researcher obtained their e-mail address.

The issues presented by "canvassing" large static Internet populations for research purposes highlights yet another area of concern for the researcher. The ease at which populations can be identified and recruited for research purposes online, while being a blessing for many market research projects, can mean that these groups become overresearched. The problems this may have are clearly dependent on the individual research project's aims and focus, yet generally it is understandable to assume that of the 544 million current users, many may become nonchalant toward the myriad of questionnaires, interviews, and focus groups they are asked to partake in on a weekly basis (NUA, 2002).

On several occasions while conducting online observation within the Virtual Reality (VR) community, Williams (2003) discovered that on the same day one entire class from an American university entered the community in a practice session of online participant observation, while the previous evening a Master's student from a university in the United Kingdom was gathering chat data for their thesis. It would be naive to assume such an invasion on a social setting would not affect respondents' behavior. Further issues of access are altered in light of the above. As is commonly known, gaining access to setting is hierarchical process, first gaining approval from the so-called gatekeeper, followed by ground-level negotiations with the actual research participants. Although Williams adhered to this process, it became apparent that many other researchers had conducted their research without such safeguards. Granted, many of these individuals may have been student researchers, but the status of the researcher cannot negate the ethical dilemmas of "harvesting" data.

As these ethical dilemmas hinder research online, so do the problems of response rates. In tandem with offline recruitment for focus groups, it is recommended that more individuals be approached that are needed to make up a viable number for the group. Reasons for this include possible group atrophy and no-shows (Bloor et al., 2000). One benefit of the online environment is the relative ease and speed at which a researcher can identify and contact a large group of individuals. With this advantage and the relative inexpense of sending e-mails, Witmer, Colman, and Katzman (1999) were able to canvass over five hundred possible respondents for their research. Similarly, Williams (2003) had access to over one thousand possible respondents. Yet, such voluminous numbers do not guarantee good response rates. While Witmer, Colman, and Katzman (1999) received an overall response rate of those wishing to participate of 20.7 percent, Williams's rate was a mere 5 percent. However, this disparity can be explained by examining the types of research conducted. Witmer, Colman, and Katzman (1999) were disseminating online questionnaires, which involve less commitment and time in contrast to Williams's participants, who would be involved in the research for over two months. More so, Witmer, Colman, and Katzman (1999) required a statistically viable sample, whereas such concerns are less important for focus group research.

Although it has been established that statistical representativeness is of little importance in focus group research, this does not mean group size and composition can be ignored. Most research texts advocate group sizes between six and eight participants, warning that if a group is too large, moderation and transcription becomes complex (Bloor et al., 2000). Such concerns have to be recast when engineering focus groups in asynchronous online settings. The method of communication and mediation alters drastically from offline to online environments in which conversation becomes digitized making transcription redundant and mediation less problematic. This ultimately means groups can comprise larger numbers allowing for longer and more involving discussion, often resulting in threading (see later). While Murray (1997), in a study of health professionals online, opted for the conventional offline number of participants for the asynchronous online focus group (6–8), it was later acknowledged that a larger group may have yielded richer and more detailed discussion. This assumption was corroborated in Robson's research of inflammatory bowel disease sufferers. With an asynchronous online focus group subscription of 57 respondents, Robson encountered threading in discussions with multiple topics simultaneously discussed. Furthermore, the larger number ensured that participants remained open, responsive, and familiar with each other that encouraged a hands-off approach with minimal guidance and questioning from the researcher.

In light of both Murray's (1997) and Robson's (1999) findings, Williams (2003) compared two online asynchronous focus groups of different size compositions. The first group (which we call here "AW") was comprised of 45 respondents in comparison to 15 in the second group (called here "vzones"). The same discussion starter questions were disseminated to both groups simultaneously beginning on day one, with the last question delivered on day 55 (see Figure 1.1).

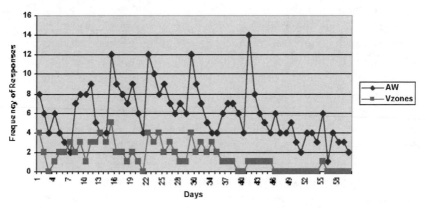

Figure 1.1

While it was expected that the larger group (AW) would generate more postings, one of the more interesting observations was the difference in group cohesion. As can be identified from Figure 1.1, postings from the vzones group diminished substantially even though questions were still being asked of the group. An explanation for this arises from the group's lack of identity and enthusiasm due to their low number. In contrast, the AW group, with its larger subscription, continued to post throughout the two-month period. While it is prudent to acknowledge the exploratory nature of Williams's (2003) research and hence the differing nature of the focus groups to other health-oriented forums, it remains evident that smaller compositions within asynchronous online focus groups may lead to rapid group atrophy, characterized by a lack in posting, the absence of group identity, and a nonchalant attitude toward the research.

While it seems that recruiting participants online for research purposes has its advantages over offline equivalents, the researcher must be aware that not all research projects have a potential Internet population to draw on. The nature of Robson's (1999) and Williams's (2003) research naturally leads them to use Internet populations as a valuable source of information. This is also mirrored in several health and market research studies in which Internet populations were easily identified. The Internet as a mediation tool for research methods might be less useful to someone conducting research into homelessness, for example, where those to be interviewed are unlikely to have a definable online population.

Asynchronous Group Communications

The earliest and most widely used forms of computer-mediated group interaction are asynchronous, text-based message board or e-mail facilities. Advances in the capacity to incorporate graphical or animated elements in computerized communications have largely bypassed asynchronous forms of interaction, and they have remained resolutely text-based.

The desire to introduce physical elements into online communications has been irresistible, and is testament to how important physicality is to interpersonal communications (Selwyn and Robson, 1998). From "smiley faces" created with standard ASCII characters, to conventions of describing physical movements in parentheses ("action words"), to more sophisticated avatars, the inclusion of physical elements in online encounters has increased as the technology has advanced. However, text-based group interactions should not be viewed as the poor cousin to newer, flashier, prettier media that allow sound or graphical images (moving or still, cartoonlike or photographic) to be exchanged by participants. As McLaughlin (2000) argues, text-based interactions can be as experientially real as graphical VR interactions, if not more so, in just the same way that a reader can be as emotionally and experientially involved in a novel as in its big screen adaptation. In many ways, he argues, our capacity to immerse ourselves in the text, where we are active participants in the text with limitless capacity to interpret it, is much greater than our capacity to involve in graphically presented images of the same activity, where our role is as the observer, and the interpretations of form and movement are given to us. As Markham (1998, 210) states, "Just as the text cannot capture the nuance of the voice, the voice cannot capture the nuance of the text."

The earliest forms of online group communications were dial-up bulletin board services. Prior to the accession of the World Wide Web, these were services that were directly dialed to, and therefore were highly geographically concentrated because of the dial-up costs of accessing a particular location. In addition, because access did not require subscription to an Internet service provider, or browser software, for some years bulletin boards were accessible to a more socially diverse population than were Internet facilities. In many ways, bulletin boards have evolved into the web board services available today. Unlike other forms of text-based asynchronous group communications, web boards are entirely web-based rather than primarily e-mail–based. Located at web sites, and requiring the use of browser software to visit, contributors compose messages on online forms that are submitted through the browser. Some web boards require users to register before reading or contributing to discussions, while others allow anyone to read or contribute unchecked.

As a research tool, web boards that require registration have many strengths, particularly with regard to identification issues.[2] The registration process allows the researcher to retain control of the composition of the research sample, and also gather relevant background information on them by including it on the online registration form. Having registered to contribute to the web board, and surrendered their anonymity to the researcher, contributors need only then identify themselves on the board by a username, withholding from general view identifying information such as their real name, e-mail address, or IP address. Thus, researchers can retain greater control over protecting the identities of research participants, without having to resort to an open free-for-all. Web boards can be confusing to use, with e-mail–based forms of group communication still being a far more familiar medium. Setting up and running the board also requires a greater degree of technical competence than other e-mail–based forms of discussion do. As contributions are composed online, there is a time pressure on those paying dial-up costs for Internet connection, which is not present when composing e-mails offline.

Newsgroups are the other main form of "open access" asynchronous group communication, in the sense that you can visit them and read their contents without being "seen" as present or subscribed as part of a group. As newsgroups are e-mail–based, they are easy to use, and as with other e-mail–based forms of communications allow contributions to be composed offline, affording participants time to refine their contributions before submission. Visually, newsgroup discussions are very user-friendly: contributions are organized into conversational "threads" that are easy to navigate, allowing readers to follow (or avoid) discussions on topics of their choice. However, new newsgroups are much harder to set up than other forms of online group communication, discussions can't be closed off, and contributions can't have identifying information of the source of the contribution removed. Thus, in practical terms, newsgroups do not offer a viable option for the administration of online focus groups.

Distribution lists are e-mail–based discussion groups, with a single central e-mail address to which contributions are sent before they are automatically bounced off to the inboxes of those subscribed to the list. Although lacking the visual niceties of newsgroup threads, distribution lists have the user familiarity of e-mail, and a number of administration options that make them particularly attractive for research purposes. Subscription to the list can be closed off, allowing the list owner to specify who can take part in the discussion, and who has access to information about the discussion and its subscribers. Contributions can be sent in digest form, whereby individual e-mails are pooled and sent out as a single compilation of e-mails at specified intervals. The lists can be moderated, which allows the researcher to remove identifying header information, organize the order of messages into threads, and interject with their own prompts or questions as a "real-life" focus group moderator might. Distribution lists are relatively straightforward to set up and run, requiring no specialist software or expertise, and are similarly easy for research participants to contribute to.

Synchronous Online Focus Groups

Most market research that has taken advantage of online focus groups has primarily employed asynchronous technologies for mediation. As detailed above, asynchronous forms of online communication include e-mail, listserv mailing lists, and USENET Newsgroups. Similarly Murray (1997), Robson (1999), and Williams (2003) utilized asynchronous online focus groups in their research. More recently, however, synchronous or temporally co-present communications technologies have been used in mediating online focus groups (Stewart, Eckermann, and Zhou, 1998). Synchronous forms of online communication vary greatly and are advancing at an exponential rate; some of the more popular include Internet Relay Chat (IRC) and America Online's infamous chatrooms.

Perhaps less familiar are those synchronous forms of online communication that allow for both text-based and graphical interaction that have emerged because of higher bandwidths and faster processor speeds. These "communities" emerged from the MUDs (Multi User Dungeons or Domains) and MOOs (Object Oriented MUDs) that were, and still are, very popular forms of text-based "real-time" communication. Mediating a focus group in "real time" has several benefits over alternative asynchronous methods. First, temporal co-presence intensifies online interactions, creating an atmosphere in which discussions can flourish. The immediacy of synchronous communication online makes it akin to that of offline communication within focus groups. This heightened sense of immediacy in chat leads to the expression of more emotion and more heated exchanges. Emotion can be readily expressed within synchronous forms of communication, because of the realization that IRC is more oral than literate—the latter being characteristic of asynchronous communication.

Although synchronous communication is written and not spoken, many of its linguistic characteristics mirror the spoken word. This is seen in the increased used of phatic communication,[3] such as "gee," "hmm," and "lol" (laughing out loud), which is typical of speech, not of writing (Sternberg, 1998). Such inferences can help judge the mood of the group and aid in more fruitful interpretation of group dynamics, processes, and meaning. The findings of Kiesler and Sproull (1992) also are of importance when interpreting data from synchronous online focus groups. In their study of decision making via Computer-Mediated Communication (CMC), it was found that the temporal duration of discussion was increased; that status barriers were subject to atrophy; that the groups decision was affected by the equalizing of high and low status; that the influence on the group decision of the group member who first advocated a decision proposal is attenuated; that individual participation in the group discussion is equalized; and that the shift between aggregate opinions held by group members before, during, and after discussion was exaggerated. Whereas Kiesler and Sproull's experiments were conducted in an asynchronous environment, we advocate that the above effects are amplified in synchronous discussion online. These effects clearly hold consequences for the interpretation of the data attained from online focus groups. While the equalization of group participation is a welcome effect, the exacerbation and attenuation of opinions and decisions as a result of the medium may place questions on the reliability and validity of group responses.

The heightened sense of immediacy produced by synchronous communication online also creates a more complex set of interactions, often resulting in real-time "threading," in which multiple conversations overlap and interweave, presenting a seemingly chaotic script. For those creating the script, this chaos is easily managed and interpreted, but for an outsider the interactions are confusing and often frustrating. This led both Stewart, Eckermann, and Zhou (1998) and Williams (2003) to conclude that the task of mediating these discussions is both challenging and wearisome. Greater moderator skills are then needed if synchronous online focus groups are to be employed, meaning the researcher not only requires the skills of a conventional moderator but also a familiarity with the technology used to mediate the discussions.

Yet, before such concerns plague the researcher, the potential difficulty of organizing the time and place of a real-time online focus group must be addressed. The first advantage of using computer-mediated discussions is the collapse if geographical restrictions. International online focus groups can be achieved with little stress on resources and costs. Yet, while the international element in Williams's (2003) research allowed for rich cross-cultural discussions, setting up a time and place for synchronous online focus groups proved problematic because of differing time zones. When times were set, Williams also was aware of the possible disparity in responses from participants. Those starting their day may have responded differently from those who had just finished lunch, or those who were tired after a long day. While the VR world had its own virtual time, it was clear that many in the group were suffering from a form of virtual jetlag.

Online Focus Groups in Virtual Graphical Environments

While it has been identified that synchronous forms of online communication differ significantly from asynchronous modes in content, form, and style, a more recent development in CMC technology may herald a completely new way for social interaction. Networked VR or Graphical MUDs (as they are more commonly referred to) are to some degree platforms where multiple users are not only able to communicate via text in a synchronous fashion, but are also presented with a graphical representation of the world within which they are communicating (Schroeder, 1997). This "world," which was until recently only "imagined" within textual MUDs, varies in its visual representation between the dozen or so platforms that currently exist online (see Roehl, 1996, 1997).

The networked VR platform used by Williams to conduct his graphical online focus group was 3-D, allowing participants to navigate and move around in a space akin to an offline environment. In this system, participants were represented by avatars, a graphical version of the person behind the home computer. If preferred, each participant could alter the appearance of their avatar by choosing from a list containing a myriad of alternative forms. These forms ranged from male to female avatars of differing dress and demeanor to inanimate and fantasy characters more analogous to the gaming genre that inspired the creation of many of these worlds. Once a suitable visual representation had been chosen, communication occurred via text, which was displayed in a window beneath the graphical interface. This combination of graphics and text in a communications medium led to an entirely different experience of conducting an online focus group.

At the outset, it was recognized that by stimulating more of the senses networked VR created the feeling of "being somewhere," coexisting in a locale both physically (graphically/visually) and textually (and in some cases verbally/auditory), which allowed for more engaging discussions. As Schroeder comments "the combined effect of using text, navigating in a 3-D environment and engaging with others via avatars...is greater than the sum of its parts" (1997, 8). So, to claim that networked VR is simply a MUD plus pictures is a gross oversight. Not only are discussions heightened in the textual sense but also forms of visual communication, until recently void in online communication, allow for a richer form of social interaction. Of the many concerns that have plagued Internet research is that of the lack of proxemical (use of space) and kinesical (body movement) features that aid in interpretation and analysis in the offline setting. Yet, the graphical environment goes a long way toward eradicating these concerns. Each avatar is ascribed a detailed set of animated emotions, so if someone in the group was in disagreement with an opinion they could shake their head, likewise if someone agreed with another avatar's statement they could jump for joy. Such forms of communication through gesture and body language adequately mirror their offline equivalents allowing for a more thorough interpretation of emotion and opinion within the online group.

Yet, while there are clear advantages in conducting online focus groups in a graphical environment, Williams (2003) had to contend with a quite unique set of issues that had to be addressed before any discussions took place. While it was recognized that the successful recruitment for the focus group would not depend upon the accessibility of the venue to the participants—with the venue being brought to their own living room or study via a modem—the setting for the discussions was still paramount. As Bloor et al. (2000) comment, there is no such thing as a neutral venue for a focus group, and that whatever setting is chosen, it needs to be recognized that the venue itself will impact on the data collected. A virtual setting is no different in this respect in that whatever graphical environment is chosen, it may, like an offline equivalent, hold several connotations that could affect the way participants interact. Given the "flexible" nature of many networked VR platforms, Williams was able to choose from an array of possible environments, ranging from the conventional four-walled virtual seminar room (with virtual tea and biscuits for that added comfort) to a quiet open field on a bright sunny day, or to the extreme an underwater fantasy world.

In adhering to the naturalistic notion that the research should be carried out in ways that are sensitive to the nature of the setting, a set of requirements was needed (Hammersley and Atkinson, 1995). First, it was decided that the chosen environment should be private, only those participating in the group and the researcher should be present; second, the setting should be free from surveillance—many of the worlds are subject to constant supervision by behavior monitors, which can create an atmosphere tension and suppression; third, there should be as little distraction as possible—many worlds provide avenues for distraction such as games and virtual shopping malls, while being fun to navigate such amusements may distract from the discussion; and, finally, the environment would not represent an institutional or unwelcoming atmosphere. The eventual discussions took place in an open field, where each participant was informed that only those involved in the discussions were present (some cunning and mischievous individuals have been known to create avatars that consist of one pixel, granting them relative invisibility within the graphical world).

While the above environment was effective in fostering a dynamic discussion, Williams (2003) concluded that further steps could be taken to improve the setting. Although researchers might have to contend with the issues of selecting a venue in the real world, conducting online focus groups within VR environments grants us the opportunity to enter more comfortable surroundings with little disruption in geographical terms. Yet, even these environments are not without their drawbacks. In this case, Williams advocates the engineering of an online setting from scratch bearing in mind the research participants' wishes and opinions. Many networked VR platforms encourage their members to "build" property within existing worlds, and to some extent advocate the building of entirely new worlds for whatever purpose. This poses the researcher with a unique opportunity to generate a setting that mirrors both their and the participant's requirements, ideally reducing the setting's influence on the data collected. However, in acknowledging the above, it is ultimately the technology that is being used to mediate the communication that will affect the data gathered (see above on synchronous online focus groups).

Interpreting Forms of Online Data

Reservations about online communications and research often focus on the lack of nonverbal data such as setting, expression, movement, phatic noise, and the like. Text-only online data are "all-inclusive text," making it harder to identify its different elements. These elements are easily distinguishable in conventional face-to-face interactions, allowing them to become primary targets for analysis. In traditional offline settings, the convention is to see these separate elements contributing to a whole meaning. By imposing such separation on the all-inclusive text of online data, while delineation is less rigid, it is useful to tease out these elements in order to counter arguments about the depthlessness of textual online communication. To this end, three features can be identified that have comparable characteristics with accepted offline data categories:

1. Form—comparable to "context" in offline research. E-mail, web board messages, chatrooms, and the like all have particular background expectancies and shared understandings.
2. Style—comparable to nonverbal cues in offline research. The conveyance of meaning through idiomatic forms of expression (emoticons, line width, use of capitals, color, and font).
3. Content—comparable to the verbal elements of offline data—the words participants use to express themselves.

All three elements have considerable bearing on where online research might take place, how research is conducted in these settings, and what kind of analyses are used. For example, setting up a focus group within a chatroom holds quite distinct challenges from holding a focus group over a distribution list. The kinds of data generated in both settings also are significantly different. Data collected in a chatroom will exhibit features associated with synchronous forms of textual communication. Overly stylistic content, disrupted adjacency (temporal lag between responses), overlapping exchanges, and topic delay all have to be contended with during mediation and analysis. Asynchronous modes, such as e-mail, are less likely to be littered with stylistic responses, with more focus on content, fostering more considered narratives. Whereas both modes of communication are viable for research purposes, the kinds of data produced are significantly different to warrant careful consideration when planning the use of online focus groups.

Ethical Considerations of Conducting Online Focus Groups

The speed, ease, and low cost of computer-mediated social research makes it an appealing option. However, the ethical considerations of online focus groups must temper the enthusiastic rush. Old ethical guidelines and procedures must be revisited and reframed in this new style of focus group, and anticipated carefully in the design stage of the research. Such considerations must take account of both codes of conduct relating to behavior in computer-mediated communities, and the codes of conduct relating to the practice of social research.

The acceptable behavior of Internet users is governed by a combination of service providers' acceptable use policies (AUPs), codes of conduct, and the implications of certain laws. AUPs are contractual agreements made between users and service providers that to some degree define how the user can use the network. Largely similar in what they cover, these AUPs outline what is and isn't allowed on the particular network, usually with a strong emphasis on responsible use of the network and not affecting the availability of the network to others. Informal codes of conduct developed naturally by online communities as the Internet grew and developed. These outline standard practices for the various services available over the Internet (e-mail, newsgroups, IRC, etc.) and define what is acceptable behavior within these areas. These codes are known as "netiquette" and should be required reading for anyone new to the Internet. These codes of conduct along with civil and cyber rights issues are continually being discussed, developed, and defended by the online community through organizations such as Computer Professionals for Social Responsibility (CPSR), the Electronic Frontier Foundation (EFF), Cyber Rights and Cyber Liberties, and the Association of Internet Researchers (AoIR). The document *RFC1855*, produced by the Internet Engineering Task Force (IETF) provides a minimum set of netiquette guidelines, in a format that allows organizations to take and adapt it for their own use. Covering one-to-one communications, one-to-many communications, and information services, these guidelines have a strong emphasis on observing the specific guidelines and culture of the group or medium you are participating in. It also highlights that the Internet is a global community constituted of a diversity of cultures, religions, and lifestyles that users should be tolerant of and open-minded about. Beyond broader general netiquette guides many Internet communities have created their own specific set of rules or guidelines that apply just to that particular group.

There are a variety of laws that relate to the use of computers and communication technology (for example, in Britain, the *Data Protection Act 1998* and the *Computer Misuse Act 1990*). The laws that are of particular relevance to conducting research are primarily the data protection and privacy laws, as these address an individual's right to privacy and protection of personal information that they give to companies or organizations. The *Data Protection Act 1998* requires those storing personal information about people on a computer to have adequate security in place to protect that data, and to be registered. Although attention to legal issues pertaining to computerized communications is important, usually adherence to AUPs and netiquette will meet with legal requirements.

Although contracts with service providers and laws are the most structured, more informal codes of conduct seem to hold more weight, especially regarding what is deemed as acceptable behavior. This is partly because they have been created by the communities themselves, but also because they are more widely known and understood by users than AUPs and relevant laws.

When planning online focus group research, these considerations must be combined with requirements of ethical guidelines of social research. While these guidelines may be more familiar to social researchers, they need rethinking in their application in an online context. Seeking consent from those who are recruited for an online focus group is relatively straightforward and comparable to eliciting consent in more traditional situations. Ostensibly, the idea of the confidentiality of identifying information in any written report of the research seems fairly straightforward. However, the risk of deductive disclosure is very real in research in computerized settings, and must be carefully anticipated during the planning of an online focus group and the identification of potential populations to be researched.

"Arguably, the Internet is a computerized nation of cyber-Springdales, where in order to retain their character and viability, small towns never grow into Metropolises, instead spawning more small towns, each in some way characteristically distinct from the other.... To describe and convey the character of a computer mediated community or group, in so very many cases, is to identify it in all but name" (Robson and Robson, 1999, 234).

In CMC, complete anonymity is almost impossible to guarantee, as information about the origin of a computer-transmitted message is, for most users, almost impossible to remove. Although the absence of anonymity in research does not mean researchers cannot guarantee confidentiality to research subjects, in computer-mediated research this is also more difficult to achieve, especially in online focus groups. Traditional procedures for storage of data and anonymizing participants are complicated in a medium where the original data are routinely available to other participants. Any research quoting or explicitly referring to an article posted in any kind of group discussion cannot prevent some level of identification of the author of that message by others in the group. If discussions are set up in a way that disguises the headers of a message, this identification need only be confined to the username chosen by the author, but if headers are left on, the situation is comparable to sending offline focus group participants home with a full transcript of the discussion together with the names and addresses of all those present. One research participant in Williams's research took up the issue of anonymity and disclosure in the early stages of the study, highlighting the awareness of these issues to Internet users generally:

Dear Matthew Williams,
This is your reply though you did NOT clearly state to participants which "role" they will play in the project"; I believe I have a fairly clear understanding. I think my input may be helpful. Enrol me please. But please note:
Remy :}) [<---notice distinctive mark...others recognize me by this. Many of us

know each other so well that even with removing sexual etc. inferences in our speech, we can still figure out who it is. In my case, I have found that few recognize me without my smiley at the end of sentences. Other personal marks such as my constant typo of remeber instead of remember and ..... long run on sentences etc...styles, are almost impossible to completely disguise and still be able to reply in our own words. Is anonymity to protect us?]
Remy

The known or foreseeable risks of participating in any research project must be outweighed by the potential or probable benefits of the research findings, but the ability to do this can be undermined in a setting where the research process and data can be so easily shared by others.

The idea that research is a two-way process, which should benefit both the researcher and the researched, is no longer a principle confined to academic feminism, where it had its roots (Reinharz, 1983). The ease and speed of transmitting information by computer lends itself to the fulfillment of this principle. Participants can review and reflect on data much more easily than in traditional, terrestrial research, where such tasks are time consuming and costly, and practical constraints of doing research may prevent the fulfillment of such good intentions. The ethos of computer-mediated communities contributes to the importance that should be placed on realizing principles relating to this issue: principles of nonhierarchical information sharing that pervade Internet communities make sharing and disseminating of research findings to participant groups singularly appropriate.

Focus Group Methodology

Conventional focus group methodology lends itself to the online setting in several ways. Focus groups aim to generate responses to questions or stimuli that are framed in the interactions of those in any given group (Bloor et al., 2000). The advent of the Internet and networked communications allows large groups to either be approached or formed for such purposes. Questions and stimuli can be provided over e-mail or accessed via web pages. Focus group methodology is also advanced by the advent of networked communications. Participants can be questioned over longer periods of time, given the ephemeral nature of Internet communications. Larger numbers can be managed in asynchronous settings, allowing for a broader understanding of the subject matter. Asynchronous communications also allow for participants to construct more considered narratives, providing a depth that might be absent in uttered data. Yet, along with these advantages come complications that may prove too cumbersome for the researcher: primarily, identifying and recruiting individuals for online focus groups is problematic. Many Internet users might initially agree to take part, but quickly withdraw acquiescence before research begins. This may be because of the transient nature of Internet populations, and a lack of face-to-face communication. The choice of "venue," times of interviews, and duration are all complicated by the international nature of some Internet groups. Also, the analysis, interpretation, and representation of digital data are yet to be fully explored, and hence any claims made from online research may be subject to question. Finally, the advent of new broadband technologies, increased use of graphical content, and an expanding online population will require an online method that is both responsive and adaptive in order to utilize and navigate a rapidly changing environment.

Notes

1   For a review, see Joinson (1998).

2   See the MGH project described by Prandy et al. (2001).

3   "Phatic" language is language used more for the purpose of establishing an atmosphere than for conveying information or meaning.

References

Baym, N. "The Emergence of Community in Computer-Mediated Communication." In *CyberSociety*, ed. S. Jones, 138–163. Newbury Park, CA: Sage, 1995a.

———— "The Performance of Humor in Computer-Mediated Communication," *Journal of Computer-Mediated Communication 1*, No. 2, 1995b.

Bloor M., Frankland J., Thomas M., and Robson K. *Focus Groups in Social Research*. London: Sage, 2000.

Correll, S. "The Ethnography of an Electronic Bar: The Lesbian Café," *The Journal of Contemporary Ethnography 24*, No. 3, 1995.

Hammersley, M., and Atkinson, P. *Ethnography: Principles in Practice (2nd ed.)*, London: Routledge, 1995.

Hine, C. *Virtual Ethnography*. London: Sage, 2000.

Joinson, A. N. "Causes and effects of disinhibition on the Internet." In *The Psychology of the Internet*, ed. J. Gackenbach, 43–60. New York: Academic Press, 1998.

Kiesler, S., and Sproull, L. "Group decision making and communication technology," *Organizational behavior and human decision processes*, 52 (1992), 96–123.

Markham, A. *Life Online: Researching Real Experience in Virtual Space*. Walnut Creek, CA: AltaMira, 1998.

McLaughlin, J. "The Name Still Remains the Same." *WebNet Journal 2*, No. 1 (January–March 2000).

Merton, R. K. and Kendall, P. L. "The Focused Interview." *American Journal of Sociology 51* (1946): 541–557.

Murray, P. "Using virtual focus groups in qualitative health research." *Qualitative Health Research 7*, No. 4 (1997).

NUA. (2002) Internet Survey, http://www.nua.com/surveys/how_many_online/index.html

Prandy, S. L., Norris, D., Lester, J., and Hoch, D. B. "Expanding the Guidelines for Electronic Communication with Patients: Application to a Specific Tool," *Journal of the American Medical Informatics Association 8*, No. 4(2001).

Reinharz, S. "Experiential analysis: A contribution to feminist research." In *Theories of Women's Studies*, eds. Gloria Bowles and Renate Duelli Klein, 192–209. London: Routledge and Kegan Paul, 1983.

Robson, K. "Employment Experiences of Ulcerative Colitis and Crohn's Disease Sufferers." Unpublished Ph.D. diss., Cardiff University, 1999.

Robson, K., and Robson, M. "Your Place or Mine? Ethics, the Researcher and the Internet." In *Exploring Cybersociety: Social, Political, Economic and Cultural Issues (Volume 2)*, eds. J. Armitage and J. Roberts. Newcastle: University of Northumbria, 1999.

Roehl, B. "Shared Worlds," *VR News 5*, No. 8 (1996): 14–19.

——— "Shared Worlds," *VR News 6*, No. 9 (1997): 10–15.

Schroeder, R. "Networked Worlds: Social Aspects of Multi-User Virtual Reality Technology," *Sociological Research Online 2*, No. 4 (1997).

Selwyn, N., and Robson, K. "Using e-mail as a research tool," *Social Research Update 21*(1998), http://www.soc.surrey.ac.uk/sru/SRU21.html.

Sharf, B. "Beyond netiquette: The ethics of doing naturalistic discourse research on the Internet." In *Doing Internet Research: Critical Issues and Methods for Examining the Net*, ed. S. Jones, 243–256. Thousand Oaks, CA: Sage, 1999.

Sternberg, J. "It's All in the Timing: Synchronous Versus Asynchronous Computer-Mediated Communication," paper presented at 3rd Annual Conference of the New Jersey Communication Association, Montclair, New Jersey, 1998. http://homepages.nyu.edu/~js15/p-time.htm.

Stewart, F., Eckermann, E., Zhou, K. "Using the Internet in Qualitative Public Health Research: A Comparison of Chinese and Australian Young Women's Perceptions of Tobacco Use." *Internet Journal of Health Promotion*, 1998. http://www.monash.edu.au/health/IJHP/1998/12.

Williams, M. "Virtually Criminal: Deviance and Harm within Online Environments." Unpublished Ph.D. diss., Cardiff University, 2003.

Witmer, D. F., Colman R. W., and Katzman S. L. "From Paper-and-Pencil to Screen-and-Keyboard." In *Doing Internet Research*, ed. S. Jones, 145–161. London: Sage, 1999.

Researching OURNET: A Case Study of a Multiple Methods Approach

ॐॐ

Sharon S. Kleinman

PEOPLE ARE INCREASINGLY using the Internet to participate in online groups. These groups, which range from soap opera fan clubs (Baym, 1997) to professionally oriented groups for women in science and engineering (Kleinman, 1998) to health-oriented support groups for people with cancer (Turner, Grube, and Meyers, 2001), are gaining researchers' attention because of the diverse and evolving activities that are taking place in them. Researchers from a variety of disciplines, including communication, anthropology, sociology, psychology, linguistics, and science and technology studies, are facing the challenges of devising reliable, valid, and ethical methods for studying interactions in computer-mediated contexts. These contexts differ from face-to-face on several dimensions that have important implications for the research process, including time and space constraints, modes of communication supported (both one-to-many and one-to-one), and a blurred distinction between public and private domains. This chapter explores the methodological and ethical challenges of researching an online group using a case study approach. The research process of a four-year qualitative case study of an online group is reviewed. Rationales for methodological choices are discussed, and suggestions are provided for researchers interested in studying online groups using the case study approach.

Case Study Approach

The case study is a productive and rewarding approach for investigating a wide range of social phenomena within online groups, including issues concerning community, interpersonal relationships, information exchange, and social support. Case studies of online contexts, like case studies of face-to-face contexts, are typically conducted when the researcher is interested in studying particular contextual conditions in order to investigate multiple issues of interest in depth. Case studies of online contexts, like case studies of face-to-face contexts, can be explanatory, exploratory, or descriptive.

Conducting a case study entails collecting, analyzing, and triangulating data from multiple sources. The data can be quantitative, qualitative, or a combination of both. The researcher uses data from the case study to establish a logical chain of evidence that supports an analysis. An appropriate theoretical framework informs the data collection and analysis processes.

In case studies of online groups, computers function as research assistants to a degree that is not possible in case studies of face-to-face groups. Computers can be used to access, manipulate, archive, and analyze data. Because computers can collect and store massive amounts of data quickly, inexpensively, and unobtrusively, a potential pitfall of automated data collection is that an overabundance of data is sometimes collected. As with any research approach, it is up to the researcher to appropriately define the boundaries of the data collected.

The evolving population of online groups, with their different goals, characteristics, and reasons for existence, represent a fertile realm for social research using the case study approach.

OURNET Case Study

The context for my case study was an online mailing list (listserv) called OURNET (a pseudonym), which had approximately eight hundred members worldwide who discussed issues of interest to women in science and engineering. The OURNET case study explored how some women in science and engineering are using an online group as a resource for social support, information, role models, and mentors (Kleinman, 1998). An online mailing list is an asynchronous one-to-many communication system. People who subscribe to the list receive all messages posted to it. OURNET was unmoderated and had no membership restrictions.

Of the many research approaches possible, conducting a case study of OURNET using a combination of several methods was most appropriate, because I was interested in exploring the benefits that this online group provided its members, rather than in testing hypotheses about online groups or computer-mediated communication. In other words, I was interested in studying "contextual conditions" (Yin, 1994, 13),[1] as the following research questions from the study illustrate:

1. What are people's reasons for joining an online discussion that identifies a marginalized group?
2. What are the perceived benefits of participating in an online discussion for members of a marginalized group?
3. How does people's level of identification with an online discussion group relate to their level of public participation?

4. What is the nature of the postings to an online discussion that identifies a marginalized group? (Kleinman, 1998, 28)

When I designed the OURNET study, I considered issues raised in a series of articles about online social research that appeared in a special issue of *The Information Society* (King, 1996; Reid, 1996), ideas presented in an article comparing the development of online social research to the development of anthropology (Kilker and Kleinman, 1997), guidelines proposed in an article about ethical research in the information age (Schrum, 1995) as well as discussions about the research process outlined in texts focusing on social research in traditional (non-online) contexts (Allport, 1942; Babbie, 1995; Fetterman, 1998; Krippendorff, 1980; Reinharz, 1992; Yin, 1994).

Three methods were used in the OURNET study—online participant observation, interviewing, and content analysis. Methodological issues that were addressed included: choosing appropriate data collection methods; obtaining representative samples of participants to interview and e-mail messages to content analyze; developing valid content analysis categories; assessing the reliability of the content analysis coding; and addressing copyright and fair use issues regarding e-mail messages posted to a public listserv.

Ethical issues that were addressed included: gaining access to the research site; obtaining consent from the fluctuating population of participants in the online group; engaging participants as coresearchers in the data analysis process; and giving back to participants by making the research findings available to them.

Data Sources

Case studies of online groups, like case studies of face-to-face groups, draw on multiple sources of data. There were four sources of data for the OURNET study: e-mail messages; interviews; online participant observation; and the membership roster. Each of these data sources has a different set of strengths and weaknesses, as Table 1.1 summarizes. Some of the strengths and weaknesses of the sources of data used for a case study of an online group parallel the strengths and weaknesses of these sources of data for a case study of a face-to-face group. In instances where the strengths and weaknesses diverge depending on whether the context is online or face-to-face, it is because of the role that the computer plays in a case study of an online group. For example, as Table 1.1 indicates, one strength of online participant observation is that it is unobtrusive because the researcher is visually anonymous to online group participants. In contrast, face-to-face participant observation generally would not be unobtrusive and would not allow the researcher to be visually anonymous.

Using the four data sources in consort allowed me to benefit from their varied strengths and also tended to minimize the effects of their weaknesses. Participant observation over a four-year period allowed me to become familiar with the group's customs and members, and it allowed me to unobtrusively experience the events of OURNET as they unfolded. During subsequent telephone interviews, I was able to converse about OURNET with a purposive sample of members in a focused and informed manner. E-mail messages provided an accurate, chronological record of OURNET discussions. They were downloaded easily and unobtrusively and then content analyzed. Similarly, the membership roster provided an accurate snapshot of the OURNET population. It also was downloaded easily and unobtrusively and then content analyzed.

Table 1.1: OURNET Case Study Data Sources

Data Source	Strengths	Weaknesses
Participant observation	* Researcher can experience context of events as they unfold in real time or use computer to archive online interactions for later analysis * Researcher can contribute to and/or influence discussion threads * Unobtrusive * Researcher is visually anonymous to participants	* Time consuming * Researcher might influence events because participants know they are being observed, though this effect is generally ameliorated by the visual anonymity of computer-mediated communication
Interviews	* Interviewer can focus on issues of research interest using closed and open-ended questions * Interviewees can be selected based on specific criteria * Interviews can be audio-taped and transcribed for later content analysis * Interviewees contribute to interpretation and analysis, commenting on their experiences and observations	* Selection bias * Inaccuracies due to interviewees' poor recall * Bias due to poorly constructed questions or interviewer's inadequate knowledge of group * Interviewees control which and how much information they reveal

Table is continued on the next page.

E-mail messages	* Downloadable for multiple reviewing and contentanalysis * Unobtrusive * Exact, containing names, references, details of events * Chronological record of many events over a long time period * Can be quantified * Can be keyword searched * Can be sorted and analyzed by computer or by hand	* Accessibility—access to ongoing discussions and/or archives might be restricted * Archives could be incomplete * Latent content of messages subject to interpretation
Membership roster	* Downloadable for analysis * Unobtrusive means of assessing demographics of the group * Can be quantified * Might indicate members' geographic locations, especially those with accounts from foreign countries in which the e-mail address suffix indicates country of origin	* Personal e-mail addresses (as contrasted with work e-mail addresses) do not indicate member's institutional affiliation * Accessibility—might be restricted

Interviewing Procedures

At the beginning of the OURNET project, I posted a message to OURNET in which I identified myself as a long-term OURNET member, explained the research project, and asked for permission to study the group and for volunteer interviewees. My e-mail address and home telephone number were included in the message so that anybody with questions or concerns could contact me easily. Dozens of people volunteered to be interviewed, and nobody expressed concern about my presence in the group as a researcher.

In-depth, semistructured interviews were conducted with OURNET members in order to learn about the insiders' perspectives about OURNET. Interviews were conducted over the telephone because the interviewees lived all over the world. With the interviewees' permission, the interviews were audiotaped. The recordings were transcribed for analysis.

The pool of interviewees represented the range of participation levels—lurkers (those who did not post public messages to the listserv), occasional contributors, and frequent contributors. The interviewees' self-reports of participation were compared with the number of messages that they posted during the data collection period and no discrepancies were found. Interviewing lurkers was necessary for investigating their motivation for joining the online group and perceived benefits. These topics are particularly interesting from the perspective of lurkers, because one of the most commented-on aspects of the Internet is its interactivity, even though many more people lurk than participate in online environments (Kiesler, 1997; Rojo and Ragsdale, 1997; Sproull and Faraj, 1997).

Although dozens of people volunteered to be interviewed, 21 interviews were conducted. I stopped interviewing OURNET members when I reached the point of data saturation—when many different people were providing me with the same or similar information. Nineteen of the interviews were with current OURNET members and two were with former members. Interviewing former members allowed me to address the limitations and utility of online group membership with people who might have different perspectives on the group that led them to leave.

Content Analysis Procedures

All of the e-mail messages posted to OURNET during a consecutive 125-day period that included one summer month (August) and two fall months (September and October) were archived. These three months were chosen because I anticipated variations in people's participation in OURNET during the summer months because many OURNET members were academics working on a nine-month schedule. In selecting the months for collecting messages, the goal was to ensure that the messages sampled were representative of the larger population from which they were chosen. This was an instance in which having been a long-term participant observer in OURNET provided insights into which months had typical participation levels.

As a systematic examination of the OURNET discussions, content analysis was used to assess how frequently OURNET members addressed various topics and in which contexts and to identify patterns and conventions in message postings. These data were triangulated with information that the interviewees reported about the content and purposes of OURNET messages.

Assumptions underlying the content analysis were that the content of the e-mail messages could be categorized inductively and that online discussions evolve over time. The implication of the second assumption was that the e-mail messages should be studied in the context of conversation threads—clusters of messages with interrelated content composed of seed messages that catalyzed at least one response message. The unit of analysis was threads (Sproull and Faraj, 1997). The threads were discerned by reviewing the messages in the archive in chronological order. Messages to which nobody in the discussion group replied publicly were categorized as solo messages.

The archive of OURNET messages was analyzed in chronological order three times. The first review of the messages focused on their manifest content, what was directly in the text of the messages, as contrasted with their latent content, the underlying meaning of the messages (Babbie, 1995; Krippendorff, 1980). Demographic information about the message senders that was indicated in their e-mail addresses and signature files also was compiled during the first review.

E-mail addresses and signature files often provide demographic information that is useful for the researcher. For example, an e-mail address with the ".edu" domain, which is an abbreviation for education, typically indicates affiliation with an academic institution as student, staff, or faculty. Other common domains include ".com," an abbreviation for commercial, ".gov," an abbreviation for governmental, ".org," an abbreviation for nonprofit organization, and ".mil," an abbreviation for United States military. A signature file consists of several lines of text identifying the e-mail account owner. It sometimes includes the person's name, institutional affiliation, job title, and links to personal or professional web sites. If the signature file feature has been activated, these lines of text are automatically appended to the end of each message sent from the e-mail account. Because people sometimes subscribe to online groups using their personal e-mail addresses from commercial Internet Service Providers, such as AOL, rather than their work e-mail addresses, it is not always possible to discern institutional affiliation information from e-mail addresses and signature files.

Also during the first analysis, categories of messages were discerned inductively. Key informants who had been long-time OURNET members were then asked to review the categories to check for construct validity. Key informants are participants in a study who go beyond providing the researcher with facts and opinions about the research issue under study. Key informants share insights that lead the researcher to further inquiry or alternative interpretations. They also often provide evidence and/or access to information sources. In Whyte's (1955) famous face-to-face case study *Street Corner Society: The Social Structure of an Italian Slum*, the key informant was "Doc." A case study's comprehensiveness, accuracy, and depth of interpretation are often dependent on having good key informants, like Doc. I knew my two key informants from face-to-face contexts before I began the OUR-NET study. However, it is not necessary to know people from the context that is being studied beforehand—a particularly interested and helpful participant will often evolve into a key informant.

During the second analysis, the messages were coded into categories. In cases in which the content of a message fit more than one category, the message was coded based on the predominant content of the message. Another computer-mediated communication researcher coded a subset of the archived messages into the content categories to check the content analysis reliability. The intercoder reliability was 93 percent, so the coding was determined to be highly reliable.

The third analysis of the messages focused on discerning the topics of messages and patterns in discussion threads. The entire texts of the messages were analyzed, rather than just the subject header lines, because subject headers do not always reflect message content.

Methodological and Ethical Issues Addressed During the OURNET Study

Ethical issues that pertain to all forms of social research, such as obtaining informed consent from research participants, maintaining their privacy, and protecting them from harm, can be slippery in research about online groups because research standards for studying these groups have not yet been codified and because of the relative ease of data collection (Kilker and Kleinman, 1997; King, 1996).

The first methodological and ethical issue that every researcher must address involves gaining access to the research site. Because OURNET was a public listserv with no membership requirements, gaining access was not difficult; I subscribed to the list by sending an e-mail message to a computer that automatically added my e-mail address to the list of addresses that received all OURNET messages.

I had been an informal participant observer in OURNET for three years before I commenced the research project. However, once I began the project, I needed to obtain informed consent from OURNET participants to study their interactions and the content of their postings. Gaining informed consent from all participants in an ongoing online group can be a challenge, because online groups often have fluctuating populations; new members, including researchers, can join a public group without the group's knowledge or consent. (This would not necessarily be the case in online groups with restricted membership.)

Data concerning online groups can be collected relatively easily, inexpensively, and efficiently: a computer can be used unobtrusively as a research assistant to collect, archive, and even analyze e-mail messages without the group's knowledge or consent (Fetterman, 1998; Kilker and Kleinman, 1997). Unlike a sociologist studying a neighborhood, a researcher studying an online group might never meet face-to-face with the members of the online group that is being studied because the group members could be spread all over the world. Thus, even when the data collection process is interactive—involving telephone or e-mail interviews, for example—a researcher could forget on some level that they are dealing with real people who could be positively or negatively affected by the research process. This is less likely to occur in face-to-face case studies, because the researcher usually has opportunities to literally see the research participants as individuals.

One study of an online group for sexual abuse survivors (Finn and Lavitt, 1994) exemplifies researchers' insufficient attention to ethical issues concerning informed consent, confidentiality, and privacy in a manner that is reminiscent of Humphreys's (1970) infamous face-to-face *Tearoom Trade* study: Finn and Lavitt

> downloaded, analyzed, and published notes, making no request to the individuals of the group for permission. This occurred even though Finn reported the existence of a note from the moderator of the group saying that interested professionals who were not sexual abuse survivors were discouraged from joining the group. The exact dates and times that sample notes were posted, as well as the name of the group, appear in the published results. Finn states that since "messages posted on a BBS (bulletin board system) are public information," changing the names on the sample messages they reprinted would insure the privacy of the BBS users. (King, 1996, 122)[2]

While using pseudonyms might protect the privacy of the individual message posters, the researchers' actions in this case could have destroyed the group members' perception of the group as being a safe and private space for discussing personal issues (King, 1996). Because published reports could have had deleterious effects on the functionality of the group, it seems obvious that these researchers did not take adequate precautions to protect the people studied from harm.

Issues of informed consent, confidentiality, and privacy can be further complicated when a researcher is studying the archived e-mail messages of an online group that no longer exists.[3] It is still incumbent on the researcher to ensure confidentiality and to protect the privacy of those who wrote the e-mail messages. This is especially imperative when the research concerns a controversial topic or if reports about the research could in any way negatively affect those who were studied.

To address the issue of informed consent in the OURNET study, I posted a message to the group explaining the project and encouraging anyone with questions or concerns about it to contact me. In this message I also asked for volunteers to be interviewed about their experiences in the group. Dozens of people volunteered, and nobody expressed concern about my presence in the group as a researcher. It is possible that the fact that I mentioned in my e-mail message that I was a long-time OURNET member helped the participants to feel comfortable with the project. Nevertheless, someone who joined OURNET after I posted the message might have had concerns had they known about the project. I decided to take this risk because I thought that a daily message about the project requesting consent from new members would have been disruptive. To strengthen the informed consent, I announced the study again at the conclusion of the data collection period to see if any members who were new since my initial posting had any concerns.

Maintaining OURNET members' confidentiality and privacy was important because members often discussed controversial issues and revealed personal information in their messages to OURNET. As a first step toward protecting OURNET members' confidentiality and privacy, I used a pseudonym for the group (OURNET) and pseudonyms for all participants in reports about the project. In addition, all identifying information was stripped from excerpts of interview transcriptions and e-mail messages in reports about the project. However, an interested (and motivated) person might be able to discover the real name of the group and could then access the publicly available archive of OURNET messages and perform keyword searches using quotes from e-mail messages that were reprinted in research reports. At that point, it might be possible for the "researcher" to identify the sender of a message and the sender's institutional affiliation based on the signature file at the end of the message or the e-mail address from which the message originated. As I selected excerpts to reprint in reports, I was mindful of this potential breach of OURNET members' confidentiality and privacy and therefore refrained from reprinting some quotes (cf. Reid, 1996).

Addressing Issues of Copyright and Fair Use

Another methodological issue in this project involved the copyright ownership of e-mail messages posted to OURNET. "Under the Copyright Act of 1976 (title 17 of the *United States Code*) an unpublished work is copyrighted from the moment it is fixed in tangible form—for example, typed on a page.... Until the author formally transfers copyright...the author owns the copyright on an unpublished manuscript, and all exclusive rights due the owner of the copyright are also due the owner of an unpublished work" (American Psychological Association, 1994, 299).

The "tangible form" does not have to be permanent, but the "medium must be sufficiently permanent or stable to allow it to be perceived, copied or otherwise communicated for more than a transitory duration" (Moore, 1999, 501). This means that the author of an e-mail message owns the copyright, unless the author transfers it, or the e-mail message was a work for hire, or the author prepared the e-mail message within the scope of their job. There are other exceptions to copyright ownership that might apply to some e-mail messages, including works in the public domain, such as U.S. government works, or works on which copyright has expired.

Educators and students should exercise caution when downloading materials from the Internet for use in scholarly or instructional works "because there is a mix of works protected by copyright and works in the public domain on the network. Access to works on the Internet does not automatically mean that these can be reproduced and reused without permission or royalty payment and, furthermore, some copyrighted works may have been posted to the Internet without authorization of the copyright holder" (Moore, 1999, 631).

Although only a court of law can authoritatively determine on a case-by-case basis whether a particular use of copyrighted material is a fair use or not, there are guidelines concerning the fair use of copyrighted materials:

> Section 107 of the Copyright Act sets forth the four use factors which should be considered in each instance, based on the particular facts of a given case, to determine whether a use is a "fair use": (1) the purpose and character of use, including whether such use is of a commercial nature or is for nonprofit educational purposes, (2) the nature of the copyrighted work, (3) the amount and substantiality of the portion used in relation to the copyrighted work as a whole, and (4) the effect of the use upon the potential market for or value of the copyrighted work. (Moore, 1999, 626)

This section of the Copyright Act provides "examples of purposes that can involve fair use of copyrighted material, including criticism, comment, news reporting, teaching (including multiple copies for classroom use), scholarship, or research" (Moore, 1999, 524). Considering these stipulations, it seems likely that a court would consider the judicious quoting in an academic article of e-mail messages that had been posted to a public online group to be a fair use.

Determining Population Demographics

Determining the population demographics of an online group can be challenging. For one thing, people can add or remove themselves from an online group easily and often invisibly. The list's owner, administrator, or moderator might be willing to provide a copy of the membership roster to a researcher who has obtained informed consent from the group. This roster would be a snapshot of the population at one point in time. In the OUR-NET study, I e-mailed my request to the list administrator, and she told me which commands to use to download a publicly available membership roster that included members' e-mail addresses and names. Cross-referencing this information with information contained in archived e-mail messages enabled me to discern the gender distribution of OURNET members as well as their institutional affiliations (e.g., colleges, military, government), and to some extent their geographic locations.

To determine the gender distribution of OURNET members, the membership roster was examined. This process involved taking most names at face value as being typically masculine or feminine. However, some names are androgynous, some people use only their initials, and some people use nicknames. In addition, some online groups allow members to suppress their names and e-mail addresses from publicly available rosters. All of these permutations can make it difficult for a researcher to determine the gender distribution of the population in an online group or the gender of an individual member, without triangulating with other data or asking members directly on a questionnaire or during an interview. In addition, it can be difficult to judge the gender of a person in an online group based on a name if the name is foreign. Again, data triangulation—which might include reading messages the person posted to the group—can often solve this problem. I determined that one OURNET member with an Asian name that was unfamiliar to me was a woman when I read one of her postings about an experience that her husband had at work.

Obtaining Representative Samples

Obtaining representative samples of participants to interview and e-mail messages to content analyze were additional challenges in the data collection process of the OURNET project. Although in a qualitative, exploratory case study like the OURNET study it is not necessary to interview a random sample, it is still important to interview a representative sample. To address the issue of selection bias resulting from having volunteer interviewees, several interviewees were recruited based on the recommendations of others in the group. For the purposes of my study, it was important to interview members with diverse institutional affiliations, varied job statuses (professors, graduate students, and scientists working in industry) and diverse levels of participation in the group (lurkers and nonlurkers). To ensure that the interviewees were representative of the online group in terms of participation levels, the interviewees' self-reports of their OURNET participation were compared to their actual participation level, which was determined by examining the message archive. To ensure that the interviewees represented the diversity of institutional affiliations and job statuses, they were asked a series of demographic questions about their education level attained, age, institutional affiliation, job title, employment history, and the nature of their work.

Involving Group Members as Coanalysts and Giving Back to the Group

Engaging OURNET members as coanalysts was important for checking construct validity (Yin, 1994). Key informants who had been long-term OURNET members reviewed the content analysis categories and drafts of research reports. These informants helped refine content analysis categories, enhance interpretations of the diverse meanings and benefits of OURNET membership, and ultimately improve reports about the findings of the study (cf. Sharf, 1999).

At the end of the study, I made a report summarizing the findings available to OURNET members. This was my way of giving back to the group that had generously shared their experiences and insights and had allowed me to examine their online interactions.[4]

Concluding Thoughts on Triangulation and Research Ethics in Online Case Studies

This examination of the OURNET case study illustrated two main points in particular: (1) the importance of methodological and data triangulation in case studies of online groups for fostering a comprehensive and accurate analysis, and (2) the necessity of taking extra precautions to ensure that online social research is conducted in an ethical manner. In the OURNET study, I found that long-term participant observation provided the opportunity for me to become familiar with OURNET's members and its history (cf. Baym, 1997; Cherny, 1995). This familiarity enabled me to discuss past conversation threads and controversies in an informed manner with the interviewees. The in-depth interviews provided an opportunity for me to explore members' experiences in and perspectives about OURNET in a depth and with a sensitivity that other research approaches, such as surveys, would not necessarily allow. As a complement to the interviews, content analysis provided a systematic examination of members' participation patterns and the content of the messages.

Interview and content analysis data were iteratively analyzed and triangulated. Methodological and data triangulation were critical because any one research or data collection method developed for studying other social contexts is likely to be inadequate for online social contexts, especially at this relatively early stage of online social research (Kilker and Kleinman, 1997). This is the case for a variety of reasons, including that interactions in online contexts have reduced and different social cues, and communicators have reduced social presence in comparison to other communication contexts, such as face-to-face (Sproull and Kiesler, 1991; Walther, 1992; also cf. Short, Williams, and Christie, 1976). Moreover, people who join online groups have different levels of computer competence and "computer reticence" (Turkle, 1984, 1988). Just as people are variably comfortable in face-to-face contexts, in online environments people are variably comfortable both socially and technically, and their comfort level affects what they write, and even if they write anything at all. Data collection and analysis techniques need to take into account people's different levels of comfort and competence online.

The OURNET study also highlighted another quality of computer-mediated communication that should be factored into research designs: computer-mediated communication can be public or private (one-to-many or one-to-one). Public e-mail messages sent to an online group might only be a fraction of the interactions among group members. Members interact using private e-mail for a variety of reasons and in a variety of circumstances. Some of the circumstances include: when a topic is sensitive or controversial; when a person wishes to disclose personal information to a restricted audience; when a person's immediate goals or concerns differ from the group's; and when a person avoids public posting because of privacy concerns or fear of being flamed in response to what they write. Private e-mail conversations took place among members of OURNET—they were alluded to in public postings to the group. I was able to find out about these types of interactions during interviews with OURNET members.

Eighteen of the 21 interviewees reported that for various reasons at times they preferred to respond to people's messages via private e-mail rather than post messages to the entire discussion group. For example, one interviewee, a 45-year-old pharmaceutical consultant, reported that she rarely posted public messages to OURNET:

> I'm more likely to respond privately to people to issues that they raise that I don't
> think the whole group necessarily wants to read the answers to. There's a lot of pri-

vate e-mailing that goes on....
I will admit that I won't post sometimes because I don't want to deal with the has-
sle of dealing with a controversial subject. I might reply privately in that case
because I don't want to be deluged with messages.

As is the case in most online groups, in OURNET lurkers greatly out-
numbered those who contributed public messages. Eighty-one percent of
OURNET members did not post any public messages to the discussion
group during the observation period. The research design took into account
this typical online group participation pattern.

In sum, studying online groups using the case study approach is still a
relatively new endeavor, and the implications of this work as well as
researchers' ethical responsibilities are not always clear. As online groups
continue to evolve in ways we haven't yet imagined, researchers will
undoubtedly face methodological and ethical issues not touched on in this
chapter that will challenge us over and over again to refine our methods and
clarify our ethical responsibilities.

Notes

1   See Yin (1994) for a comprehensive description and rationale for the case study approach.

2   I apologize to the members of the group Finn and Lavitt (1994) studied for the additional attention. I bring up this case because since King's (1996) article was published, other
researchers have used the actual names of computer-mediated groups that they have studied in their reports.

3   "Archived e-mail and Usenet records represent an increasingly accepted source of data for
research, but these materials are becoming inaccessible as the technology to read old computer formats disappears and the computer tapes themselves decay," as Kilker (1999, 263)
found in examining a group from the 1970s.

4   See Reinharz (1992) for discussions of reciprocity in feminist social research that
informed the OURNET study.

References

Allport, G. *The Use of Personal Documents in Psychological Science*. New York: Social Science
    Research Council, 1942.
American Psychological Association. *Publication Manual of the American Psychological Association*.
    4th ed. Washington, DC: American Psychological Association, 1994.
Babbie, E. *The Practice of Social Research*. *7th ed*. New York: Wadsworth Publishing Company,
    1995.
Baym, N. K. "Interpreting Soap Operas and Creating Community: Inside an Electronic Fan
    Culture." In *Culture of the Internet*, ed. Sara Kiesler, 103–120. Mahwah, NJ: Lawrence
    Erlbaum Associates, 1997.

Cherny, L. "The MUD Register: Conversational Modes of Action in a Text-Based Virtual Reality." Ph.D. diss., Stanford University, 1995.

Fetterman, D. M. *Ethnography: Step by Step. 2nd ed.* Thousand Oaks, CA: Sage, 1998.

Finn, J., and M. Lavitt. "Computer Based Self-Help Groups for Sexual Abuse Survivors." *Social Work with Groups 17* (1994): 21–46.

Humphreys, L. R. A. *Tearoom Trade: Impersonal Sex in Public Places.* Chicago, IL: Aldine, 1970.

Kiesler, S. *Culture of the Internet.* Mahwah, NJ: Lawrence Erlbaum Associates, 1997.

Kilker, J. A. "Networking Identity: A Case Study Examining Social Interactions and Identity in the Early Development of E-Mail Technology." Ph.D. diss., Cornell University, 1999.

Kilker, J. A., and S. S. Kleinman. "Researching Online Environments: Lessons from the History of Anthropology." *The New Jersey Journal of Communication 5*, no. 1 (1997): 66–83.

King, S. A. "Researching Internet Communities: Proposed Ethical Guidelines for the Reporting of Results." *The Information Society 12* (1996): 119–127.

Kleinman, S. S. "Membership has its Benefits: Computer-Mediated Communication and Social Identification in an Online Discussion Group for Women in Science and Engineering." Ph.D. diss., Cornell University, 1998.

Krippendorff, K. *Content Analysis: An Introduction to its Methodology.* Newbury Park, CA: Sage, 1980.

Moore, R. L. *Mass Communication Law and Ethics. 2nd ed.* Mahwah, NJ: Lawrence Erlbaum Associates, 1999.

Reid, E. "Informed Consent in the Study of On-Line Communities: A Reflection on the Effects of Computer-Mediated Social Research." *The Information Society 12* (1996): 169–174.

Reinharz, S. *Feminist Methods in Social Research.* New York: Oxford University Press, 1992.

Rojo, A., and R. G. Ragsdale. "A Process Perspective on Participation in Scholarly Electronic Forums." *Science Communication 18*, no. 4 (1997): 320–341.

Schrum, L. "Framing the Debate: Ethical Research in the Information Age." *Qualitative Inquiry 1*, no. 3 (1995): 311–326.

Sharf, B. F. "Beyond Netiquette: The Ethics of Doing Naturalistic Discourse Research on the Internet." In *Doing Internet Research: Critical Issues and Methods for Examining the Net*, ed. S. Jones, 243–256. Thousand Oaks, CA: Sage, 1999.

Short, J., E. Williams, and B. Christie. *The Social Psychology of Telecommunications.* Chichester: John Wiley, 1976.

Sproull, L., and S. Faraj. "Atheism, Sex, and Databases: The Net as a Social Technology." In *Culture of the Internet*, ed. S. Kielser, 35–50. Mahwah, NJ: Lawrence Erlbaum Associates, 1997.

Sproull, L., and S. Kiesler. *Connections.* Cambridge, MA: The MIT Press, 1991.

Turkle, S. *The Second Self: Computers and the Human Spirit.* New York: Touchstone, 1984.

———. "Computational Reticence: Why Women Fear the Intimate Machine." In *Technology and Women's Voices: Keeping in Touch*, ed. C. Kramarae, 41–61. London: Routledge, 1988.

Turner, J. W., J. A. Grube, and J. Meyers. "Developing an Optimal Match within Online Communities: An Exploration of Computer-Mediated Communication Support Communities and Traditional Support." *Journal of Communication 51*, no. 2 (2001): 231–251.

Walther, J. B. "Interpersonal Effects in Computer-Mediated Interaction." *Communication Research 19*, no. 1 (1992): 52–90.

Whyte, W. F. *Street Corner Society: The Social Structure of an Italian Slum.* Chicago, IL: University of Chicago, 1955.

Yin, R. K. *Case Study Research: Design and Methods. 2nd ed.* Thousand Oaks, CA: Sage, 1994.

Managing Visibility, Intimacy, and Focus in Online Critical Ethnography

࿔࿔

Kathleen LeBesco

HISTORICALLY, ETHNOGRAPHIC RESEARCHERS have been drawn to discourse communities in order to gain a better understanding of the meanings that community members generate through conversation. This process typically involves extensive participant observation on the part of the researcher, which necessitates sharing considerable time and space with the community of interest, as well as the ability to step outside one's own agenda as a researcher. Critical ethnography puts a new spin on this qualitative interpretation of data, in that it is both rigorously scientific and functions as a tool for critiquing culture itself. Recently, critical ethnographers find themselves especially interested in the world of online discourse communities, where they have interpretive access to participants and conversations that might be otherwise restricted in the "real world." They also recognize that since the mid-1990s, with the boom in e-mail and Internet usage, a truly significant amount of important conversation is happening online that would be neglected if researchers were to take the place-sharing edict of traditional ethnography literally.

This chapter explores methodological issues I encountered in utilizing discourse analysis and critical ethnography in understanding conversations on two fat-related Internet sites (one newsgroup, one listserv). I describe the dilemmas I encountered while using these qualitative methods in the online environment, including: (1) how to navigate the issue of ethnographer visibility as participant/researcher in a text-only space; (2) how to handle the transition from group interviews (with which most participants are very comfortable) to individual interviews (which often arouse a sense of illicitness among participants used to public conversation); (3) how to deal with the exponential data overload generated by the ability to record all conversation electronically; and (4) how to reinvent the ethnographic notion that ethnography need involve the sharing of physical space and time with one's research subjects, to make room for asynchronous, virtual communication.

I draw on an extended research project—"Revolting Bodies? The Online Negotiation of Fat Subjectivity"—in order to illustrate the management of these methodological issues. The project investigates the embodied experience of fatness in spaces between subjectivity and subjection on one Internet newsgroup and one listserv. Literature on identity politics, computer-mediated communication, and the social construction of the body was reviewed as it relates to the possibility of individuals with shared characteristics and/or interests utilizing technology to transform meanings for their corporeal experience. Using the methods of critical ethnography, I provided an interpretation of the ways in which site participants fluidly invoke and reject dominant meanings for the fat body within their project of resignifying fat bodies. Emergent themes included narratives of personal fat experience, comparisons of fat within cyberspace and "real" space, discussions of the pleasures and pains of fat bodies, attempts at guarding borders of identity and community, explorations of the mutual constitution of identities and oppressions, and, finally, strategies for reconceptualizing fat.

My methodologies required the use of group interviews, individual interviews, and observations of the communicative practices of participants on two fat-related Internet sites. One site is a newsgroup (hereafter referred to as FAS), an electronic "bulletin board" where users interested in discussing certain topics may simply "lurk" (read postings without responding), respond to postings, or create their own threads of discussion. This type of site generally receives many cross-postings about fat advocacy. The other site under examination was a listserv (hereafter referred to as FD), which functions as an electronic mailing list that deposits all site postings into members' e-mail accounts. The listserv is a forum for discussion pertaining to fat lesbians. The method I used did not require a scientifically designed random sample; the results are not meant to be a generalizable "truth" valid for all participants in the fat-related sites. Instead, I utilized cooperative[1] members of a self-selected and stably constituted group in order to make some theoretical suggestions.

As I undertook the project of trying to understand the negotiation of fat subjectivity online, a number of key methodological issues arose. First and foremost, how would I situate myself in relation to the speech communities under investigation, where I bounced between identities of researcher/not-fat and researched/formerly-fat? How would I account for the fact that I did not work in the service of fat subjectivity at the time when I was indeed considered physically fat? How would I hold myself responsible for entering fat-positive reality into discourse, thus subjecting it to the social surveillance of scholarly practice (Fine, 1994, 73)? Would I be able to get away with cutting and pasting choice parts of various methodologies, or would I have to stick with something road-tested to ensure odd-sounding issues like validity and reliability? Would I be able to meet the challenge of writing about fat discourse communities without resorting to dichotomous "good/bad" characterizations of their speech acts? Given that I was working online, what were the rules for human subjects? Was I working with human subjects, or rather public documents, given that their "conversations" were written and accessible[2] to the general public? How would I present myself to other members of the online groups? Would they trust me enough? Would I be able to gain rapport? What follows is an analysis of my experience negotiating many of these issues while carrying out my online research project.

Being Acknowledged: Establishing Researcher Visibility and Intimacy

A key issue in ethnographic practice is building trust with one's research subjects, which typically means that they are aware of one's involvement as a researcher. In text-only sites such as newsgroups and listservs, an ethnographer must take special precautions to render oneself visible to one's subjects, in that one cannot literally be seen. On the one hand, more interesting data may be recorded from subjects who have forgotten about an invisible ethnographer. On the other hand, the ethnographer faces an ethical dilemma concerning subjects' ongoing awareness of the researcher's presence. In this section, I explore different options for balancing researcher visibility with researcher unobtrusiveness.

Text-only sites typically involve participants conversing, although in delayed-response mode, about subjects of common interest; thus, most research subjects are comfortable discussing their views or interests in a public forum. However, an invitation by an ethnographer to participate in a private conversation, away from the eyes of other group members, can raise suspicions among group members. In this section, I explain reasons for these suspicions as well as tactics for successfully gaining individual interview access based on a shared sense of intimacy.

In my project, I began by taking a cue from Correll's (1995) ethnographic work in online discussion groups, and introduced myself and my project on the sites through postings and discussions with site moderators. For FD, I notified the listwrangler via private e-mail of my interest in studying the group; she suggested I post generally, which I did. From that point, I negotiated my presence there as researcher from an initial position of "Here I am; please tell me if you don't want to be quoted, even anonymously" to verifying via private e-mail that I had individual permission from any poster I wanted to anonymously quote. For FAS, I simply reposted a message every two months to remind them that I was observing the exchanges for the purpose of my study, rather than merely participating like the rest of them. After lurking for approximately three months, during which time I made descriptive notes about the threads and articles posted on the sites, I began to thematize some of their posts and ask many of my own questions. Thus, I was simultaneously observing, engaging in unstructured and creative interviewing (Douglas, 1985), interpreting, and practicing self-reflection.

I gained entree, organizational and individual, to these sites as a researcher, partly, I suspect, because I committed early on to a fat-positive perspective. Part of my introduction, aside from my academic credentials, explained my interest in studying online conversations about fat as stemming from my personal experience of corpulence. I positioned myself as someone who had lost weight and would no longer be considered "fat" by what I imagined to be their standards, but as someone who respected and still wished to participate in many of the struggles waged in fat communities.

In my project, being a good researcher meant being attentive. This meant paying attention to what my research subjects expected from me: for some, it was simply fun to voice their opinions and experiences and to have a good listener—an occasion that can speed the pace of bonding in online relationships (Smith-Stoner and Weber, 2000). For others, it was an abiding sense that their participation in the project would further their larger goal of celebrating or politicizing fatness. Once I had established some initial connection, it was vital that I continue to nourish those bonds by letting my research subjects know about the idiosyncrasies of my life and my schedule. This helped them to understand why it would seem that I wasn't listening, for instance, on long weekends when I went on computer-free vacation. I went into the project with good social skills, if not polished technical ones,[3] and my ability to maintain a long-term sense of personal familiarity with subjects, to self-disclose as necessary, and to provide support ended up paying off in the long run.

This act of identification helped me to gain rapport with group participants. It is noteworthy that in the month of March 1997, eight different researchers (other than myself) attempted to initiate various studies (using questionnaires and group surveys) on these sites, and all but one were rejected. The users of these sites expressed little interest in filling out surveys for faceless researchers, but were willing to engage in conversation that could be interpreted by pro-fat researchers whom they trusted as a result of long-term participation on the sites.

My way of fitting in initially was to ask follow-up questions after posts I found interesting, but it was not until six months into the study that I began introducing my own topics online. I had mistakenly been convinced that lurking was the most respectful way to acknowledge my bond with, yet difference from, the "real" participants. After delurking, though, I found that participants preferred other participants "speak up" rather than hide in the shadows where they could not be "seen." I had been cautious about not wanting the users to feel like guinea pigs, and they responded by telling me that it was exactly my reticence and invisibility as a researcher that made them feel like lab rats. Instead, they suggested, I should just jump in and post what I wanted to—which would put us all on more equal footing. Thus began my regular posts.

In conducting my research, I also borrowed from phenomenological interview techniques, which employ open-ended and follow-up questions to explore issues important to research subjects. One move that helped to establish intimacy and connection with my research subjects reflected the concern of feminist phenomenology about the hierarchical relationships present during interviews, especially in the beginning and when other status markers such as variances in age, race, or class are noticeably present. Thus, I tried to frame my interviews in the speech style I encountered on the sites, which was often (but notably, not always) nonhierarchical. "Nonhierarchical relationships are characterized by, for example, reciprocal questions between the interviewer and the interviewees, by interviewees' taking the lead in the interview, and by interviewees' taking the interviewer into their confidence and risking self-disclosure" (Nelson, 1989, 215).

Nonhierarchical relationships also come from the self-disclosure of the researcher, whose voice is traditionally supposed to be unheard, lest it be manipulative. In phenomenological research, according to Nelson, "the researcher approaches the interviews by placing herself as nearly as possible in the concrete situation and assuming personal responsibility for the choices to be made" (1989, 231). In my work, this was accomplished by intensively describing, thematizing, and interpreting the essences of experience that emerged during my lengthy data-review process. In building rapport with my research subjects, I realized that my personal experiences as a participant in online negotiations of fat identity were not data to be bracketed out. Indeed, the questions in fat-related discussions I had faced as a formerly fat, presently fat-identified user were the very motivation for undertaking this project.

After a solid year of "living with" the data, by which I mean I reviewed the downloaded material frequently, I attempted a description of the interviews and interaction based on topics which began to make sense to me intersubjectively. This was done, following Nelson, by listing thematic topics brought to light by participants, and then checking among interviews to see how topics were interrelated.

While my use of these phenomenological elements did help to increase the level of intimacy between research subjects and researcher, the study nonetheless retained more traits that would identify it as ethnographic. There are many features of ethnography that I found attractive, given my ontological orientation toward my topic and research subjects. The practice of intensively sharing lifeworlds and presence with research subjects is appealing, especially given that I entertained many of the same concerns as they regarding the resignification of the fat body. Yet, because of my removal from the strictly defined realm of fat identity and from the geographic space occupied by my research subjects, I also was attracted to ethnography's means for dealing with the "stranger in a strange land." In addition, I found solace in the ethnographic researcher's acknowledgment that his/hers is not the definitive read of the meanings held by a particular culture, especially in light of attempts by positivist researchers to make such claims.

However, one of the downfalls of such a "connected" methodology is that the researcher may suffer from overconfidence about the nature of her bond with her research subjects. Thankfully, there are some red flags raised for ethnographic researchers who are likely to suffer from these delusions of alliance. Stacey asks "whether the appearance of greater respect for and equality with research subjects in the ethnographic approach masks a deeper, more dangerous form of exploitation" (1991, 113). Because the process and the product of ethnographic research belong, in many ways, to the ethnographer, this is a serious question. The greater intimacy inherent in online ethnography—where all research subjects wear their hearts on their sleeves, so to speak—presents a greater danger of vulnerability and imposition on research subjects. It seems that the best we can do as researchers with a will to knowledge is enter our subjects into discourse responsibly, with all the attendant difficulties of the rare species of reflexivity which avoids self-important projection in the ethnographic text.

Rather than hoarding or ignoring the undeniable presence of my own authorial power in this process, I attempted to share it with the agents of my study. Following Nelson, "The researcher approaches the interviews by placing herself as nearly as possible in the concrete situation and assuming personal responsibility for the choices to be made" (1989, 231). One of those choices involved me exploring their stories without the desire for closure. This directed me to look at my research itself as an important process of creating communication, and to focus on networks of meaning about fat on the Internet instead of on self-contained individuals (Lannamann, 1995). Not incidentally, it also helped strengthen bonds with research subjects who grew to regard me as a tireless listener.

In looking back, I believe that I was able to overcome the natural suspicions faced by online posters—that researchers are nosy, exploitative, out to embarrass them—and thus move to productive individual interviews primarily because I was concerned about and considered myself a member[4] of the group that I studied. Those conditions bore on my interest in methodologies which are interactive, which account for power relationships and contradictory identities, and which fight the repressive power of science to predict and control larger groups imagined to be represented by research subjects. They also led me to online communities, where the kinds of political discussions about fat that were absent in my geographic part of the world were to be found.

Avoiding Data Overload: Maintaining Focus

In face-to-face ethnographic settings, ethnographers typically rely on their ears and their speedy handwriting ability to filter out noteworthy information for recording purposes. In text-only sites, ethnographers are both blessed and cursed by having access to complete electronically stored transcripts of all conversational transactions. The traditional ethnographer may at times feel frustrated by his or her inability to produce a "perfect" record of interaction in his or her notes due to the limits of his or her perception. However, the virtual ethnographer may feel overwhelmed by the task of thematizing from the massive amount of conversational data that have been recorded by the computer. This brief section suggests strategies for carving out the worthiest information, based on my experience with the fat discourse project.

I began the project by locating a number of interactive online sites related to fat issues, and then I had to select from among them those that I thought would best present an insider's knowledge about the issues in which I was interested. This led me to discard some sites. For instance, I decided not to work with one electronic newsgroup dedicated strictly to the posting of fat personal ads, because I believed that the highly ritualized form of such ads would not present as complex a picture of how fat individuals articulated their relationships to their bodies and their culture. I also decided to forego working with a newsgroup reserved for posting visual, highly sexualized digital images of fat people, as I was more interested in the uses of language for reconfiguring fat.

Even within the two groups I finally chose to work with, FD and FAS, I did make some decisions as to what would count as data; originally, it was everything that was posted on both sites. When that proved not only unwieldy but also uninteresting, I decided to foreground exchanges that spoke to individual or community identity. The topics I had chosen to write about in my literature review also helped me to focus my idea of what counted as data.

I collected data by means of downloading posts (known as "articles," or "threads" when in clusters) about topics I found to be of particular interest.[5] As a virtual ethnographer, it is much easier to collect and record interaction "completely" than it is in "reality," largely due to the printed nature of online interaction. However, I was careful not to be tempted into trying for a complete picture of interaction on these sites, and thus downloaded and participated discriminately.[6] In fact, rather than shooting for coherence, I was most alert to contradictions and gaps in subject narratives during data collection.

I should note that the majority of data excerpts that "made it" into the examples of conversation I chose to represent particular themes in my finished report were not the result of my questions. Instead, they were parts of conversations that had been going on while I was only lurking or reading. While I am aware that my presence as a researcher very likely affected what was said, even if I did not specifically ask a question, I would characterize my interactive participation in this project as relatively minor, as compared to, for instance, data generated exclusively from lengthy formal interviews.

The best piece of advice I can offer to first-time online researchers is to establish a set of criteria at the outset that will help you determine which information paths to follow as the project unfolds. As in my description, the criteria should be malleable, so that one is allowed to pursue interesting angles that perhaps had not occurred to the researcher before the project began. However, the flexibility of such criteria should not convince one that they are completely unnecessary, as they do assist greatly in preventing a researcher from feeling entirely overwhelmed by data overload. The recommendation is akin to suggesting that one carry a roadmap when driving unfamiliar roads, but that one keep open the possibility of turning off course should an exciting opportunity for new sights present itself.

Legitimating Online Ethnography

Much like drivers who never deviate from premapped routes, some traditional ethnographers reject the idea that ethnography can happen when the researcher is not physically co-present with his or her research subjects. Jones parses their concerns when he asks: "Although the artifactual elements of online social relationships seem readily available, in what ways is it possible for the researcher to travel to the 'place' occupied by a community, to observe, participate, to use traditional ethnographic methods?" (1999, 17). While this is a seemingly valid concern, it is perhaps a myopic one. Pratt's interesting work isolates as a fundamental problem with traditional ethnography its sense of total self-immersion. She recognizes immense jealousy on the part of ethnographers who see disciplinary outsiders encroaching on their territory of research, whose refusal to translate this realization "into the currency of the discipline that made it all possible" (Pratt, 1986, 31) is taken as a monumental betrayal. Traditional ethnographers unfortunately devalue and militate against research marked by difference, denigrating (for instance) the inclusion of personal narrative as "ethnograph-me," and online research as a shoddy substitute for the "real thing." This limited and unimaginative orthodoxy undermines ethnography's great usefulness for interpreting conversation in our fastest-growing arena, the online world. In this section, I reflect on and evaluate the methodological rigor of my fat discourse project to suggest strategies of self-definition for ethnographers invested in researching online conversation.

From the outset, my interests were not in traditional ethnography, per se. I would define my particular research tactics as stemming from critical ethnography, as defined by Thomas: "a way of applying a subversive worldview to the conventional logic of cultural inquiry" that offers "a more direct style of thinking about the relationships among knowledge, society, and political action. The central premise is that one can be both scientific and critical, and that ethnographic description offers a powerful means of critiquing culture and the role of research within it" (1993, vii). As in conventional ethnography, I engaged in qualitative interpretation of data, followed guidelines of ethnographic methods and analysis, and maintained a preference for grounded theory. I tried to speak on behalf of my research subjects to an academic audience, in order to give their own voices more authority. Also diverging from conventional ethnography was my expressed commitment to changing culture through the resignification of fat, rather than just claiming to describe culture. Finally, I tried to invoke, rather than repress, my political biases regarding this area of study.

Following Thomas's (1993, 33) guideposts for critical ethnography, it is necessary for me to explain my choices regarding research practices. Before beginning the project, I grappled with ontological questions surrounding the broad topic of fat politics. I tried to go beyond uncritically accepted, preconceived assumptions about fat bodies (e.g., that they are ugly, unhealthy, asexual), and looked to my research project as a way beyond accepted appearances to a more complicated picture of fat subjectivity.

I moved from a general awareness of fat politics to my specific study basically because of my excitement at finding an accessible population of politicized people engaging in online discussions and debates about fat. I had to be flexible in terms of design, execution, and even perspective toward studying this population; I ended up studying them for four times as long a period as I had originally intended, and I had to keep my progressive politics in check as I interpreted their contributions. Still, the critical ethnographic perspective enabled me to express my enthusiasm and passion for the topic and the subjects as I wrote about injustice, power, stratification, and allocation of cultural resources in fat communities.

After finding appropriate community discourse online and recording it for an extended period, I coded and organized data by borrowing concepts from phenomenology. I did the work by hand, rather than using a software program, because I wanted to "live" with the data in a fuller way. After coding and organization, I prepared a demonstration of particularly interesting themes in the data for analysis. Readings by colleagues helped me to spot conceptual errors, and to guard against "subtle misinterpretations that confirm some presupposition without actually demonstrating it" (Thomas, 1993, 39). Interpreting the data, I went through a process of defamiliarization. This involved my attempt to look at the nonliteral meanings of data texts and translate what I had seen into something new, an interpretation of how cultural symbols of fat create and constrain, and an identification of the ways in which alternative interpretations of cultural symbols can be enacted.

After the initial write-up came a period of reflection, marked by consideration of how my involvement in the project affected my data gathering, analysis, and the ways in which I would introduce my data to different audiences. I also considered how the research had changed my perspective on fat subjectivity, somewhat loosening my ties to a progressive agenda which might have led to a romanticization of the fat population I studied. I went back to my writing, trying to weave in explanations for how my own values and ideologies influenced the work. I also tried to think about the social and political implications of my "findings" and their presentation to both fat and scholarly audiences. I was reasonably satisfied that my study did challenge the ways in which fat was signified in the mainstream and did suggest how alternative resignificatory practices are undertaken.

Overall, I am satisfied with the work as a piece of critical ethnography, inasmuch as it "show[s] how individuals, including the researcher, constitute and are constituted by discursive fields that attempt to maintain 'continuous' narratives and that suggest a monologic form of subjectivity" (West, 1993, 218), a task taken by some to be the mandate of future critical ethnographies. Personally, I believe I have contributed to some extent to a reworking of cultural myths about fat, and perhaps this project will allow others to see new meanings for fat. I have upheld my obligations of intellectual responsibility by attempting to revitalize conceptual frameworks about not only fat bodies, but also about connections between discourses of sexuality and size. Politically, I think that this work identifies and challenges unnecessary forms of social domination around fat subjectivity, and ethically, I believe my scholarly efforts work in the service of bettering the lives of at least one disenfranchised group.

I would hate to imagine a situation in which the orthodoxies of ethnography might hinder a researcher from exploring such rich topics, simply because the conversations happen in a virtual environment. My choice to study communication about fat identification on the Internet was not incidental. Besides its obvious potential as an alternative forum for engaging in identity struggles, I was drawn to cyberspace for several reasons. I had easy interpretive access to and interaction with the weavers of the narratives, what it meant to be "real" was under negotiation, and I acknowledged that the online stories about fat held important suggestions for staging subjectivity under the rubric of postmodernism.[7] I am interested in the changes in embodiment allowed for by the use of technology, and critical ethnography in an online environment was the most obviously useful means of pursuing such lines of thought.

Following Lannamann, work that deals with online communication allows the possibility of debunking the "cultural authority of the self-contained individual" (1995, 119), instead focusing on social interaction and processes of communication. Rather than dealing with "individualist narratives [that] obscure the material conditions—including the microprocesses of power and domination—in which relationships emerge" (Lannamann, 1995, 119), online research can use the linked world system of the Internet to advance an alternative model of personhood. Such a model would "recognize the constitutive role of social interaction in the construction of personal identity" (Lannamann, 1995, 122).

Online social research is a necessary component of investigating the quality of the Internet as a forum for political work (a subaltern counterpublic, as Fraser [1992] would say), as well. Rumor has it, the Internet allows the potential to create new rules for identity membership, due to the erasure of the physical on text-based sites. In current popular lore, the Internet is a bunker for democratic struggle. In a time when power relations are no longer understood as neat "us versus them" antagonisms, when relationships of power are altered not exclusively by Washington lobbyists and Capitol Hill legislators but also by writing, performing, acting individuals and affinity groups in the form of cultural politics, an important new political arena comes in the cybernetic shape of information technologies. "The vocabulary of resistance must be expanded to include means of electronic disturbance. Just as authority located in the street was once met by demonstrations and barricades, the authority that locates itself in the electronic field must be met with electronic resistance" (Critical Art Ensemble, 1994, 24).

There is something appealing in Rushkoff's (1995) claim that users are capable of developing nongeographic communities through the creation and expression of selves. Expanding the possibilities for connection among somewhat disparate groups of users, the Internet potentially accommodates alternative political strategies. Researchers should not forego the opportunity to understand such strategies simply because they are situated in the faceless forbidden zone of the Internet; instead, now more than ever, researchers must develop sophisticated measures for interpreting online communication.

Particularly vocal are those who question the possibility of an active, engaged citizenry in cyberspace, where participants remain physically isolated from one another. Carlsson (1995) argues that our free communication spaces are currently boring because of community weakness. He believes that whereas "e-mail and electronic discussion groups are bringing together new communities around shared ideas and interests, the people involved remain very isolated. The millions of Internet users are mostly very alone as they 'communicate,' so it's difficult to see how underground communities can develop to reclaim the public space essential to a free society" (Carlsson, 1995, 243). Such a claim calls into question Carlsson's criteria for communication toward a free society; if he considers only face-to-face contact as qualifying, then such Internet isolation is a boondoggle for democracy. But if Carlsson were to recognize that meanings can be created even when the physical distance between communicators is great, he might revalue Internet listservs and newsgroups. Such venues are particularly useful in organizing people who, because of their physical size, meet with space access issues or ridicule when they appear in those old-fashioned kinds of public spaces of which Carlsson seems to be so fond.

Other critics of cyberspace take issue with the physical fragmentation that accompanies forays into electronic communication. Simmons, for instance, asks whether the "disembodied body of cyberspace, the body reduced to information, [is] a necessary artifice" (1995, 152) of progress. Is it really politically useful? Is it good to be able to take advantage of the absence of physical consequences in cyberspace? The throngs of people who populate chatrooms and online matching services obviously benefit in some way from the playful invisibility that text-only space affords. Furthermore, "necessary artifice" does not have to be invoked so regretfully. It could be argued that indeed, the maintenance of artifice is not only useful for, but integral to, the practice of cultural politics.

Many questions about identity arise when examining the negotiation of fat identity through communication on the Internet. Besides the fact that the Internet alters what counts as "everyday communication," it also alters what counts as being embodied. The Internet provides a relatively new space for engaging in what is arguably interpersonal communication. Gone are the "faces" in conventional notions of face-to-face interpersonal communication, yet many of the relationships predicated online involve frequent, sophisticated, verbal interactions among individuals, rather than traditional "mediated" (read: one-way) relationships between, say, a viewer and his/her television set. Fat narratives created and identities negotiated online provoke exciting new questions: What does it mean to claim unity as a fat person (or with fat issues) in a space that erases all physical evidence of the modern body? How does the design of Internet space affect deployments of power around specific body shapes and sizes? Assuming that cyberspace is no more free from governmentality than any other place, in what forms does policing of bodies and identities crop up in the Internet forum? Given conventional and reductive understandings of embodiment as evidence of identity, where things are exactly as they seem to be, it is important to probe communication "from the body" in spaces devoid of faces. The call for online social research has never been sounded more loudly.

If indeed "technologies are becoming better life support systems for our images than for our bodies" (Stelarc, 1996, 22), then the Internet holds much promise as a forum for constructing new meanings for fat bodies. Many scholars and activists in recent years have written about the potential of the Internet as a forum for the democratic participation of an active, politicized citizenry (Gamson, 1995; Huntemann, 1997). Sclove claims that "technologies...constitute part of a society's core political infrastructure...by establishing an intricate and pervasive network of structurally consequential social influences, opportunities, constraints, and inducements" (1995, 88).[8] It logically follows that online research methods are necessary for making sense of this relatively new space for political engagement and action.

Nancy Baym (1995), arguing for an understanding of computer-mediated communication which elevates to the status of the social what is often considered antisocial, considers the wealth of social dynamics influenced by external contexts, temporal structure, computer infrastructure, user purposes, and user characteristics. She concludes that "CMC not only lends itself to social uses but is...a site for an unusual amount of social creativity" (1995, 160). Certainly, this contention bodes well for a movement to renegotiate the meaning of fat, a task requiring a great deal of creativity in light of socially overdetermined attitudes toward abundant flesh.

Other scholars herald not social creativity, but the possibilities of physical creativity granted us by the Internet. "Invading technology eliminates
skin as a significant site, an adequate interface or barrier between public
space and physiological tract. The significance of the cyber may well reside
in the act of the body shedding its skin." Furthermore, "in this age of information overload, what is significant is no longer freedom of ideas but rather
freedom of form—freedom to modify and mutate the body" (Stelarc, 1996,
19). Indeed, for Australian performance artist Stelarc, the project of the
body is a project of redefinition: "It is no longer meaningful to see the body
as a site for the psyche...but rather as a structure to be monitored and modified...not as a subject but as an object...for designing.... The body is trau-
matized to split from the realm of subjectivity and consider the necessity of
reexamining and possibly redesigning its very structure" (Stelarc, 1996, 20).
Stelarc's contention raises interesting responses from critics: What does it
mean, then, when the bodies produced on these sites don't really seem radically redesigned?

How can Internet technology provide a place to "leave behind the bag-
gage that goes with being rated" (Spender, 1995, 244) as a fat person without losing the fat body entirely? If held back from online research by out-
moded assumptions about the co-presence of researcher and subject, one
might never be able to answer this question.

On the micro level, my project examined how the use of Internet technology, specifically e-mail, enables and constrains the formation of relationships. I considered how factors such as delayed response, perceived risk,
and lack of paraverbal cues drive users to create new ways of physicalizing
this channel of communication. The question suggested by Lannamann was
useful here: What everyday practices give rise to differences (1995, 123)
among users? It is my contention that the ways in which communication
patterns are altered on the micro level are instructive as to the ways in which
identity politics are played out in the larger picture. The mere idea that the
micro level may involve microchips needn't sign its death warrant as an area
of interest.

Against orthodoxies that demand adherence to traditional notions of
place-sharing, I believe that as long as the online researcher holds him- or
herself to clear and rigorous standards, the online environment can provide
excellent "stomping grounds." There are many methodological standards to
which I held myself accountable in this project: verisimilitude (did the interpretation I render have fidelity and coherence?); personal responsibility (was
I accountable to my research subjects for the way in which I enter them into
discourse?); political praxis (did this project work discursively to position fat
subjects more promisingly in fields of power?); multivoiced texts (did I

show the contradictions and contestations present in online dialogues?); and dialogues with subjects (did I examine how the interactive nature of this research process shaped my interpretations?) are important criteria.

Taking each in turn, I believe that my interpretation maintains fidelity to the stories I have examined in that I included quotes exactly as they originally appeared on line and tried my best to contextualize them accurately within the larger conversations of which they were part. Describing my account as coherent requires a degree of tolerance for any attempt to fuse together and extract from what originally appeared as diffuse and scattered posts and threads online. I am accountable to my research subjects for the ways in which I have entered them into academic discourse in that I remain open to argument about my interpretations, and throughout the project, I aspired to provide explanations for my choices about how to frame particular issues. It is my hope that the project will be read not just as a description of people trying to resignify fatness, but as an attempt to participate in this important resignification itself within a scholarly arena. My analysis certainly showcases the extent to which online negotiations of fat subjectivity are composed of abutted contradictions and contestations, rather than representing such negotiation as carried out by a uniform, tidily packaged entity called "the fat subject."

I want to conclude this section by indicating some of the chief questions to which I believe online researchers must be accountable during the research process: "How do you communicate with your research subjects? How does this communication position them in relation to you? What are you asking of them? What are the relations of power and control operative in your work?... What, if any, implications does your research have on your personal and professional politics?" (Hawes, 1994, 9).

I have attempted to address many of these questions in this chapter, in hopes that online researchers become more aware of the processes by which visibility and intimacy with research subjects are accomplished. I also expect that online researchers will find themselves convinced of the validity with which their work is increasingly being received as a significant contribution to knowledge.

Notes

1 "Cooperative" here means that the users were aware of and voluntarily involved in my research project. I announced my presence initially by means of postings and online conversations with site monitors, and repeated this message periodically to remind new users. I interacted as participant-observer, and when I got to the stage of interviewing users, I discussed with them the implications of their possible involvement in the project and gained their permission to quote them anonymously.

2 This is "accessible" with a small "a," in deference to the masses of people who cannot access these online conversations because of lack of computer literacy, funds for increasingly expensive computer accounts, or a plethora of other circumstances.

3 See Chris Mann and Fiona Stewart (2000, 132–144) for more on this distinction.

4 Membership is a problematic concept. I considered myself a member because I share with other participants the experience-based knowledge of what it is like to live under conditions of fat oppression, despite the fact that I was not, at the time of the study, subject to those conditions because of weight loss. Membership for me means that I do share consciousness about fat-related issues; however, I am careful to assume neither that all fat people share the same consciousness (or should they) nor that it is my physical experience as a formerly fat person that defines my ability to relate.

5 Following Emerson, Fretz, and Shaw, selecting data "is intuitive, reflecting the ethnographer's changing sense of what might possibly be made interesting or important to future readers, and empathetic, reflecting the ethnographer's sense of what is interesting or important to the people he [*sic*] is observing" (1995, 11).

6 For instance, I downloaded and participated in many discussions about identity and experience, but many fewer about requests for large-size clothing resources.

7 By examining arenas of attempted technological democratization such as listservs and newsgroups, I am trying to address what is commonly perceived as a social problem—the decline of face-to-face community in political organization—and, importantly, examining how technological democratization contributes to "the broad-based fairness and empowerment needed to begin effectively addressing technologies' other social consequences...as well as chronic societal problems otherwise not attributable to technology" (Sclove, 1995, 89, emphasis added). If we view oppressions as linked and mutually constitutive, then democracies of technologies have important consequences for democracies of bodies.

8 Interestingly, Sclove also suggests that technology has played a key role in American political disengagement, although his warrants for this claim center on electoral politics and sparse voter turnout—which may signal a move toward American interest in cultural politics rather than simple apathy.

References

Baym, N. K. "The Emergence of Community in CMC." In *Cybersociety: Computer-Mediated Communication and Community*, ed. S. Jones. Thousand Oaks, CA: Sage, 1995.

Carlsson, C. "The Shape of Truth to Come: New Media and Knowledge. In *Resisting the Virtual Life: The Culture and Politics of Information*, ed. J. Brook and I. A. Boal. San Francisco, CA: City Lights, 1995.

Correll, S. "The Ethnography of an Electronic Bar: The Lesbian Café." *Journal of Contemporary Ethnography* 24 (1995): 270–298.

Critical Art Ensemble. *The Electronic Disturbance*. New York: Autonomedia, 1994.

Douglas, J. D. *Creative Interviewing*. Beverly Hills, CA: Sage, 1985.

Emerson, R. M., R. I. Fretz, and L. L. Shaw. *Writing Ethnographic Fieldnotes*. Chicago: University of Chicago Press, 1995.

Fine, M. "Working the Hyphens: Reinventing Self and Other in Qualitative Research." In *Handbook of Qualitative Research*, ed. N. K. Denzin and Y. S. Lincoln. Thousand Oaks, CA: Sage, 1994.

Fraser, N. "Rethinking the Public Sphere: A Contribution to the Critique of Actually Existing Democracy." In *Habermas and the Public Sphere*, ed. C. J. Calhoun, 109–142. Cambridge, MA: MIT, 1992.

Gamson, W. A. "Safe Spaces and Social Movements." Paper presented at the Annenberg Scholars Program Conference on Public Space. University of Pennsylvania, Philadelphia, PA (March 1995).

Hawes, L. "Revisiting Reflexivity." *Western Journal of Communication 58* (Winter 1994): 5–10.

Huntemann, N. "Creating Safe Cyberspace: Feminist Political Discourse on the Internet." M.A. thesis. University of Massachusetts, Amherst, 1997.

Jones, S. "Studying the Net: Intricacies and Issues." In *Doing Internet Research*, ed. S. Jones, 1–27. Thousand Oaks, CA: Sage, 1999.

Lannamann, J. W. "The Politics of Voice in Interpersonal Communication Research." In *Social Approaches to Communication*, ed. W. Leeds-Hurwitz, 114–132. New York: Guilford, 1995.

Mann, C. and F. Stewart. *Internet Communication and Qualitative Research*. Thousand Oaks, CA: Sage, 2000.

Nelson, J. "Phenomenology as Feminist Methodology: Explicating Interviews." In *Doing Research on Feminist Communication*, ed. K. Carter and C. Spitzack, 221–241. Norwood, NJ: Ablex, 1989.

Pratt, M. L. "Fieldwork in Common Places." In *Writing Culture: The Poetics and Politics of Ethnography*, ed. J. Clifford and G. E. Marcus. Berkeley: University of California Press, 1986.

Rushkoff, D. "Mere Anarchy Loosed Upon the World." *Virtual City: Your Guide to Cyberculture* (Fall 1995): 13.

Sclove, R. E. "Making Technology Democratic." In *Resisting the Virtual Life: The Culture and Politics of Information*, ed. J. Brook and I. A. Boal. San Francisco, CA: City Lights, 1995.

Simmons, J. "Sade and Cyberspace." In *Resisting the Virtual Life: The Culture and Politics of Information*, ed. J. Brook and I. A. Boal. San Francisco, CA: City Lights, 1995.

Smith-Stoner, M. and T. Weber. "Developing Theory Using Emergent Inquiry: A Study of Meaningful Online Learning for Women." Ph.D. diss. California Institute of Integral Studies, 2000.

Spender, D. *Nattering on the Net: Women, Power, and Cyberspace*. North Melbourne, Australia: Spinifex, 1995.

Stacey, J. "Can There Be a Feminist Ethnography?" In *Women's Words: The Feminist Practice of Oral History*, ed. S. B. Gluck and D. Patai. New York: Routledge, 1991.

Stelarc. "From Psycho to Cyber Strategies: Prosthetics, Robotics and Remote Existence." *Canadian Theatre Review* (1996): 19–42.

Thomas, J. *Doing Critical Ethnography*. Newbury Park, CA: Sage, 1993.

West, J. T. "Ethnography and Ideology: The Politics of Cultural Representation." *Western Journal of Communication 57* (1993): 209–220.

"Seeing and Sensing" Online Interaction: An Interpretive Interactionist Approach to USENET Support Group Research

❧
Mary K. Walstrom

And thus, in our researches, we have concentrated all our attention upon what is supposed to occur "inside" isolated individuals studied "externally", from the point of view of third-person observers, socially uninvolved with them. We have failed to study what goes on "between" people as first- and second-persons, the sense-making practices, procedures or methods made available to us as resources within the social orders into which we have been socialized....

(Shotter, 1989, 143)

...those [second person "you's"] involved in joint action experience themselves not only as having a "place" or "position" in a "situation" as individuals, but also as being ethically or morally interlinked with others "in" that situation in a way quite different from those outside it. They feel answerable to, or responsible for, those within it...

(Shotter, 1995b, 54)

STUDIES OF ONLINE DISCUSSION groups are rapidly growing because of the many advantages these contexts offer researchers. Some of these advantages include expanded access to and comfort for research participants, decreased cost and time, removal of transcription biases, and simplified data organization (Mann and Stewart, 2000). Online support group research has become a prominent branch of this new field of study. One boon of this inquiry is the rich insight it offers into ways people cope with problems that are seldom publicly expressed.

There are many different kinds of USENET newsgroups based on the nature of topics discussed. They can be roughly divided into high-risk, medium-risk, and low-risk groups (Chen, Hall, and Johns, "Research Paparazzi," later chapter in this volume). Support groups belong to the high-risk category, as most of the discussions deal with highly sensitive topics, personal trauma, confidential information, and emotionally charged experiences. To gain access to such high-risk groups, and to adequately research them, require a methodology that will take into account the sensitivity of the topic and emotions of the participants. Traditional social scientific methods that require researchers to take a rational and detached standpoint do not work well in these kinds of online groups. That is, traditional methods generally exclude the forming of social relationships between researchers and participants. As Shotter (1989) argues, such relationships are key to grasping participants' sense-making practices (including both analytical and emotional) and for linking researchers to participants ethically (entailing joint responsibility for interaction). Thus, qualitative methods that feature researcher-participant relationships can enable effective study of the sensitive and emotional topics discussed in public support groups online.

In this chapter, I present an interpretive interactionist-based approach to qualitative analysis of USENET support groups. The core of this approach entails the researcher's active involvement (in Shotter's terms, "joint action") in the discussions being analyzed, drawing on the discursive resources and historical backgrounds shared by group members in sense-making practices. Moreover, this approach obliges researchers to not only participate in the support groups that they study but also to have experienced the dilemma central to the participants' discussions. From the perspective of social constructionism, these activities locate researchers in both "third-" and "second-person" positions (Shotter, 1987, 1989), to which I refer as analyst and participant-experiencer, respectively. These positions give researchers access to two rich layers of interaction in interpretive processes. The first position involves the "seen," namely, the systematic patterns displayed in interaction, and the second refers to the "sensed," that is, the emotional meanings evoked through interaction (Katz and Shotter, 1996). The "seen" becomes intelligible as researchers use methodological tools to analyze interaction, and the "sensed" is grasped as researchers affectively respond to interaction. The latter stems from the researcher's shared experience with support group participants, both as a group member and as a person coping with, or who has overcome, the same dilemma facing participants.

The interpretive interactionist-based approach to public, online support group studies presented here rejects traditional research paradigms that privilege conceptions of scientists as detached observers. Such paradigms support passive methods of Internet research (Eysenbach and Till, 2001), featuring the mining of support group discussions (or their archives) by researchers uninvolved in or familiar with newsgroup culture.[1] The prevalence of these paradigms may stem from the limitations of scientific discourse itself: "In our concern, as first-person subjectivities with only a third-person objective world, this whole category of events, in which the responsibility for an outcome is shared between a "you" and an "I," disappears.... As scientists we have lacked an intelligible vocabulary in terms of which to make sense of it" (Shotter, 1989, 16).

To amend this deficiency, I support incorporating "second-person" perspectives, of participant/experiencer, into traditional "third person"-based research paradigms. With this inclusion, researchers are jointly involved in and linked to participants, as Shotter (1989) suggests, in ways third-person researchers are not.

Thus, I assert that researchers dually positioned as analysts and participant-experiencers may richly draw on both linguistic and emotional resources to capture meanings emerging between individuals within a commonly socialized group (cf. Shotter, 1989). I seek to demonstrate that this process—central to the interpretive interactionist-based methodology proposed—yields rich "seen" and "sensed," practical-moral knowledge of online support group interaction.

I begin the ensuing discussion of an interpretive interactionist-based approach to analysis of public, online support group interaction with a brief overview of the study I recently conducted out of which it emerged. Drawing on this study, I introduce interpretive interactionism, and highlight its strengths for locating, organizing, interpreting, and reporting public, online support group interaction. I then demonstrate how interpretive interactionism may be merged with three additional methodologies to produce a rigorous, data-driven, and emotionally informed analysis. I emphasize in these latter two sections how navigating between analyst ("third-person") and participant-experiencer ("second-person") perspectives can be done, "seeing" and "sensing" online support interaction. Finally, I detail the benefits of the proposed approach for researchers and participants. Given these benefits, I claim that the following interpretive interactionist-based approach to studies of public, online support groups is especially suitable for studies of these high-risk research contexts.

An Online Support Group Study

The methodological approach I introduce below is based on an analysis I conducted of 10, two-part exchanges[2] between female participants in a USENET support group for individuals struggling with eating disorders (mainly anorexia and bulimia). The focus of this research emerged out of linguistic practices and emotional senses that became salient to me in my encounter with support group interaction, drawing on my background as a discourse analyst and as a group member also in recovery from anorexia nervosa, respectively. That is, systematic patterns I saw and affective responses I felt while reading and contributing to support group interaction informed an analysis of three of its discussion features, described below.

The features of eating disorder support group of interaction I came to study manifested over one year that I read and saved discussion posts to bolster my ongoing recovery. I began doing so after unexpectedly finding the support group listed one day among the collection offered through my university's servers. During that year, while studying qualitative methodology, I carefully reflected on and eventually launched a study of the support group interaction. This choice was shaped by my concerns about the effects on my own recovery of being reimmersed in "eating disorder talk." A desire to use my analytic training to illuminate what I saw as a deficient area of communication research overrode my hesitancy. This area involved qualitative understandings of the discursive structure and important function of eating disorder support groups, whose vital role in eating disorder recovery I had personally experienced.

With this general research direction, I began reading and systematically saving posts during a second year of following eating disorder support group interaction. I was drawn to posts featuring group participants' frequent references to and dialogues with "eating disorder voices" (both explicit and implicit).[3] These dialogues snared my attention as they resonated with my own—and many other women's—experience with the painful, intrapersonal dimension of eating disorders, such as anorexia nervosa and/or bulimia (Claude-Pierre, 1997; Hornbacher, 1998). Drawing on my academic studies of interpretive interactionism and other qualitative methodologies at that time, I progressively crafted—through extensive, multiple iterations of the interpretive process—the methodological framework I used for interpreting my empirical observations of and emotional responses to eating disorder support group interaction.

These "seen" and "sensed" interpretations yielded three layers of findings. First, I located a coherent narrative employed by support group participants to accomplish the explicitly stated purpose of the group—solving eating disorder problems (through exchanging information) and providing emotional support. These purposes served the larger group aim of facilitating eating disorder recovery.[4] Specifically, my analysis first evidenced how this narrative served as a vehicle for problem solving. For example, this narrative equipped group participants to battle and overcome critical voices that policed their eating behavior and attacked their self-worth. This genre featured a major plot line, protagonists, complicating action, and two alternative evaluative points (one in which participants conquered the voice and the other in which the voice prevailed). I conceptualized this genre as a "public" narrative (Somers and Gibson, 1994), due to how it served as a collective resource that group participants uniquely invoked in yet systematic ways.

Second, I identified the discursive practices group participants employed to supply emotional support to one another. For example, my analysis evidenced numerous, and I claim strategic, uses of politeness strategies, serving to build solidarity and protect individual and group face. Protection of group face, amid the challenges to problematic behaviors often featured in support group talk, I found to be vital to problem-solving activity. By protecting individual, and hence group, face, I claimed that support group participants created a safe context for problem-solving activity (Walstrom, 2000b).

Third, in addition to illuminating the micro-level structure of two explicitly stated support group purposes, my analysis highlighted a third process—the co-construction of eating disorder identities. This finding emerged out of an analysis of ways in which group participants located themselves and other members as protagonists in narrative activity—a discursive strategy called (self-other) "positioning."[5] Through positioning ourselves in narrative, we co-create with our interlocutors (actual or imagined) a sense of self and identity (Bequedano-Lopez, 1997; Capps and Ochs, 1995; Davies, 1992; Davies and Harré, 1990; O'Connor, 1994, 1997; Ochs and Taylor 1995).

I further claimed that the analysis featured unique analytical and ethical strengths given its emotionally informed and data-driven interpretations.[6] Central to this outcome was the dual positions of participant-experiencer and analyst I navigated between in the interpretive process. This process was driven by the interpretive interactionist-based methodology that I employed.

Social Constructionism

A key theoretical perspective that informed the methodology presented here is social constructionism (Edwards and Potter, 1992; Gergen, 1982, 1985; Harré, 1983; Shotter, 1984, 1993a, 1993b; Shotter and Gergen, 1994). This perspective takes as its focus the contingent, ongoing flow of communication jointly created between selves and others—the "self-other dimension of interaction" (Shotter, 1993a, 10; 1995a, 164). The utterances that drive this interaction are regarded as co-constructed, as are the interpretations, stances, actions, activities, identities, emotions, and other culturally meaningful realities they produce (Jacoby and Ochs, 1995). Co-construction refers to a "distributed responsibility among interlocutors" (Jacoby and Ochs, 1995, 177) for collaborative interactional processes, but does not assume affiliation or support (e.g., a disagreement is co-constructed).

The methodological approach I present is grounded in a rhetorical-responsive version of social constructionism (Shotter, 1993a, 1993c).[7] In this version, the appropriate units of analysis for studies of human interaction are "living utterances...voiced in concrete social contexts" (Shotter, 1993a, 7). A rhetorical-responsive version of social constructionism provides a rationale for seeking understandings of "living utterances," the basic units of analysis accessible to and appropriate for researchers positioned as ("second-person") participant-experiencers and ("third-person") analysts.

Interpretive Interactionism

Interpretive interactionism is a methodology that powerfully persuades and equips researchers to take up what I've referred to as analyst and participant-experiencer perspectives. Interpretive interactionism, according to Denzin (1989), delves into the everyday experiences of research participants, attending to their voices, emotions, actions. Analytical foci involve turning point events, those moments that radically alter participants' views of themselves and their experiences (Denzin, 1989, 10). The goal of interpretive interactionism is to produce thick descriptions of the social relationships being studied. These interpretations reveal meanings that inform and structure participants' experiences of dilemmas they face. Detail, context, and emotion are presented, whereby the "feelings, actions, and meanings of interacting individuals are heard" (Denzin, 1989, 83).

The thick descriptions produced through interpretive interactionism create verisimilitude—truthlike statements that create for readers the feeling that they have experienced or could experience the events being described (Denzin, 1989). These statements are considered valid in their ability to be confirmed. Such interpretive results are achieved as researchers live their way into the lifeworlds of participants. This hermeneutic process entails the reflection by researchers on their prior interpretations of and personal experiences with the dilemmas they study, acknowledging that objective, value-free inquiry is impossible. Researchers navigate between their own and participants' self-stories, seeking points at which those circles converge. As researchers seek to merge their own biographies with those of participants, shared emotionality and understanding evolves. Interpretations are acknowledged as provisional, for "[f]ull, objective, all-encompassing knowledge of a subject or situation is never possible" (Denzin, 1989, 82). In reporting findings, researchers make interpretive processes as public as possible for readers. Specifically, the multiple methods employed by the researcher are revealed. The multimethodological approach to analysis encouraged within interpretive interactionism contributes to findings that demonstrate "sophisticated rigor" (Denzin, 1989, 22).

Interpretive interactionism has both micro- and macro-level aims. The former involves the seeking of local meanings that illuminate the lifeworlds of participants, discussed above. The latter entails the connection of these local meanings, or personal troubles, to the public policies or institutions existing to address them. A critique of those policies or institutions ensues. Interpretive interactionism also critiques positivist and postpositivist research approaches by rejecting nonbiographical, ahistorical, nomothetic (seeks generalizations), and ostensibly value-free interpretations. Rather, it embraces postmodern, feminist, and critical ethnographic perspectives. These perspectives produce research accounts that problematize the gendered, situated, structural, and practical features of participants' lifeworlds in a patriarchal, political economy (Denzin, 1989).

Interpretive interactionism provides a solid rationale and framework for public, online support group studies by researchers occupying both analyst and participant-experiencer positions. For example, this method supported the ways I drew on personal biography (a 15-year struggle with anorexia) in identifying an initial research focus—support group participants' intra- and interpersonal battles with their eating disorder voices. It also encouraged the use of multiple methodologies to enhance the analytical strength of my observations (as discussed below). In short, this method guided and legitimated the "seeing" and "sensing" of prominent discursive and emotional themes in support group interaction. To recap, I saw systematic linguistic structures in women's narratives (e.g., tracing narrative positionings of group participants) and sensed the significances of group participants' accounts (e.g., responding to the affective displays in calls for help, questions, and epiphanies).

Interpretive interactionism also serves as a useful tool and vehicle for navigating a hermeneutic circle in interpretive processes. This analytical activity involves the tacking back and forth by researchers between the lifeworlds of participants and their own biographies to generate the thick descriptions, as noted above. Interpretive interactionism also allows researchers to produce accounts that seek to resist and remedy the oppressive conditions they share with research participants.

To illustrate, this latter outcome appeared in my study as a critique of the institutional discourses that shape the experience of women with eating disorders. This critique entailed a counterdiscourse to the dominant discourses of medicine (Foucault, 1979, 1980)[8] and mainstream media as they conceive of anorexia and bulimia. These discourses objectify, pathologize, and trivialize the experiences of those struggling with these conditions (Chernin, 1981; Garrett, 1994; 1998; Simblett, 1997; Szeleky, 1988a, 1988b; Walstrom, 1996). This counterdiscourse was accomplished through an analysis that highlighted group participants' competencies (e.g., problem solving and exchanging support) and fully represented participants' voices, actions, and emotions (done by quoting complete group participants' postings in research accounts). The latter practice also mitigated the power of scientific discourses to speak for group participants in two ways. First, it acknowledged the authority of women in presenting their own experiences, and second, it afforded opportunities for alternative interpretations of the provisional research findings formed. I see these critical processes as additional ways to exploit the ethical advantages available within interpretive interactionism, which I argue may be maintained when combined with additional methodologies. As noted, such merging builds sophisticated rigor of interpretations and also expands the scope and depth of inquiries that may be done. I now seek to demonstrate one way these outcomes may be achieved by discussing several methodologies that may be effectively joined with interpretive interactionism.

Supporting Methodologies

In order to recruit analyst ("third-person") and experience-participant ("second-person") perspectives in support group research, I present three methodologies that I suggest usefully enrich an interpretive interactionist-based approach to public, online support group research. In the merging of these methods with interpretive interactionism, the positivist and postpositive traditions that lie at their roots are to be rejected.[9] As noted, these traditions exclude researcher-participant relationships that constrain the analytical, emotional, and ethical dimensions of research findings.

Grounded theory (Strauss, 1987; Strauss and Corbin, 1994) may be coupled with interpretive interactionism to serve as a powerful tool for organizing and identifying major themes in massive numbers of support group posts collected for close analysis. The goal of this method is to produce a theory that explains behavior that is relevant and problematic for a group of individuals. Locating a core category in collected data is central to generating this theory. The constant comparison method is used to locate a series of possible core categories. Categories are based on empirical indicators the researcher locates in the data—the actions and events in participants' spoken or written accounts. Several types of coding can be conducted (e.g., open, axial, and selective). The researcher compares the major themes, or categories, that emerge in this process. Once a saturation point in coding is reached, a theory is formulated through iterations of sorting and writing memos that elaborate the core category.

The constant comparison method guided my initial observations and interpretations of the 823 posts and 144 threads I collected during one year for analysis. A core category emerged as I (as an analyst) observed the frequent, systematic uses of metaphor by group participants to "personify" (Lakoff and Johnson 1980, 33) their eating disorders (e.g., as a voice, monster, dictator, committee, part of me, or simply "he"), and, emotionally responded to (as a participant-experiencer) group participants' strong affective displays around these references. The constant comparison method also helped me categorize distinct functions that appeared to be accomplished through group participants' exchanges. I coded these functions as introductions, calls for help, questions, epiphanies, and success stories. These categories served as important primary lenses for my later analysis of identity co-construction—based on the self-other positionings of group participants displayed within each category—and the problem solving and emotional support participants accomplished concurrently. I turned to conversation analysis to penetrate and reveal the latter processes, an effective tool for tapping the micro-level complexities of interactional and emotional work.

Conversation analysis (Atkinson and Heritage, 1984; Goodwin, 1981; Jefferson and Lee, 1981; Psathas, 1995; Sacks, Schegloff and Jefferson, 1974; Schegloff, Jefferson, and Sacks, 1977) is a second method that may be combined with interpretive interactionism to enhance the analyst- and participant-experiencer perspectives it advocates. Conversation analysis focuses on participants' points of view in talk-in-interaction; that is, treats what participants themselves display as salient in the structure of their talk as primary grounds for interpretations.[10] Participant perspectives are ostensibly shown as conversation analysts closely chart the turn-taking and preference organization displayed in sequences of talk. Preference involves how "to deal with cases where there are non-equivalent courses of action available and the alternatives are ranked" (Sacks and Schegloff, 1979, cited in Potter, 1996, 60).[11] In other words, normative standards for social interaction, such as those governing turn-taking or the supplying of normative responses (e.g., providing a disagreement to a self-deprecation), form the backdrop of interpretations. These interpretations tend to capture meanings that lie outside the processing of individuals engaged in the ongoing flow of interaction (Taylor, 1995a, 1995b). This analytical power can directly benefit research participants, for instance, by revealing to agoraphobia sufferers ways their vocabulary and narrative structures shape (and perpetuate) their afflictions (Capps and Ochs, 1995).

Conversation analysis helped magnify and sharpen the "seen" and "sensed" views I developed of two purposes of the online eating disorder support group—problem solving and providing support. For example, in attending to the preference organization of utterances within initial post and reply sequences, the architecture of women's problem solving became apparent. This insight entailed a distinct genre, used as collective problem-solving resource, which I called a public narrative.[12] Through it, group participants readily supplied solutions to both explicitly- and implicitly-indexed problems.[13] Second, in mapping the normative rules governing politeness in support group interaction, the exchange of emotional support became apparent. For example, I traced how group participants sought to protect the "face" of recipients of their posts by weaving positive affective expressions through challenges to eating disorder behavior. Such support, I argued, created a safe context for problem-solving activity.

Discourse analysis (Fairclough, 1989, 1992; Schiffrin, 1994; van Dijk, 1989, 1993) is a third methodological tool researchers may unite with interpretive interactionism, maximizing the interpretive strength of the "second-" and "third-person" positions it supports. Like conversation analysis, discourse analysis reveals meanings that often escape the awareness of interactants themselves (Capps and Ochs, 1995). That is, researchers trace micro-level discursive features systematically displayed in interactants' exchanges. Situated understandings of the form and function of these exchanges result. One notable branch of this methodology, critical discourse analysis (Fairclough, 1989, 1992; van Dijk, 1989; Taylor, 1995a, 1995b), parallels interpretive interactionism in its ability to address macro-level, social structures. That is, critical discourse analysis exposes the hegemonic, institutional forces impacting local interactions, advancing critiques of power imbalances operating in those contexts.

Discourse analysis served as a crucial lens for analyzing the self-other positionings (Davies and Harré, 1990) displayed in eating disorder support group in narrative activity. As noted, these positionings involved action, thought, feeling, evaluation, and states of being. I wanted to more deeply explore these structural features of support group talk that had attracted my attention in their varied configurations in the initial coding process. That is, discourse analysis allowed me to deepen my analytical understanding of the problem-solving and supportive functions of women's exchanges, indexed in the categories I "saw" through the constant comparison method. Moreover, discourse analysis furthered my emotional understandings of group participants' affective displays in identity co-construction and change. For example, I "sensed" the importance of these displays for the co-creating of eating disorder and recovering identities, as respondents validated and compassionately responded to initial posters' expressions of fear and self-hatred or, alternatively, to their expressions of anger (toward their eating disorder voices) and self-love. These "seen" and "sensed" understandings shaped the stage-based framework for understanding the co-construction of eating disorder identities (from eating-disordered to recovering) in online support group narrative activity that my analysis advanced.

To merge the above three qualitative methodologies with interpretative interactionism may yield rich, data-driven, and emotionally informed interpretations of online support group interaction. These interpretations are not products of a priori conceptual models externally imposed on data analyzed. Rather, interpretations emerge out of a historically and biographically situated researcher navigating between analyst and participant-experiencer positions, "seeing" and "sensing" interaction, respectively. This dual positionality also ties researchers closely to research participants. That is, through active involvement in and shared responsibility for interactional outcome, researchers are morally linked to research participants in ways that outsiders are not.

Online Interpretive Interactionist Approach

The interpretive interactionist-based methodology, when applied to studies of public, online support groups, generates many beneficial features for the researcher and the researched. Given the highly sensitive discussions featured in online support groups, these features are crucial for the successful implementation and completion of the studies.

Interpretive interactionist-based inquiry benefits researchers as it establishes relationships between researchers and participants noted as key to effective studies of high risk online forums. For example, at the outset, researchers share research aims with group participants and elicit their feedback. This may be done in the form of a self-introduction that also displays that one is a socially competent and involved follower of the group (e.g., exhibiting knowledge of the group's purpose and norms for posting, and that one shares the dilemma being discussed). Such presentations enhance the likelihood of participant feedback on and support for research aims.

For example, in an extensive, two-part self-introduction to the online eating disorder support group, I shared my aim to illuminate the group's problem-solving and supportive processes, solicited feedback about this aim, and provided a detailed account of my personal struggle with anorexia nervosa. In doing so, I demonstrated competence for and interest in support group participation by observing norms for first-time postings (offering a self-introduction) and in showing familiarity with the group purposes. All responses I received to my self-introduction, both those privately sent and posted publicly, welcomed me to the group and heartily supported my study. These supportive responses continued during the two weeks following my posting. Also important to note is that in subsequent references to my project in the replies I privately sent to individuals and publicly posted to the group, no one protested or criticized the study. Because potentially hundreds of participants had time to read my self-introduction, I took the consensus of positive feedback I received as a reasonable index of current support group participants' approval of my project.[14]

The interpretive interactionist-based approach to online support group studies presented here also generates benefits for support group participants. These benefits result from the feminist, communitarian ethic achieved by researchers who are jointly involved in the interaction they study (as analysts and participant-experiencers). A feminist research ethic "entails a commitment to the common good and to universal human solidarity" (Denzin, 1997, 274). This ethic is based on researchers' genuine care for and shared emotionality with research participants. From these connections, analysts strive to conduct "research that makes a difference in the lives of real people" (Denzin, 1997, 268). The proposed interpretive interactionist approach enables this aim easily. For example, three participant benefits can be seen in the research accounts that this method produces. These benefits are arguably accomplished by: (1) the representing of participants' own voices, validating their perspectives; (2) a thick description of a problematic experience shared by participants, enhancing their self-understandings; and (3) a critique of dominant discourses that structure (and constrain) participants' ability to cope with this experience, fueling their potential to realize positive changes.

In the support group study I conducted, I have sought such participant benefits in the following ways. The first involved fully quoting individual postings in the analysis, and including, when possible, the complete two-part exchanges in notes or appendices. These quotings afford a public voice to a group of individuals who are largely marginalized in mainstream discourses— females, in general, and females struggling with eating disorders, in particular.[15] At the same time, such quoting mitigates the traditional power of the researcher's voice, as it enables for alterative readings of interpretations to be produced.

A second benefit was sought in emphasizing in my analysis group participants' communicative competencies (Cazden, 1988; Hymes, 1971). These skills involved participants' adept accomplishment of support group aims— problem solving, exchanging support, and seeking recovery. I claim these skills were demonstrated through a multilayered, micro-level analysis of two-part exchanges, which highlighted group participants' use of a local narrative genre and practices of self-other positioning to achieve group purposes. In short, I contend that a second benefit for support group participants may involve enriched insight into their eating disorder conditions, based on a micro-level analysis of participant communicative proficiencies.

Following from these two benefits, a third involved, as noted above, advancing a critique of dominant discourses and institutions that marginalize, pathologize, and trivialize eating disorder experience. A critique of faulty representations by dominant discourses of eating disorder experience is accomplished through the first two benefits sought. That is, in presenting group participants' own voices and perspectives (with full quotings), and in recognizing their skills in coping with their condition (their communicative competencies), an alternative discourse of eating disorders (and recovery) is created, namely one that resists dominant discourses of these experiences.

In sum, an interpretive interactionist-based approach to online support group studies features important benefits for online researchers and for support group participants. I have attempted to highlight these benefits by demonstrating the methodological and intrinsic ethical value of this qualitative approach. The core of this approach involves the taking up by researchers of both analyst ("third-person") and experiencer-participant ("second-person") positions. These positions equip researchers to richly "see" and "sense" support group interaction, which enable empirically and ethically rigorous interpretations.[16] Such interpretations feature both analytical and emotional understandings emerging from researchers' unique joint involvement in and responsibility for support group interaction. Thus, I contend that the proposed interpretive interaction-based methodology recognizes and effectively overcomes the unique challenges of high-risk, online research contexts.

Notes

1 As Eysenbach and Till (2001) note, many self-help groups have been the target of passive Internet research methods, including eating disorder groups (e.g., Winzelberg, 1997).

2 One exchange involves an initial post and one reply. Two-part must be understood as one-to-many (initial poster to all ASED participants) and then one-to-one/many (respondent to initial poster and all ASED participants).

3 In a larger analysis (Walstrom, 1999), I demonstrate how these references are indexed through shifts between direct and indirect discourses (Bakhtin, 1986) or reported speech and thought (Holt, 1996; Voloshinov, 1973).

4 These purposes appeared in the support group's Frequently Asked Questions (FAQ) document.

5 The term "self-other" positionings refers to eating disorder support group participants' taking up of protagonist positionings and the locating of group participants within such positionings by respondents.

6 I elaborate on how Bakhtinian theories ungird the ethical merits of this method in a larger work (Walstrom, 2000a).

7 See Schwandt (1994) for a discussion of other versions of social constructionism.

8 Berkenkotter and Ravotas (1997) and Ravotas and Berkenkotter (1998) powerfully demonstrate the ways in which the discourses of psychotherapy, as found in the *DSM-IV*, accomplish forms of disciplining, silencing, and power addressed by Foucault (1979, 1980).

9 See Denzin and Lincoln (1994) for a discussion of the positivist and post-positive traditions underlying the first two methods, grounded theory and conversation analysis.

10 While not typically dealing with the power relations, conversation analysis has been merged with various other postmodern methodologies to illuminate and critique inequalities situated in the structure and sequence of everyday interaction (Conefrey, 1997; Diversi, 1998; Taylor, 1995a).

11 Following Shotter (1987), I stress that what may be regarded as nonequivalent and alternative rankings must be determined within a particular social situation.

12 In another work (Walstrom, 2000a), I discuss how Bakhtinian theory was central to my interpretation of the multiple components of this genre (e.g., plot, characters, complicating action, and evaluative point[s]).

13 Implicitly indexed problems, I argue, are gleaned from group participants' shared "apperceptive" background (cf. Morson and Emerson, 1990).

14 Currently, the support group FAQ document includes a disclaimer that requests researchers to refrain from conducting studies of group interaction. At the time I introduced my research and collected data, this disclaimer was not present.

15 I thank Professor Charles Ess (personal communication, Novermber 22, 2001) for underscoring and further crystallizing this point.

16 Following Herring (2001), I claim this interpretive interactionist-based approach to studies of public, online support groups offers a viable, ethical alternative to obtaining informed consent. I elaborate and support this claim elsewhere (Walstrom, in press).

References

Atkinson, J. M. and J. Heritage, eds. *Structures of Social Action: Studies in Conversation Analysis.* Cambridge: Cambridge University Press, 1984.

Bakhtin, M. M. "The Problem of Speech Genres." In *Speech Genres and Other Late Essays,* ed. C. Emerson and M. Holquist (V. W. Mcgee, Trans.), 60–102. Austin: University of Texas Press, 1986 (Original Work Published 1979).

Bequedano-Lopez, A. "Heteroglossia and the Construction of Asian American Identities." *Issues in Applied Linguistics 8* (1997): 47–62.

Berkenkotter, C. and D. Ravotas. "Genre as a Tool in the Transmission of Practice over Time and Across Professional Boundaries." *Mind, Culture, and Activity 4* (1997): 256–274.

Capps, L. and E. Ochs. *Constructing Panic: The Discourse of Agoraphobia.* Cambridge, MA: Harvard University Press, 1995.

Cazden, C. *Classroom Discourse. The Language of Teaching and Learning.* Portsmouth, UK: Heinemann, 1988.

Chernin, K. *The Obsession: Reflections on the Tyranny of Slenderness.* New York: Harper and Row, 1981.

Claude-Pierre, P. *The Secret Language of Eating Disorders: the Revolutionary New Approach to Understanding and Curing Anorexia and Bulimia.* New York: Random House, 1997.

Conefrey, T. "Discourse in Science Communities: Issues of Language, Authority, and Gender in a Life Sciences Laboratory." Ph.D. diss., University of Illinois, Urbana-Champaign, 1997.

Davies, B. "Women's Subjectivity and Feminist Stories." In *Investigating Subjectivity: Research on Lived Experience*, ed. C. Ellis and M. G. Flaherty, 53-76. Newbury Park, CA: Sage, 1992.

Davies, B. and R. Harré. "Positioning: the Discursive Production of Selves." *Research on Language and Social Interaction 20* (1990): 43–63.

Denzin, Norman K. *Interpretive Interactionism.* Newbury Park, CA: Sage, 1989.

———. *Interpretive Ethnography.* Thousand Oaks, CA: Sage, 1997.

Denzin, Norman K. and Yvonna S. Lincoln, eds. *Handbook of Qualitative Research.* Thousand Oaks, CA: Sage, 1994.

Diversi, M. "Street Kids in Search of Humanization: Expanding Dominant Narratives Through Critical Ethnography and Stories of Lived Experience." Ph.D. diss., University of Illinois, Urbana-Champaign, 1998.

Edwards, D. and J. Potter. *Discursive Psychology.* London: Sage, 1992.

Eysenbach, G. and J. E. Till. "Ethical Issues in Qualitative Research on Internet Communities." *British Medical Journal 323* (2001): 1103–1105.

Fairclough, N. *Language and Power.* London: Longman, 1989.

———. *Discourse and Social Change.* Cambridge, MA: Polity, 1992.

Foucault, M. *Discipline and Punish: The Birth of a Prison.* New York: Random House, 1979.

———. *The History of Sexuality, Vol. 1.* Translated by R. Hurley. New York: Vintage Books, 1980.

Garrett, C. "The 'Eating Disorders' Smorgasbord." *Australian Journal of Communication 21*, no. 2 (1994): 14–30.

———. *Beyond Anorexia: Narrative, Spirituality, and Recovery.* Cambridge, UK: Cambridge University Press, 1998.

Gergen, K. J. *Toward Transformation in Social Knowledge.* New York: Springerverlag, 1982.

———. "The Social Constructionist Movement in Modern Psychology." *American Psychologist 40* (1985): 266–275.

Goodwin, C. *Conversational Organization: Interaction Between Speakers and Hearers.* New York: Academic Press, 1981.

Harré, R. *Personal Being: A Theory for Individual Psychology.* Oxford: Basil Blackwell, 1983.

Herring, S. "Ethical Challenges to Doing Research on the Internet: The CMDA Perspective." Presented at the Second International Conference of the Association of Internet Researchers, Minneapolis-St. Paul, MN, October 2001.

Holt, E. "Reporting on Talk: the Use of Direct Reported Speech in Conversation." *Research on Language and Social Interaction 29* (1996): 219-245.

Hornbacher, M. *Wasted: A Memoir of Anorexia and Bulimia.* New York: Harper Flamingo, 1998.

Hymes, D. "Competence and Performance in Linguistic Theory." In *Language Acquisition: Models and Methods*, ed. R. Huxley, and E. Ingram. New York: Academic Press, 1971.

Jacoby, S. and E. Ochs. "Co-construction: An Introduction." Research on *Language and Social Interaction 28* (1995): 171–183.

Jefferson, G. and J. Lee. "The Rejection of Advice: Managing the Problematic Convergence of a 'Troubles-telling' and a 'Service Encounter'." *Journal of Pragmatics 5* (1981): 339–422.

Katz, A. M. and J. Shotter. "Hearing the Patient's 'Voice': Toward a Social Poetics in Diagnostic Interviews." *Social Science and Medicine 43* (1996): 919–31.

Lakoff, G. and M. Johnson. *Metaphors We Live By*. Chicago: University of Chicago Press, 1980.

Mann. S. and F. Stewart. *Internet Communication and Qualitative Research: A Handbook for Researching Online*. London: Sage, 2000.

Morson, G. S. and C. Emerson. *Mikhail Bakhtin: Creation of a Prosaics*. Stanford, CA: Stanford University Press, 1990.

O'Connor, P. "'You Could Feel it Through the Skin': Agency and Positioning in Prisoners' Stabbing Stories." *Text 14* (1994): 45–75.

———. "'You Gotta Be a Man or a Girl': Constructed Dialogue and Reflexivity in the Discourse of Violence." *Pragmatics 7* (1997): 575–599.

Ochs, E. and C. Taylor. "Managing the Therapeutic Institution." In *Gender Articulated: Language and the Socially Constructed Self*, ed. K. Hall and M. Bucholtz. New York: Routledge, 1995.

Potter, J. *Representing Reality: Discourse, Rhetoric, and Social Construction*. London: Sage, 1996.

Psathas, G. *Conversation Analysis: the Study of Talk in Interaction*. Thousand Oaks, CA: Sage, 1995.

Ravotas, D. and C. Berkenkotter. "Voices in the Text: The Uses of Reported Speech in a Psychotherapist's Notes and Initial Assessments." *Text 18* (1998): 211–239.

Sacks, H., E. Schegloff, and G. Jefferson. "A Simplest Systematics for the Organization of Turn-taking for Conversation." *Language 50* (1974): 696–735.

Schegloff, E., G. Jefferson, and H. Sacks. "The Preference for Self-correction in the Organization of Repair in Conversation." *Language 53* (1977): 361–382.

Schiffrin, D. *Approaches to Discourse Analysis*. Oxford: Blackwell, 1994.

Schwandt, T. S. "Constructivist, Interpretivist Approaches to Human Inquiry." In *Handbook of Qualitative Research*, ed. Norman Denzin and Y. Lincoln, 118–137. Thousand Oaks, CA: Sage, 1994.

Shotter, J. *Social Accountability and Selfhood*. Oxford: Basil Blackwell, 1984.

———. "The Social Construction of an 'Us': Problems of Accountability and Narratology." In *Accounting for Relationships: Explanation, Representation, and Knowledge*, ed. R. Burnett, P. Mcgee, and D. Clark, 225–247. London: Methuen, 1987.

———. "Social Accountability and the Social Construction of You." In *Texts of Identity*, ed. J. Shotter and K. J. Gergen, 133–151. London: Sage, 1989.

———. "Becoming Someone: Identity and Belonging." In *Discourse and Lifespan Identity*, ed. N. Coupland and J. Nussbaum, 5–27. Newbury Park, CA: Sage, 1993a.

———. *Conversational Realities: Constructing Life Through Language*. London: Sage, 1993b.

———. "Harré, Vygotsky, Bakhtin, Vico, Wittgenstein: Academic Discourses and Conversational Realities." *Journal for the Theory of Social Behavior 23* (1993c): 459–482.

———. "Dialogical Psychology." In *Rethinking Psychology*, ed. J. A. Smith, R. Harré and L. Vanlanganhove, 160–178. London: Sage, 1995a.

———. "In Conversation: Joint Action, Shared Intentionality, and Ethics." *Theory and Psychology 5* (1995b): 49–73.

Shotter, J. and K. J. Gergen. "Social Construction: Knowledge, Self, Others, and Continuing the Conversation." In *Communication Yearbook 17*, ed. S. Deetz, 3–33. Thousand Oaks, CA: Sage, 1994.

Simblett, G. J. "Leila and the Tiger: Narrative Approaches to Psychiatry." In *Narrative Therapy in Practice: The Archaeology of Hope*, ed. G. Monk, J. Winslade, K. Crocket, and D. Epston, 121–157. San Francisco: Jossey-Bass, 1997.

Somers, M. R. and G. D. Gibson. "Reclaiming the Epistemological 'Other': Narrative and the Social Constitution of Identity." In *Social Theory and the Politics of Identity*, ed. C. Calhoun, 37–99. Oxford: Blackwell, 1994.

Strauss, A. *Qualitative Analysis for Social Scientists*. Cambridge, UK: Cambridge University Press, 1987.

Strauss, A. and J. Corbin. "Grounded Theory Methodology: An Overview." In *Handbook of Qualitative Research*, ed. Norman Denzin and Y. Lincoln, 563–574. Thousand Oaks, CA: Sage, 1994.

Szeleky, E. "Reflections on the Body in Anorexia Discourse." *Resources for Feminist Research 17*, no. 4 (1988a): 8–11.

———. *Never Too Thin*. Toronto: The Women's Press, 1988b.

Taylor, C. Sources of the Self. Cambridge, MA: Harvard University Press, 1989.

Taylor, C. E. (1995a). "Child as Apprentice-narrator: Socializing Voice, Face, Identity and Self-esteem amid the Narrative Politics of Family Dinner." Ph.D. diss., University of Southern California, 1995a.

———. "You Think it Was a Fight?: Co-constructing (The Struggle For) Meaning, Face, and Family in Everyday Narrative Activity." *Research on Language and Social Interaction 28* (1995b): 283–317.

van Dijk, T. A. "Structures of Discourse and Structures of Power." In *Communication Yearbook 12*, ed. J. A. Anderson, 18–59. London: Sage, 1989.

———. "Principles of Critical Discourse Analysis." *Discourse and Society 4* (1993): 249–283.

Voloshinov, V. N. *Marxism and the Philosophy of Language*. Trans. by L. Matejka and I. R. Titunik. Cambridge, MA: Harvard University Press, 1973 (Original Work Published 1929).

Walstrom, M. K. "'Mystory' of Anorexia Nervosa: New Discourses for Change and Recovery." In *Cultural Studies: a Research Annual (Vol. 1)*. ed. Norman K. Denzin, 67–100. Greenwich, CT: JAI Press, 1996.

———. "'Starvation...Is Who I Am': from Eating Disorder to Recovering Identities Through Narrative Co-construction in an Internet Support Group." Ph.D. diss., University of Illinois, Urbana-Champaign, 1999.

———. "'The Eating Disorder Is Not You': Applying Bakhtin's Theories in Analyzing Narrative Co-construction in an Internet Support Group." In *Studies in Symbolic Interactionism 23*, ed. Norman K. Denzin, 241–260. Greenwich, CT: JAI Press, 2000a.

———. "'You Know, Who's the Thinnest?': Combating Surveillance and Creating Safety in Coping with Eating Disorders Online." *Cyberpsychology and Behavior 3*, no. 5 (2000b): 761–784.

———. "Ethics and Engagement in Communication Research: Analyzing Public Online Support Groups as Researcher-participant." In *Virtual Research Ethics: Issues and Controversies*, ed. E. A. Buchanan. (In press).

Winzelberg, A. "The Analysis of an Electronic Support Group for Individuals with Eating Disorders." *Computers in Human Behavior 13* (1997): 393–407.

Part II

Issues of Online Social Research

Introduction: Opportunities and Challenges in Methodology and Ethics

🙞🙜

Amy S. Bruckman

THE COMPUTER STANDS "betwixt and between" normal categories, Sherry Turkle noted (Turkle, 1984, 24). For example, it is between alive and not alive, challenging us to rethink what it means to be "alive." The computer's liminal status poses fundamental questions, not just about itself but about us. This is even more true of computing in the age of the Internet. Internet-based communications are between public and private, published and unpublished, identified and anonymous.

Dennis Waskul and Mark Douglass note that, "the labels of 'public' and 'private' are metaphors applied to the context of cyberspace.... The blurring of public and private experience is particularly characteristic of on-line research. What is 'public' and 'private' is not always clear in conception, experience, label, or substance" (Waskul and Douglass, 1996). Clearly the front page of cnn.com is public. But what about my personal web page? What about a web page I post that is unlinked to any other page, that contains HTML tags telling search engines to please ignore it, and whose URL I send only to close friends? What about a web page on a password-protected site? Does it matter how easy it is to obtain a password to access the site, or whether the site has a posted policy on appropriate use of material there?

In physical space, "public" versus "private" is not a binary distinction, but a question of degree. The architect William Mitchell notes that front porches are an example of a transitional zone in between public and private. Conventions for how to behave appropriately in this transitional zone have evolved over thousands of years, and differ across cultures. Mitchell comments that we need to come to better understand the privacy equivalent of front porches in the digital realm (Mitchell, 2001).

Just as "public" and "private" are blurred online, so are "published" and "unpublished." The concept of "published" versus "unpublished" seems on the surface like a clear, binary distinction: a work is either published (in which case scholars may comment on it without permission), or not.

However, even in the preelectronic age, the distinction is in fact more of a continuum. Consider, for example, a self-published leaflet. Suppose an author makes one hundred copies of a document and distributes them in a public square. Intuitively, this document seems to be "published," even though it is not accessible in libraries or stores. What if the author distributes only ten copies? What if the author distributes only one copy? Does it matter if that one copy is handed to a friend or a stranger? One copy handed to a friend is an instance of personal correspondence, but what about one copy handed to a stranger? "Published" and "unpublished" is not as clear of a distinction as it may seem at first. There exist gray zones where material is "semipublished."

While examples of semipublished material are rare in the world of print media, they are common in the world of electronic publication. For example, consider a public e-mail list with open subscription and a widely announced open web-based archive of past discussions. We can reasonably argue that posts to this list are like publications. However, contrast this to a private list. For example, suppose a group of friends start a private e-mail list to discuss basketball and arrange their weekly basketball game. The list is not archived and membership is only by personal invitation. It is reasonable to argue that posts to this list are not publications. However, now suppose that one member of the list decides to create an archive of their conversations, and puts it up on his web page. Are posts to the list still unpublished? Does it matter whether the list members know of the existence of the web archive? The status of the list is now less clear.

What if one of the list members finds out about the archive and asks that it be taken down? Can information be "unpublished" after it has been published? Suppose the researcher has kept a copy of the archive, even though it is no longer available online. Should research on this material stop? Does the reason the archive was removed matter? For example, is it different if the archive was removed simply due to computer failure? What if the archive was removed because list members found they were being studied and did not wish to be? Complicated, ambiguous situations are not only possible but common in practice.

"Published" versus "unpublished" is a continuum, and the status of each individual piece of information found online must be determined on a case-by-case basis. The mere presence of information on the Internet does not automatically grant it "published" status.

Finally, a third example of categories that are blurred online is "anonymous" versus "identified." Most Internet-based communications are pseudonymous. Users chose made-up names for the purposes of a particular electronic forum. However, they may use the same pseudonym over an extended period of time and ultimately care about the reputation of that pseudonym. They may use that pseudonym on multiple sites. The pseudonym may in fact contain part or all of their real name. Furthermore, people engaging in serious conversation with one another online tend to continually reveal little bits of information. If the forum is archived, these accumulated small pieces of information often eventually begin to identify the individual. For all these reasons, pseudonyms often function rather like real names (Frankel and Siang, 1999). Julian Dibbell (1998) comments that the environment he studied, a MOO [a graphically represented multiuser domain], "happens to be a world in which, for technical reasons, knowing a person's name is the approximate virtual equivalent of knowing that person's phone number, home address, and social security number as well." Both technological and social factors contribute to how identified or anonymous an individual is in a given situation.

These ambiguities—public and private, published and unpublished, anonymous and identified—often make it difficult to apply existing human subjects rules to Internet-based communications. For example, current human subjects regulations in the United States state that unobtrusive observation of unidentified individuals in a public place is exempt from regulation. But what "places" online are "public"? When are users "unidentified"? As we have seen, these questions are more challenging to answer than it may seem on the surface. Similarly, human subjects regulations do not apply to material that is published. I do not need consent from the author to comment on or analyze a published book, paper, letter to the editor, and so on. But what material online is "published"? Existing regulations do not give adequate guidance on these issues.

Given the complexity of the issues, it's not surprising that extensive scholarly debate has taken place on these issues. In the papers that open and close this section, authors Mark Johns, Jon Hall, and Tara Crowell, do something long overdue: they approach the underlying issues empirically. In so doing, they make a more substantive contribution to our understanding than any amount of argument and counterargument could ever accomplish. In Lori Kendall's engaging chapter, the author reflects on what it means to do ethnography in this new medium. She narrates the process of negotiating multiple identities, expectations, and audiences in her professional practice. Finally, Annette Markham poses fundamental questions about what it means to study online versus face-to-face communication. Together, these pieces extend our understanding of this liminal medium and what it means to do research there.

References

Dibbell, J. *My Tiny Life: Crime and Passion in a Virtual World.* New York: Henry Holt and Company, 1998.

Frankel, M. S. and S. Siang. *Ethical and Legal Aspects of Human Subjects Research on the Internet.* Washington, DC: American Association for the Advancement of Science (AAAS), 1999.

Mitchell, W. Personal communication to A. Bruckman, April 2001.

Turkle, S. *The Second Self: Computers and the Human Spirit.* New York: Simon and Schuster, 1984.

Waskul, D. and M. Douglass. "Considering the Electronic Participant: Some Polemical Observations on the Ethics of On-Line Research." *The Information Society 12* (1996): 129–139.

Surviving the IRB Review: Institutional Guidelines and Research Strategies

か。

Mark D. Johns
G. Jon Hall
Tara Lynn Crowell

WITH THE EMERGENCE OF the Internet and the advancement of various online technologies, researchers are no longer limited to traditional means of information gathering and data collection. However, online environments have introduced a new set of variables to the research context and, as a result, researchers are struggling as they seek to adapt traditional methodologies and compliance rules to the online setting. Part of this struggle involves satisfying the requirements of those charged with overseeing the way in which research is being conducted in a particular setting.

Before the actual investigation commences, the research process begins with a research design. The design requires forethought by the researcher related to myriad factors and review by an oversight officer or board prior to implementation. In the United States, these oversight agencies are conventionally called Institutional Review Boards or IRBs. Compliance with federal guidelines, and the local or institutional interpretations of those guidelines, are critical considerations to the design process. The purpose of this chapter is to briefly trace the historical foundations of this system and to explore ways in which experienced Internet researchers have approached the review process in designing their research.

Issues being discussed here are not uniquely American, as social science researchers around the world share common concerns and confront analogous problems, and the Internet expands beyond national borders. A number of countries also have oversight agencies using the same general guidelines and principles as does the United States.[1] It also should be noted that one might expect to see cultural differences as to the way in which the principles are interpreted and applied.[2] However, the authors address the issues surrounding institutional review from an American context, hopeful that researchers in other contexts will find points of similarity to their own circumstances.

Historical Perspective[3]

Concerns for responsible treatment of human subjects grew out of bio-medical research, specifically the notorious "experiments" perpetuated on concentration camp prisoners under the pretext of "medical research" by scientists and physicians in Nazi Germany during World War II (Berger, 1990; Burns and Grove, 1993, cited in Berg 2001; Lifton, 1986). These atrocities prompted judicial decisions leading to development of the *Nuremberg Code* (1949), which laid down the first principles for guiding research on human subjects. The first and most notable principle was that subjects must voluntarily consent to participation (Lifton, 1986). This principle, the precursor of informed consent, was the foundation of the *Declaration of Helsinki* adopted by the World Health Organization in 1964 and revised in 1975. Although designed for the biomedical community, it later served as a guiding principle in the development of subsequent guidelines by various agencies and organizations in the United States, as well as many other countries.

In addition to human rights violations in Nazi Germany, the *Tuskegee Syphilis Study*, which began in 1929 and ended in 1972 (Brandt, 1978, cited in Berg, 2001; Jones, 1981), the *Brooklyn Jewish Chronic Disease Hospital Study* in the mid-1960s (Levine, 1986, cited in Berg, 2001) as well as other biomedical experiments conducted during the same period (Hershey and Miller, 1976, cited in Berg, 2001) were instrumental in raising the collective conscious as to the need for stringent guidelines.

During this period, there were virtually no federal or state statutes regulating research, nor had discipline-related associations seen the need to establish codes of conduct. It was 1966 before the American Medical Association developed its *Ethical Guidelines for Clinical Investigation*. In the same year, the U.S. Surgeon General issued the first set of rules as it related to public health research. These guidelines mandated the establishment of the review committee system and charged them with the responsibility of protecting human subjects and to ensure informed consent (Berg, 2001). In 1971, the U.S. Department of Health, Education, and Welfare (DHEW) published a policy that expanded the principles of institutional review and informed consent to all DHEW grant and contract activities involving human subjects.

In 1974, the U.S. Congress passed the National Research Act (NRA). The NRA created the National Commission for the Protection of Human Subjects of Biomedical and Behavioral Research. The commission was noteworthy in several respects. First, the inclusion of "behavioral" in the title extended the scope beyond the biomedical community to social research. Second, it directed all institutions that conducted sponsored research—including colleges and universities-to establish IRBs. Third, the Commission was charged to identify the basic ethical principles that should govern conduct and to develop appropriate and responsible guidelines to ensure compliance. The product of the Commission work was the *Belmont Report* (DHEW, 1979),[4] which, for all intents and purposes, continues to serve as the ethical foundation for the practice and regulation of research in the United States.

In 1991, the successor to DHEW, the Department of Health and Human Services (DHHS) issued a second set of regulations for protecting the welfare of human subjects. Included in this revision was a second set of guidelines, known as the *Common Rule*,[5] with which research institutions must comply if funded by federal monies. These compliance regulations empowered IRBs to approve, require modification, or disapprove research. More recent DHHS action suggests that there may be moves toward even sharper scrutiny and expanded authority for IRBs (AAUP, 2000). During the fall of 2000, a policy was enacted requiring educational meetings for all researchers, designed to assure understanding of participant protection issues (Thomas, 2002). Known as the *Responsible Conduct of Research* (RCR) policy,[6] it called for institutions to develop and provide training for researchers, regardless of discipline and whether federally funded or not. The RCR adds a new dimension to research preparation and, at this writing, it is not yet clear what impact the RCR policy might have.[7]

Hence, various oversight mechanisms have multiplied rapidly in recent decades.[8] It is the researcher's responsibility to be familiar with the guidelines and regulations, and to keep abreast of changing developments.

Role of the IRBs

As previously discussed, IRBs were established by statute with the mandate to protect the rights and welfare of human subjects. Each IRB is responsible for the development of local guidelines and procedures to carry out the provisions of the law. These guidelines and protocols vary from one institution to the next, yet adhere to the *Common Rule*. Researchers may look at the IRB Forum website (http://www.irbforum.org) for procedures of various institutions.

It is estimated that in 2000, there were more than four thousand IRBs in universities, hospitals, and private research facilities. Latest figures available, from 1995, report that 35,000 to 45,000 research projects were conducted annually under the auspices of these IRBs (AAUP, 2000, 2). As one might expect, the two most common research venues are from biomedical/clinical and higher education. Both undergraduate and graduate research projects are potentially subject to IRB review, but this practice varies from one institution to the next.

Although the central focus of IRBs has been on biomedical community, social science research was included almost from the outset. IRBs, particularly in colleges and universities, tended to require IRB review of all research involving human subjects, whether funded by government monies or not. According to a report in 2000, approximately 75 percent of the largest research institutions in the United States have voluntarily extended the IRB review to all research (AAUP, 2000, 2).

The *Belmont Report*, which formulated the framework for guiding the development and review of research proposals, recognized three "Basic Ethical Principles"—respect, beneficence, and justice—that became the criteria by which the IRBs are to evaluate research proposals (*Belmont Report*, Part B).[9] Respect was a response to the concern over involuntary participation. It championed the belief that potential subjects had the right to make their own decisions as to be involved in a study, and that those unable to make such decisions need to be protected. Beneficence relates to the evaluation of benefits derived from the research when weighed against the risks (physical, psychological, emotional personal/professional) incurred. Justice dictates that all participants be treated equally and fairly in both the recruitment stage and during the course of the investigation. And in those cases where the intent is not to do, an explanation is required.

These three principles are not the prescription of a set of ethical rules but goals on which the research should focus. By laying out these three ethical principles, the *Belmont Report* provided not only goals for researchers but also yardsticks for the IRBs. The three principles of respect, beneficence, and justice must be satisfied for successful review. It is the varied application of these principles, and differing perceptions as to what is meant or intended by the IRBs, which causes problems for researchers. The "local" IRB has jurisdictional oversight by mandate and may, depending on how it interprets the principles as they apply to a specific project, approve, require modification, or reject.

In 1991, DHHS softened the regulations as they related to research in educational institutions by exempting studies related to certain preapproved categories of research, so long as the research design poses "minimal risk" (Department of Health and Human Services, 2001). That is, the risks of physical, emotional, or economic harm would be no greater than those encountered in the course of normal daily activities for the study population. This expedited review was, for many years, the way in which most proposals outside the biomedical/clinical community were handled.

In recent years, a number of factors have contributed to greater reluctance on the part of IRBs to utilize expedited review. Among these may be the emergence of the Internet, with its worldwide reach, incredible number of users of all ages, cultures and backgrounds, ease of use, and concerns about misuse and abuse. In June 1999, the American Association for the Advancement of Science (AAAS), in collaboration with the National Institute of Health's Office for the Protection from Research Risk, convened a conference to explore the relevant issues related to Internet research and make recommendations for future action. The conference was prompted by the wide-ranging kinds of research that were taking place on the Internet (Frankel and Siang, 1999).

The report of the committee reflects the struggles of the online researcher and the reservations many hold toward conducting research in these new venues.[10] The Internet, simply put, poses issues, problems, and concerns that were not anticipated when regulations were established. A key factor contributing to the lack of guidelines is that several controversial issues involving online research have yet to be resolved and there are widespread differences of opinion as to what constitutes appropriate online ethical conduct and respect for human subjects. As examples, there still is no agreement as to whether messages found online constitute human interactions (private correspondence) or published texts (open to public analysis), whether lurking is a defensible research technique, or whether seeking consent is required in all venues. One need only read postings on the AoIR and CRTNET listservs,[11] or attend academic conferences in various disciples, to observe both the level of concern on such issues, and to see how groups of this type are attempting to address them in a responsible way. Lacking an understanding of how online research is similar to, or different from, traditional contexts has left many IRBs uncertain as to how to review proposals.[12]

Experiences from the Field

In order to document how researchers have attempted to comply with the essential principles of the *Belmont Report* while negotiating the panoply of differing IRB standards, a survey of veteran online researchers was conducted. Notes were posted to the CRTNET and AoIR-L listservs, inviting Internet researchers with experience in seeking IRB approval for online social research to log onto a web site that had been specially established for the purpose of this study. The web site allowed respondents to answer several open-ended questions while enabling responses to be completely anonymous. However, any respondents who wished to do so were invited to identify themselves, separately from their responses, so that they might be contacted for additional follow-up questions.

After completing a screen providing information about the study, informed consent was indicated by clicking a link to a subsequent survey page. There, respondents were asked to briefly share the nature of their research, and the manner in which they had proposed to protect human subjects. In particular, they were asked to explain how they had proposed to deal with issues such as anonymity, privacy, and informed consent. Furthermore, respondents were asked to describe any difficulties they had experienced in obtaining IRB approval for their research.

The survey findings show that each respondent had an awareness of issues related to the protection of human subjects. In describing their proposals, all indicated that they had made intentional provisions to gain informed consent and to maintain the anonymity of subjects participating in the research. One researcher explained the use of wording introducing an online survey that would be very similar to that used in a more traditional "paper-and-pencil" instrument:

> The information collected here is for research purposes only. All responses are treated as confidential, and in no case will responses from individual participants be identified. Rather, all data will be pooled and published in aggregate form only. Participation is voluntary, refusal to take part in the study involves no penalty or loss of benefits to which participants are otherwise entitled, and participants may withdraw from the study at any time without penalty or loss of benefits to which they are otherwise entitled.

Another indicated the use of some typical procedures for maintaining the security of online responses: "I stipulated that I alone would be handling the 'data,' it would be downloaded to a separate stand-alone computer, and all 'data' would be destroyed upon completion of the project. I offered them results from the study as well as copies of their personality inventories which was also data I collected in exchange for their cooperation." Others proposed maintaining participant anonymity in similarly straightforward fashion. Some handled this manually; "When we sent out the survey and received responses, we physically blocked out the e-mail address from the sender. On a separate list, we kept track of who did and did not respond, so we could send a reminder." Others made use of technology: "At no time did the survey ask for name or other types of identification. Also, the data were directly sent to a different website. We were the only ones with access to this web site."

These provisions did not always meet with the approval of the IRB. As noted, the lack of consistent interpretation and application of federal IRB standards can lead to very different responses to the same proposal from different review boards. One researcher wrote, "It went smoothly [on my own campus].... I submitted the information to another campus as I originally planned on gathering data at two different schools, but they denied it flatly." Another respondent noted, "I think our main problem was that the IRB review team changed in the middle of our review.... When we first applied, we submitted a consent form almost identical with the one used in a previous, related deception study, and at first there was no criticism of the consent form; then the [IRB] team changed, and suddenly all kinds of new problems were found."

In at least two cases, the relative anonymity, which is a characteristic of computer-mediated communication, was considered by the IRB not to be a means of protection for the human subjects but, rather, a detriment to the quality of the research data. One respondent was challenged by their IRB because there was no way that the researcher could verify that subjects taking part in an online survey were, in fact, of legal age. Similarly, the mechanisms used in cyberspace to make such determinations was, in at least one instance, a source of confusion. One respondent wrote, "Because I was interviewing people whom I'd never meet, I wanted to ensure that I was not interviewing people who were under 18. So, I added to the standard consent form two buttons. They had to check one of the two stating if they were over 18 or under 18. My reviewer thought this meant that I also wanted to interview people who were over 18.... It took two months to learn that was the problem with my proposal."

Another respondent described a complaint from an IRB based on the fact that an e-mail survey, once completed, would be transmitted in its entirety the instant the "send" button was pressed. "They wouldn't have a choice to stop/ not participate." The researcher had to explain that not responding to the e-mail at all was an option for the subjects who received the survey, or that an e-mail may be deleted without being sent, even after it has been written.

By contrast, some IRBs were quite willing to be flexible in accommodating the mechanics of online research. A respondent mentioned, "My University's IRB did not have a problem with me not getting physical signatures. It was enough for them that they typed their name in a form field, and that I recorded that." Another remarked, "The informed consent was the same as a paper-pencil, just with two buttons 'I agree to Participate' or 'I do not agree to Participate.' If they clicked the first then they were forwarded to the survey; if they clicked the latter, they were sent to [an alternate web site]."

Clearly, what the issue here is varied levels of understanding among IRB members of the formal features of the online environment, and varied levels of trust concerning the integrity of human interactions taking place online. Online research methods may be subject to particular misunderstandings on the part of IRB reviewers, or may be held to standards beyond those normally exercised in face-to-face research. Although it is doubtful that an IRB would require formal verification of identity, age, or status for a mail or telephone survey, suspicion of the online environment brings the possibility of deception more readily to mind. A web link button or other mechanism typically used by a researcher to guide or select human subjects online, while quite similar to the design of typical paper questionnaires, may or may not be judged a satisfactory safeguard by the IRB.

An IRB Encounter

Lack of understanding of the formal features of computer-mediated communication has left some IRB members confused when evaluating research proposals which seek to apply traditional research methods in the virtual realm. The following case study illustrates some of the questions and confusion generated when an IRB is confronted with a research proposal which represents an interface between research methods and Internet technology. This case is highlighted here, not because it is unique, or because it predicts what every Internet researcher is likely to encounter, but because it serves as an illustration of some typical issues that may need to be addressed by online researchers as they prepare research designs and proposals for IRB consideration.

The research was designed to identify the characteristics of individuals who acquired HIV through heterosexual activities. The research objective was to link the attitudes/behaviors of individuals living with HIV with those who are not infected. By uncovering accurate information about individuals living with HIV and illustrating the similarities between these two groups, the researcher hoped to decrease the false sense of invulnerability among those not infected, and increase their safer sexual communication and behavior.[13]

Because of the specific criterion that participants be HIV-positive heterosexuals who obtained the virus through hetero(sexual) contact and the sensitive nature of the subject matter, the researcher believed that collecting data online would be an effective way to obtain this information. Participants were to be solicited from online newsgroups, AIDS hotlines and support groups, AIDS chatlines, and AIDS organization web pages. Participants were to be asked to provide information on their knowledge of HIV, perceived risk of HIV infection, safer sex communication, and safer sex behaviors prior to infection. Participants' responses to closed- and open-ended questions were to be analyzed to identify the specific attitudinal and behavioral characteristics of heterosexuals living with HIV and to determine if HIV-positive and HIV-negative individuals have similar characteristics. Additionally, participants were to be asked to provide suggestions and/or advice to HIV-negative individuals based on their experience in living with HIV.

Preparing for IRB Review

Given that the researcher was using a survey method, she first provided the IRB with an "exempt status" proposal, which was quickly denied. As stated in the university's IRB guidelines, survey research or interview procedures are exempt, except where all of the following conditions exist:

* Responses are recorded in such a manner that the human subjects can be identified, directly or through identifiers linked to the subjects.

* The subject's responses, if they became known outside the research, could reasonably place the subject at risk of criminal or civil liabilities or be damaging to the subject's financial standing or employability.

* The research deals with sensitive aspects of the subject's own behavior such as illegal conduct, drug use, sexual behavior, or use of alcohol.

On receiving word that her study was not approved by the board, the researcher was informed that her study had failed each of the above three conditions. More specifically, the board indicated that:

* With online data collection, there are ways to identify participants and to link them to their responses.

* If someone discloses that they had "illegal" sexual relations, the researcher would have a legal obligation to report it to the authorities.

* The questions on the survey dealt with sexual behavior.

The researcher was then instructed by the IRB office to submit a "full board review" proposal.

The second proposal submitted by the researcher was also rejected, with the board citing numerous concerns and problems. More specifically, the IRB's comments expressed concern with six issues concerning logistics of the survey:

Informed Consent Form. The IRB had problems with the inability of the researcher to obtain participants' signatures online. Or, more precisely, there was disagreement concerning what constitutes a legitimate signature online. Being oriented to writing and printing technologies, IRB members were untrusting of the various forms of electronic signatures commonly employed on the Internet. No clear standards yet exist for such signatures in a research context, and different technologies afford varying levels of security. Electronic signatures utilized for online banking, for example, are more secure than those used to sign informal e-mail messages. What level of signature security is adequate for the "signing" of an informed consent document?

Voluntary Participation. The IRB voiced concern about whether or not participants would have "freedom of choice" to discontinue the survey once they had begun. As print-oriented individuals, members of the IRB were unaware of technologies available to allow research participants to be in control of their responses to specific survey questions, or to simply not respond at all.

Subject Anonymity. The IRB expressed concern for subject autonomy in two somewhat contradictory ways. The IRB was concerned with protecting subject autonomy in the online environment. Yet, at the same time, the board members wanted to know how the researcher would ensure participants met the specific sampling requirements—that they really were who and what they claimed to be. Even though the Introduction Page and Consent Form stated that participants must be HIV-positive heterosexuals who were infected through heterosexual activity, some IRB members were concerned that the researcher would have no way to monitor the identities of those filling out the survey. Therefore, IRB members questioned the validity of this type of online data because the researcher could not be sure that participants were, in fact, HIV positive.

Data Confidentiality. The IRB's criticism of online research and data confidentiality was simply that no online study could guarantee confidentiality, but that data would always be vulnerable to some sort of "hacking" or unauthorized access. In fact, all research data, whether kept on paper in a locked file or kept on a computer disk, is vulnerable to unauthorized access. The question is what level of security is reasonable in relation to the potential risks to research subjects if confidentiality were compromised. But the IRB saw electronically gathered and stored data as inherently less secure than traditional paper files. Again, IRB members needed to be made aware of the various security technologies available, and a determination needed to be made as to what level of security would be adequate for this particular set of data.

Debriefing of Participants. The IRB was concerned with the type of debriefing procedures that could be given online, because no researcher would be present to answer questions or provide further information. However, once again technologies exist online both for providing information at least as effectively as in print, and for facilitating questions and answers via e-mail.

Value of the Study. The last major objection the IRB had regarding the proposal was the value of the study. Many universities and colleges are now extending the role of the IRB not only to the protection of human subjects but also to assessing the value of the research being conducted. Obviously, the IRB has always weighed the risks versus the benefits, and if the risks outweighed the benefits, the study was not "worth" the risk. The IRB questioned the value of the study because some members did not believe it should be conducted at all.

Strategies for IRB Approval

Once the researcher addressed each of these six issues in writing and made the required changes to the instructions, consent form, survey, and debriefing page, the IRB approved the study. The specific strategies used to deal with each of the concerns raised by the IRB are highlighted in this section. The primary strategic goal was to provide information to the members of the IRB about the capabilities of the technology and its applicability for online research.

Informed Consent Form. With a traditional paper-and-pencil survey, researchers are able to keep a hard copy of the consent forms with participants' signatures. This is necessary in order to prove that informed consent was actually obtained should there be later questions or legal action. However, with online research, the researcher can obtain participants' consent but without a signature. Participants can either click on "I Agree to Participate" or "I Do Not Agree to Participate." If individuals click on the first it takes them to the survey; therefore, the only way they can access the survey is if they "agree to participate." If individuals click on the second, it sends them to an alternate web site, thereby not allowing them to access the survey. As stated by John Mueller (1997): "By clicking the link the participant accepts the terms of the consent form and proceeds to the actual survey. Although this could be seen as problematic, in fact, this format is widely used in lieu of a signature, for example, when entering credit card information online, or when accepting the terms of a software license prior to installation. So there are ample precedents for its use."

Voluntary Participation. One IRB member noted that "if people change their mind, they won't be able to quit half way through." However, with online surveys, individuals may feel less pressure to either begin or complete a survey. When individuals log onto the Internet, they are free to "surf" anywhere. If they do not want to participate in a research project, they can simply visit another web site. Similarly, if they begin filling out a survey and wish to stop, they can click on the "X" button at the far right corner of their screen or change the web address in the address window. With traditional pencil-and-paper surveys, participants may not feel free to withdraw due to perceived penalties or may refrain from expressing their desire not to participate because of face-to-face social pressures. Neither of these factors influences a researcher and subject in a "virtual encounter." Despite the above explanation, the IRB insisted that the following statement appear on the Introduction/Instruction Page: "My participation in this study is entirely voluntary, and I may terminate my participation at any time prior to the completion of this study without penalty."

Subject Anonymity. Generally, researchers protect subject autonomy by instructing participants not to place their names or any type of identifying number or information on their questionnaire. Researchers also keep participants' signed consent forms separate from the questionnaires. Thus, the researchers are unable to put a "name" with a "data set."

The present online study dealt with subject autonomy in the same manner. Participants were instructed not to provide their name or contact information, and the survey did not provide a "Name" or "Address" field. The IRB, however, required the following directions appear on the Instruction/Introduction page:

> I realize that the informed consent form will be kept completely separate from the raw data. I will not put my name anywhere on the questionnaire, and I realize that my name will not be associated with the data. I realize that publication of this data will not enable identification of me in any way. I realize that data will not be available to non-project personnel and that it will be put into locked cabinets. I understand that the Informed Consent forms will be destroyed once the identifiable data is no longer needed.

Unlike paper-and-pencil surveys, there are ways that a computer can track who has visited/logged on to a web site. Yet, researchers should keep in mind that just because someone visited the site does not mean that they completed the survey. Some domains are associated with personal addresses, and therefore may provide information that identifies participants. Thus, in this case, the researcher explained to the IRB that she would edit the data files periodically, deleting the headers. Although the possibility existed that subject autonomy could be potentially breached in this online research, the IRB accepted the above procedures; but they raised a second concern that contradicts the very nature of subject autonomy.

The board members wanted to know how the researcher could be sure that subjects were HIV positive. The researcher responded to this issue in several different ways. First, by requiring verification of individuals' HIV status, researchers would be exposing participants' identity and possibly putting them at risk. Given the prejudice and discrimination associated with AIDS, exposure of someone's HIV status could cause mental, physical, relational, professional, and/or financial harm. Second, as stated in the study's rationale, participants are more likely to disclose personal and sensitive information about themselves online because of the anonymity of online surveys (i.e., absence of face-to-face interaction). If the researcher were to require or ask for verification of an individuals' status, this would certainly bias the type of people who would participate. This type of systematic subject bias would likely have a greater influence on the validity of the sample. Third, all survey research is susceptible to participant deception. Just because a researcher is able to physically see his/her subjects does not ensure participants' honesty. A participant could engage in deception just as easily filling out a pencil-and-paper survey. In most cases, this type of error is random, not systematic, and therefore will not impact the validity of the study (especially if the study involves a sufficient number of subjects). Finally, IRB members were provided with a detailed description of the recruitment of participants to illustrate the extent to which the researcher targeted the desired population.[14]

Data Confidentiality. Researchers conducting traditional paper-and-pencil surveys usually are required to keep signed consent forms separate from any raw and/or redefined data and to keep data gathered strictly protected from any nonproject personnel by storing the data in a locked cabinet. Finally, once the identifiable data (i.e., the signed informed consent forms) are no longer needed, they must be destroyed.

With online data collection, there are no signed consent forms; and the data are still "locked" away, just on a computer rather than in a file cabinet. To ensure participants' responses would remain confidential, the researcher provided the IRB with the following statement: "To ensure participants' responses are confidential, online surveys are constructed to send data to a separate CGI bin that is accessible only by the researcher."

Thus, the data are still on the web, but at an address only known to "project personnel." Additionally, the researcher provided the IRB with the following quote and citation: "For online data files, confidentiality is achieved in that the data are stored on a computer in a personal account that is accessible only to someone who knows the account user ID and password, which should again be just the researcher (in truth, cracking a UNIX account password is probably much more secure than a file cabinet that yields too often to a bent paper clip!)" (Mueller, 1997).

Given the above explanation, the IRB insisted the following statement appear on the Informed Consent Form: "As with any study conducted via the Internet, confidentiality cannot be guaranteed."

Debriefing the Subjects. Unlike personally administered surveys, with online surveys no researcher is present to debrief participants, provide participants with additional information, or to provide future information about the study's findings. This is why it is very important to provide participants with a "Thank You" page at the end of an online survey. This page lets participants know they have successfully completed the survey and provides them with follow-up material if desired. The researcher submitted such a page to the IRB. The page included (1) thanks for participating, (2) restated the purpose of the study, (3) web sites that provide additional information on HIV and AIDS, (4) where and when they could find a brief report of the results of the study, and (5) researcher's contact information. If researchers provide the above information, these debriefing procedures should be equal, if not superior, to the verbal/written ones provided during paper-and-pencil surveys.

Value. The researcher received the following verbal feedback: "Some of the committee members do not think the study is worthy of conduct." The IRB requested part of the researcher's literature review and rationale. They also wanted the original articles that the scales were taken from to verify reliability and validity. In addition, the IRB recommended changing some of the wording on the survey.

Again, the IRB questioned the validity of gathering this type of data online, because the researcher could not be sure the participants were really HIV positive. The board suggested that it would be better to collect the data with face-to-face interviews or at least with pencil-and-paper surveys. One suggestion made by the IRB was to visit public organizations that provide services to HIV-positive individuals. The researcher responded by explaining that given the demographic similarities of many of these individuals, this sample would not be an adequate representation of the desired population. Not to mention, these procedures (i.e., presence of the researcher) would ensure less autonomy than online surveys.

Online Research and the IRB

The case presented here is somewhat extreme because of the nature of the research and the response of the IRB. Because the research involved an investigation of sexual attitudes and behaviors, and because it focused on a disease that continues to carry a negative social stigma, the IRB was correct in exercising caution in assuring that the human subjects involved would be protected. The IRB was acting responsibly in asking the researcher to fully explain her procedures for acquiring informed consent, protecting subject anonymity, and maintaining the security of the collected data. The sensitive nature of the research also made it appropriate that the IRB give attention to the availability of debriefing information.

What this case does demonstrate, however, is that IRB regulations, and those who interpret them, are firmly grounded in the literate culture of paper and print. The arrival of electronic media requires a redefinition of what constitutes legitimate research and acceptable methodology. Medium theorists (Meyrowitz, 1985; Ong, 1982) often point out that, in the first phase of the introduction of a new medium of communication, individuals are preoccupied with fitting old content and preexisting formats for information into the new medium, often without regard to the differing capabilities and limitations of the new medium. This well describes the current situation with IRBs, which insist that research procedures in the online medium must be identical to those used with "paper-and-pencil" research. Procedures that are parallel with, similar to, or congruent to those utilized offline are not considered valid because they are different. Methods that are adapted to the online environment are held in suspicion because they are not "tried and true." This is not a matter of ignorance on the part of the IRB, but an understandable bias in favor of that which is familiar and against that which is less familiar.

Thus, until online research enters the mainstream, Internet researchers must ask themselves how they might demonstrate to their IRB not only that methods and procedures are as good as those used in traditional environments but also in explicating why and how these methods and procedures are effective in providing adequate means of gaining informed consent, providing data security, and supplying consistent follow-up information to research subjects. Furthermore, online researchers should consider whether there are instances in which online methods actually fulfill the fundamental goal of protecting human subjects more adequately and more thoroughly than is possible through traditional means.

The issue of identity, which became a locus of concern in the present study, serves as an example. Deception is always a possibility in social research. When conducting surveys by mail, researchers are not in a position to verify that the instrument has been completed by the intended recipient. Conducting surveys or interviews by telephone provides only slightly greater assurance of the identity of the respondent. Even when conducting a survey or interview in person, it is always possible that the research subjects are not actually who they present themselves to be unless unusual measures are taken to verify identities. Still, identity validation is not generally considered a problem in these methodologies. In most instances, researchers simply trust that research subjects have no real reason to misrepresent themselves, and that the rare cases in which misrepresentation occurs will have minimal impact on the study when diluted in the larger pool of legitimate data. However, there is never absolute certainty that the researcher is not being deceived in some respect and, in the end, researchers rely on the good faith of those who volunteer to be research subjects.

Identity has become an issue in online research because of the frequent and generally accepted use of pseudonyms and the ease with which computer users are able to assume multiple identities online. Yet, behind most online identities (other than automated "bots") is a real person with real social experiences. These persons are available to the researcher only through the persona presented online. Thus, online researchers will have to ask themselves what might motivate such a person to construct a false persona and to practice deception. Particularly in instances such as in the case illustrated above, the nature of the disease and its social stigma would provide very little incentive for someone to pretend inclusion among those affected. Researchers also will wish to ask themselves whether there are means, through careful and systematic construction of survey or interview questions, to detect and exclude any possible fraudulent personas. Absolute certainty that the researcher is not being deceived is not possible, but the researcher must determine whether the chances of deception are really significantly greater than would be the case using traditional methodologies. IRBs may need to be reminded that, in the end, researchers rely on the good faith of those who volunteer to be research subjects, both online and in "real life."

Ultimately, the concern here revolves around the question of control. In traditional research, the researcher goes to the subjects (as was suggested, in the case above, that the researcher ought to visit local public organizations that provide services to HIV-positive individuals, rather than utilizing the Internet), or possibly advertises the research and invites potential subjects to apply for admission to the study. The researcher, thus, is in active control of which subjects will be included and which will be excluded from the study.

In cyberresearch, the role of the researcher is more passive. The researcher does not go to the subjects but instead selects an appropriate online venue in which to invite the subjects to come to her. Thus, control over who will participate is shifted from the researcher to the participants themselves. As noted by the IRB in this case, this situation may call into question the integrity of the research in that subjects may not actually be who and what they represent themselves to be. However, by careful selection of the venues in which an invitation to participate is issued, researchers reduce this potential considerably, as noted, because it would be a rare individual who would choose to devote the time and energy to participate in a USENET group, listserv, MUD, or other online forum devoted to a subject in which they had no interest or stake.

Offering control over the choice to participate is precisely the point of the requirement for informed consent, and anonymity is the main concern of data security. It is, therefore, ironic that the online environment, which affords the subjects both an extra level of anonymity and control, should be held suspect by an IRB. Only when the online researcher is able to demonstrate that the features of computer-mediated communication enhance, rather than inhibit, the protection of human subjects, by shifting power from the researcher to the researched, is a smooth path to IRB approval ensured.

This chapter provides a brief overview of the historical evolution of the IRB and the role of IRBs in social research, as well as a report of a survey of veteran online researchers about their experiences with IRB applications, and a discussion of a case in which difficulty in gaining IRB approval was experienced. In presenting this information, we hope that readers have a better understanding of the rationale for establishing IRBs as well as for the currently understood functions of IRBs in the United States-and, by extension, in other parts of the world as well. The report of the survey will hopefully prepare future online researchers to consider how to construct their research proposals for IRB review, specifically about how to handle important issues such as informed consent, protection of privacy, data security, and subject debriefing. The case study serves to alert online researchers to possible difficulties in obtaining IRB approval. The historical understanding of the IRB, advice for technical preparation, and the forewarning of possible obstacles hopefully will prepare online researchers for a smooth and problem-free IRB review. More important, we hope this information will be helpful as the online research community and IRBs work together toward establishing clearer guidelines for the review of online research proposals.

Notes

1 As an example, see the UK Data Protection Site at: http://www.dataprotection.gov.uk and the European Commission site at: http://eu.int/comm/internal_market/en/dataprot/wpdocs/wpdocs_2K.htm.

2 See Ess and the Association of Internet Researchers (2002) for a good introduction to the issues related to cultural differences as well as insights to the human subjects issue internationally. A formal statement is expected to be adopted by the AoIR membership in 2003.

3 The authors are indebted to Berg (2001) for his historical commentary, which was instrumental in the preparation of this section.

4 The *Belmont Report* may be found at: http://ohrp.osophs.dhhs.gov/humansubjects/guidance/belmont.htm.

5 The *Common Rule* is part 46 of Title 45 (45CFR46) of the Code of Federal Regulations. It may be found at: http://ohrp.osophs.dhhs.gov/humansubjects/guidance/45Ccfr46.htm.

6 The RCR policy may be found at: http://ori.dhhs.gov/html/programs/finalpolicy.asp.

7 See Thomas (2002) for a good discussion on the RCR and potential implications for social science research.

8 Codes for associations may be found as follows:

American Psychological Association—http://www.apa.org/ethics/code.html

American Computing Machinery—http://www.acm.org/constitution/code.html

American Anthropology Association—http://www.aaanet.org/committees/ethics/ethcode.htm

American Sociological Association—http://www.asanet.org/members/ecoderev.html

American Political Science Association—http://www.apsanet.org/pubs/ethics.cfm

9 Readers are encouraged to read the *Belmont Report* narrative on the three basic ethical principles (see note 4). Also, see Keyton (2001, 83–84) for excellent analysis of the principles.

10 The AASA report may be found at: http://www.aasa.org/spp/dspp/sfrl/interes/main.htm.

11 Mailing lists may be found at: AoIR—Air-l@aoir.org;
CRTNET—http://lists1.cac.psu.edu/cgi-bib/wa

12 In August 1999, the University of Illinois-Chicago was one of several institutions that had suspended all human subjects' research until protocols were re-reviewed and the OHRP lifted restrictions.

13 For more information on some of the specifics of the results found in this study, see Crowell and Emmers-Sommer (2001).

14 During the online study, over 30 percent of the participants contacted the researcher via e-mail after completing the survey. Many of them wanted to provide more information, to explain their situation in greater detail, or to offer thanks for doing this type of research. Others indicated that they would forward the URL of the research web site to someone they knew; while still others wanted to complain about the survey or to offer suggestions on how to improve the study. Although the information in these e-mails, obviously, could not be used in any way in the research, in many ways it provided the researcher with a better personal understanding of HIV-positive heterosexuals than realized from the actual data. This type of insight will be useful in directing

future HIV/AIDS research. Finally, after looking over the answers participants provided (especially answers to open-ended questions), it seemed very unlikely to the researcher that anyone fabricated living with HIV.

References

American Association of University Professors (AAUP). *Protecting Human Beings: Institutional Review Boards and Social Science Research.* Washington DC: 2000. Available on the World Wide Web at http://www.aaup.org/statements/Redbook/repirb.htm.

Berg, B. *Qualitative Research Methods for the Social Sciences.* 4th ed. Boston: Allyn Bacon, 2001.

Berger, R. L. "Nazi Science: The Dachau Hypothermia Experiments." *New England Journal of Medicine 322*, no. 20 (1990): 1435–1440.

Brandt, A. M. *Racism and Research: The Case of the Tuskegee Syphilis Study.* Hastings Center Report (December, 1978): 21–29.

Burns, N. and S. Grove. *The Practice of Nursing Research.* 2nd ed. Philadelphia: W.B. Saunders, 1993.

Crowell, T. L. and T. M. Emmers-Sommer, "'If I Knew Then What I Know Now': Seropositive Individuals' Perceptions of Partner Trust, Safety, and Invulnerability Prior to HIV Infection." *Communication Studies 52*, no. 4 (Winter 2001).

Department of Health, Education, and Welfare (DHEW). *Report of the National Commission for the Protection of Human Subjects of Biomedical and Behavioral Research. Ethical Principles and Guidelines for the Protection of Human Subjects of Research.* Washington, DC: 1979. Known as the *"Belmont Report,"* it is available on the World Wide Web at http://ohrp.osophs. dhhs.gov/humansubjects/guidance/belmont.htm

Department of Health and Human Services. *Code of Federal Regulations (45 CFR 46). Protection of Human Subjects.* Washington, DC: National Institute of Health, Office for the Protection from Research Risks. June 18, 1991, Revised November 13, 2001. Known as the *"Common Rule,"* it is available on the World Wide Web at http://ohrp.osophs.dhhs.gov/humansubjects/guidance/45cfr46.htm

Ess, C., and the Association of Internet Researchers. "Ethical Decision Making and Internet Research: Recommendations from the AoIR Ethics Working Committee." 2002. Available from World Wide Web at http://www.aoir.org/reports/ethics.pdf

Frankel, M.S. and S. Siang. Ethical and Legal Aspects of Human Subjects Research on the Internet: A Report of a Workshop. Washington, DC: American Association for the Advancement of Science, November, 1999. Available on the World Wide Web at http://www.aasa.org/spp/dspp/sfrl/projects/inters/main.htm

Hershey, N and M. Miller. *Human Experimentation and the Law.* Germantown, MD: Aspen Systems, 1976.

Jones, J. H. *Bad Blood: The Tuskegee Syphilis Experiment.* New York: Free Press, 1981.

Keyton, J. *Communication Research: Asking Questions, Finding Answers.* Mountain View, CA: Mayfield Publishing, 2001.

Levine, R .J. "Declaration of Helsinki." *Ethics and Regulations of Clinical Research.* 2nd ed. Baltimore: Urban and Schwartzenberg, 1986.

Lifton, R. J. *Nazi Doctors.* New York: Basic Books, 1986.

Meyrowitz, Joshua. *No Sense of Place: the Impact of Electronic Media on Social Behavior.* New York: Oxford University Press, 1985.

Mueller, John. "Researcher On-line: Human Participants Ethics Issues." Calgary, AB: University of Calgary, Department of Psychology, October 13, 1997. Available on the World Wide Web at http://www.psych.ucalgary.ca/Research/ethics/online.html

Ong, Walter J. *Orality and Literacy: The Technologizing of the Word.* New York, Methuen, 1982.

Thomas, J. "'Big Brother' or Allies? In Defense of the IRBs and RCR." *Society for Study of Symbolic Interaction Notes 29*, no. 1 (March 2002): 4–6.

Participants and Observers in Online Ethnography: Five Stories About Identity

ॐ

Lori Kendall

Story One: The Narrator

ETHNOGRAPHERS OF ONLINE social spaces confront many of the same problems as researchers practicing more traditional ethnographic methods, as well as some new ones. Like traditional ethnographers of face-to-face groups, online ethnographers must find ways to understand the culture and practices of the group under study. They must then find ways to explain those practices to others. Studying interaction that occurs primarily through text among geographically dispersed people presents special problems for ethnographers, who must come to terms with how participants communicate meaning without the use of such nonverbal communication channels as tone of voice, gesture, facial expressions, and so on. When telling stories about their research to others, online ethnographers also confront audiences with varying degrees of knowledge and experience with the Internet, and often must provide explanations about online interaction that go beyond the particular practices of the studied group.

The stories I tell herein come from ethnographic research I did on an online social forum I'm calling BlueSky.[1] BlueSky is a type of interactive, text-only, online forum known as a "MUD." MUD originally stood for Multi-User Dungeon (based on the original multiperson networked dungeons and dragons-type game called MUD). As in other online chat programs, people connect to MUD programs through Internet accounts and communicate through typed text with other people currently connected to that MUD. There are hundreds of MUDs available on the Internet and through private online services. Many MUDs serve as gaming spaces for adventure or "hack-and-slash" games. MUDs also operate as locations for professional meetings, classes and other pedagogical purposes, and as social spaces. Although participants have programmed various toys and games for use within BlueSky, BlueSky functions primarily as a social meeting space.

I spent over two years doing participant-observation research on BlueSky, supplemented by face-to-face interviews with 30 BlueSky participants and various other sources of information about MUDs. Like other participant-observers, I became a member of the group (and still hang out online with that group), and participated in the same activities as other group members. My dual identity—as academic and as MUDder—enables me to act as a translator of BlueSky's culture to interested others. It also places me in a liminal position with regard to both groups; MUDders may be suspicious of my academic status and my use of them as research subjects, while academics may be suspicious of my activities as a MUDder and may wonder if I can maintain sufficient objectivity to accurately analyze the culture and interaction of a group of which I'm a member.

Every story I tell about BlueSky takes its shape through consideration of three overlapping groups: the people of BlueSky; the audience (which may be composed of academics or the general public; Internet savvy or relatively inexperienced, or blends of these); and myself (with all of the sometimes contradictory interests I have in how I come across to these various groups). When I speak to an audience or present a written article that purports to be "about BlueSky," the stories I present are never only about BlueSky. Close reading of ethnographic stories reveals much about the ethnographer and their (understanding of) their audience, as well as about the research "subjects."

The stories that follow, unlike stories I have told elsewhere, are more explicitly about these three groups (if I can refer to myself as a "group"). I first discuss reactions to stories about BlueSky and examine what these reactions tell us regarding assumptions about and understandings of online socializing. I next provide two different views (Story Three and Story Four) of one of my most often told stories—regarding my first contact with BlueSky—and examine what my way of telling that story reveals about myself and my relationship to my audience. Finally, I discuss some of the reactions of BlueSky participants to my research. In Story Five, I attempt to look through their eyes at the academic world rather than through academic eyes at their world. In the closing section, I return to this identity of the Narrator, an identity that, like the other identities here, is constructed based on (in this case) (1) cultural conventions regarding academic writing, (2) assumptions about the audience, and (3) my own interests in how I wish appear as a scholar and as an authority on online research.

Story Two: The Reviewer

Most ethnographic stories, as the word ethnography itself implies, are told in writing. Being an aspiring academic (most of my articles about BlueSky were written while I was still a graduate student or just after I received my Ph.D.) meant attempting to publish "stories" about BlueSky in academic, peer-reviewed journals. Although the eventual audience for these stories comprises a wide range of academics and other interested parties, the initial audience for a submitted manuscript usually consists of four people: the editor and three anonymous reviewers. The subject of Internet research was relatively new to most of the journals I submitted work to, meaning that my translation of BlueSky's culture to these audiences required engaging with existing understandings of ethnographic and other forms of social research, as well as existing understandings of the Internet and online interaction. Comments that recur repeatedly in reviews I've received over the years highlight several important issues involved in the study of online interaction: (1) the question of what "participant observation" means when all interaction occurs through text; (2) dominant cultural ideas about mediated interaction in general; and (3) how these ideas reflect on the researcher's presentation of self and thus on veracity of the researcher's accounts and analysis of research.

Given the nature of the blind review process, comments I received on submitted manuscripts were not intended for publication, and the identities of the authors are in most cases unknown to me. Therefore, I present below a fictionalized, composite "review" that draws on actual comments received from reviewers.[2] (Many of these same comments occur in face-to-face question-and-answer sessions as well.)

> While I agree that connections between gender performance and the reproduction of inequality need to be explored through research, I can't see the importance of such performances in chat rooms. I wonder if the author knew these people prior to doing research. I'm also bothered by the description of the methodology. The author claims to have engaged in "participant observation," yet the article really consists almost solely of textual analysis. Participant observation doesn't just mean that the author "participated" in the group, but that they were able to interpret meaning through the understanding of facial and bodily gestures, as well as physical and social context. The author apparently interviewed participants in person, but appears to make no distinction between online and face-to-face communications. These two very different data sets should be separated in the analysis. In addition, I am quite troubled by the fact that the author changed the participants' pseudonyms. This seems dangerously close to falsification of data. What assurance do we have that BlueSky actually exists? Finally, I find problematic the claim that the dialogues presented herein can even be considered social interaction in any conventional sense.

Some of the above comments resulted from inadequate methodological discussion on my part. Now that I am as often the reviewer as the reviewed, I notice this same problem in other articles about Internet research. This highlights the importance of full and careful description and disclosure of the process of information gathering and analysis. However, some of the comments above reflect more specifically on issues relating to the type of interaction being researched.

For instance, several of the comments above refer to the relative unimportance of online social interaction. Audiences raise such concerns regarding other types of interaction as well. Most of us who have studied social interaction in semipublic places such as bars or coffee houses, or who have engaged in other forms of microsociological analysis such as conversation analysis, have heard similar complaints that such forms of interaction are trivial and not worth studying. The type of online interaction I studied, involving as it did members of a particular subculture of young people whose interactions were primarily sociable, invites such criticism not entirely because it occurred online, but also because it consists of people "just hanging out." This is no doubt one of the reasons I tend to mention the fact that a significant portion of the communication on BlueSky concerns the exchange of job-related information. If my research subjects aren't just goofing off, then I'm not just goofing off either.

That BlueSky's communications occur online adds further to the tendency to see them as trivial, as the Reviewer's comment concerning chatrooms indicates. Reviewers and other social researchers are not the only people who tend to view online socializing as not really social interaction. Popular accounts of the Internet reflect this assumption as well and, in fact, many online participants themselves feel similarly. Comments made by BlueSky participants during my research reflected a belief that online interaction was not real socializing.

For instance, in my interview with RaveMage, a BlueSky participant and psychiatrist, he talked about BlueSky and other similar MUDs as, in a way, training wheels for the socially impaired:

> RaveMage: It's almost like a day hospital for people who have social difficulty. First you interact in a literally faceless and completely defended way with people that if anything upsets you, you just disconnect, no big deal. And you can do it without having to worry about, unfortunately, things like personal hygiene and stuff like that. [In the early days] we were going around yelling "mud naked, mud naked" because you can! So after all that what comes out next is that then you try to go to a [face-to-face] get-together.

Lori: [So] it's sort of a training [ground].

RaveMage: Exactly.

Lori: And then you can use those same skills with other people.

RaveMage: First you learn to do it on the muds, and then often [when] you try to do it in person the first time you get a really rude shock, but that's okay because that also is educational and they learn that and then after that they move [on]. [He mentions two BlueSky participants.] They are just terribly nice people, great to be around [but] if we hadn't had the chance to talk to them [online] first and realized that, we wouldn't have put up with [them face-to-face].

While RaveMage's comments may in part simply reflect a recognition of the differences between online and face-to-face communication—especially the lack of physical presence—to some degree his comments also represent online communication as less fully social than face-to-face communication.

Similarly, Beryl, another long-time BlueSky participant, described a previous participant in terms which did not grant full social status to online communication:

Lori: Were there people that you liked online and you'd meet them and you wouldn't like them?

Beryl: Yes. Like Cap turned out.... He's not bad online.... But he's never mastered being social. So he was a totally different person in real life.

As described by a variety of BlueSky participants, Cap had many annoying habits that interfered with his offline presentation of self, including a tendency to tickle people without warning. There are many personal habits that can seriously disrupt offline communication (interrupting, talking too loudly, etc.) that don't affect text-based online communication. But significantly, Beryl's evaluation of Cap as having "never mastered being social" nevertheless enables him to be "not bad online." BlueSky participants also reported that they tended not to fully trust others unless they had met face-to-face, although their descriptions of what was missing online tended to be vague. Whatever that intangible something is that enabled BlueSky participants to only feel that they fully knew someone else if they had met face-to-face, it also appears to be a required ingredient for evaluating an interaction as truly social. Even my own question, as to whether Beryl felt differently about people after "meeting" them—although made in the context of an interview in which it was clear that "meeting" people meant face-to-face meetings—suggests that the (often lengthy) interaction she had online with people did not qualify as "meeting" them.

For my audiences as well, the information that most BlueSky participants have met several others (often as many as 20, and for a few well-traveled and high-status people, anywhere from 50 to 150) changes the tone of the questions I receive. Prior to explaining that I met many BlueSky participants face-to-face and that they have often met each other, audiences tend to object that I can't "really know" who these people are. My analysis of gender and other aspects of identity remains suspect while it is based solely on online data.

In addition to reflecting a particular cultural understanding of online interaction, the Reviewer's suggestion that my methodology was more content analysis than participant observation also fails to recognize both the amount of social context that can be conveyed through text, and the importance of ongoing participation to understanding the social context of an online group. On BlueSky, joking rituals, formulaic expressions, repetition, and continual references to shared history tend to substitute for some of the missing richness of face-to-face communication. Their years of shared online interaction allow BlueSky participants to add nuance to their textual communication.

My own process of learning the technical aspects of MUDding, as well as BlueSky's cultural conventions and history, gave me important insight not just into BlueSky as it existed while I was studying it, but also to the processes BlueSky's participants had to go through to arrive at their current understandings and beliefs. For instance, although almost no one on BlueSky "masqueraded" with an identity substantially different from their offline identity, my own experience on other MUDs with this phenomenon enabled me to understand the hostility of BlueSky participants to anonymous guests and to masquerades in general.

In addition, having a stake in the ongoing conversation changes one's understanding of that conversation. Reading a log of someone else's discussion, unless it for some reason directly affects the researcher (by happening to refer to a "hot button" topic, or mentioning someone the researcher knows), is not the same as reading a log of a conversation about which the researcher can remember "that's the first time anyone really laughed at a joke I made," or "I wish I hadn't brought that topic up, because the argument caused some tensions between people." The memory of how interaction felt at the time it occurred comes back to me when I read through logs (and my notes regarding those logs), and those feelings become part of my analysis, as they do in other types of ethnography. This provides a richer analysis than does content analysis, in which the words themselves, and perhaps their latent thematic material, are the only sources of information for analysis.

This also means that when reproducing logs of online interaction in my writings, I must intersperse small sections of log with my own commentary. I have found that, otherwise, readers find these logs boring. I must supply analytical information that connects their own interests (in what online interaction means, in particular theories about the Internet, etc.) with conversations in which they did not take part and in which they therefore have no stake.

The question of the relative worth of ethnography as compared to other social research methods emerges again in the Reviewer's comment about "falsification" of data and the real existence of BlueSky. The social research methods that more closely resemble the methodology of the natural sciences—experiments and survey research—can usually provide greater protections for subjects' privacy, often guaranteeing complete anonymity. Ethnographers, by contrast, come to know their subjects quite well. The ethnographic use of narrative and description in research reports sometimes risks revealing too much about the people under study. Therefore, ethnographers routinely change the names of their informants to protect their privacy. The Reviewer's objection to this may simply reflect the divides that exist between practitioners of various types of social research.

However, as with the concern about whether or not online socializing is truly social, I believe the concerns about falsification and reality reflect ideas about online social spaces in general. If such spaces exist only through words, then changing any of those words represents a more problematic step than it would in reporting about other types of social spaces.

Finally, the stray question—a seeming non sequitur—as to whether I knew the BlueSky participants prior to beginning my research occurs often enough in both reviews of my work and questions following oral presentations to warrant further analysis. Like the negative evaluations of online socializing, this comment suggests that online interaction, and chatrooms in particular, may not be worthy of study. The interest in my personal MUDding history suggests that I chose my research topic and "field site" for personal, rather than analytical, reasons. While many, if not most, researchers choose their topics out of personal interest, the particular mention of that possibility in this case suggests that if I'm one of "those people" who hang out online, this reflects on my own social competency and by extension perhaps on my analytical competency as well. This comment asks me to account for myself as possibly a member of a low-status group, and to account for my choice of topic and field site in terms that justify their analytical interest. Such comments suggest that I may not have fully bracketed the "participant" half of my participant-observer self when making my analytical "observations." The fact that I was not a participant on BlueSky prior to beginning my research enables me to easily sidestep this question. The many online ethnographers who do study sites with which they had previous familiarity may have to work harder to justify their choice of topic and site.

Story Three: The Audience

A Partygoer: So, how did you pick BlueSky? How did you find them?

The Ethnographer: Well, actually I just stumbled across the group when I was exploring a variety of different muds. BlueSky was the first mud I encountered where it seemed that people treated me rudely. They were very obnoxious and vulgar; I was insulted and logged off in a huff. But hey, I'm supposed to be doing research, right? I can't let a little rudeness bother me! [with self-mocking false bravado]: So I mustered up my ethnographic courage, picked a poisonous name for my character, and logged back on. Once I had hung out there for a bit longer, it became clear that the people on BlueSky had been participating online for several years and had very well-developed relationships with each other and a complex subculture. I got interested in seeing what kind of relationships they had and how they integrated online socializing into their lives and work schedules.

This is my "first contact" story, which I often tell both to informal groups at parties and as part of more formal presentations in classrooms or professional meetings. Told in an ironic and self-mocking tone, the story can be summarized like this: researcher meets 'natives'; natives revile and abuse researcher; after a brief retreat, researcher returns to the field in a more culturally appropriate guise; researcher then gains the trust of the natives and successfully completes the research project. This story plays on stereotypes of the colonial anthropologist as bold adventurer while also exposing the level of my naivete in the early stages of my research. How I tell this story, and even that I tell it at all, reveals the multiple and overlapping relationships between the ethnographer, the "subjects" of research, and the various audiences for reports of that research.

One way to view ethnography is as a process of "translation." As an ethnographic researcher, I immerse myself in a culture and then write up reports or give presentations that expose, explain, and interpret that culture for diverse audiences. One of the implications of this is that the process of research does not end with a neat and distinct "exit" from the field. As long as I continue to talk about my experiences, to translate them for new audiences, I continue the process of interpretation and reinterpretation that began when I first started learning about MUDs. This process purports to represent the culture and beliefs of the people on BlueSky, but it also involves negotiation of my own culture and beliefs, as well as those of my audiences. Navigating the shifting overlaps between these different groups and relationships can sometimes reveal the tensions and struggles between and among these different research "participants."

Arriving at the version of my "first contact" story recounted above required numerous reinterpretations of my first visit to BlueSky. Over the months of my participation on BlueSky, I periodically reread the log of my first visit, each time understanding things I had completely misinterpreted on the previous reading. My increasing knowledge about how MUDs work, as well as about BlueSky's culture and personalities, afforded me greater understanding with each reading but, more than that, my own ideas and perceptions changed over time. Not only did I better understand the events of my first visit to BlueSky but I also felt differently about those events, having forged relationships with people who on that first day were strangers.

But in addition to increasing my own understanding of those first-day events, I had to find a way to convey that understanding to others who in most cases have no experience on MUDs, but who often do have very strong ideas and opinions about the Internet and what kind of socializing occurs there. Whether the "how did you find these people?" question occurs in the context of a professional discussion of research techniques or a friendly exchange of "what do you do for a living?" stories, in order to translate my BlueSky experiences to other audiences, I have to understand the culture of those audiences almost as well as that of BlueSky. In addition, I have to make decisions about how I as researcher wish to appear in my stories.

Story Four: The Newbie

The following are excerpts from my first log from BlueSky, dated May 5, 1994. I provide these excerpts to enable a comparison between my "first contact" story and what "really" happened. Of course, the commentary I provide in between the excerpts necessarily leads the reader to a particular interpretation of the logs themselves. I have attempted as much as possible to provide an "objective" account of the events, but in fact no such account is possible. An unedited log would provide the reader with even less information than I had during this encounter. My own interpretation—the one I believe to be "true"—required months of experience on BlueSky.

WELCOME TO BlueSky.
The Falcon

> This spacious tubular chamber is furnished with myriad tables and chairs of every conceivable material, height, and design, as though a used furniture store had exploded. Booths tucked against the walls offer a modicum of privacy. Panels in the curving walls provide diffuse lighting for the patrons who sit about drinking and talking. At the far end of the chamber, a vertical extension provides room for a very tall high-diving platform.

The above description is an abbreviated version of what I saw after logging on to BlueSky and making my way to the "room" where most people hang out, described as a bar called The Falcon. My experience on other MUDs had taught me the basics of finding where people were on the MUD and making my way to that room; however, I had only been visiting MUDs for about a week, and my skills were still extremely limited. BlueSky required an e-mail registration process to acquire a character (with a unique name and password). This process usually took about a week, so for the moment I was using the "Guest" character available on most MUDs. Guest provides an anonymous, and usually technically limited, interface for interacting with others. On most MUDs, it is usually used by first-time visitors, but it can also provide anonymity for regular participants.

Upon entering the Falcon, I found myself in the middle of an ongoing conversation. (The BlueSky MUD program does not number lines; I have added numbers preceding each line in each of the following excerpts to aid in discussion.)

1. Spot nods. Beer is up there.
2. Spot says "Also blowjobs."
3. woozel can be wooed with beer.
4. woozel . o O (BJ = Spot)

Whereas on other MUDs, the entrance of a new participant was usually acknowledged, no one appeared to notice my arrival, and no one greeted me. At the time, I lacked the crucial fact needed to interpret this seeming lack of interest: BlueSky had only one Guest character. When additional people logged on as Guest, they shared control of the Guest character with anyone previously logged on as Guest. The other BlueSky participants did not notice my arrival because I—or Guest—was already there. BJ, a regular BlueSky participant, had previously logged in as Guest and had been engaged in conversation for some time before I arrived. From my perspective, this meant that anything the other person using "Guest" typed now appeared on my screen as if I had typed it.

5. You say "blowjobs work"
6. Spot nods.
7. woozel cannot be wooed with blowjobs

8. You say "hello"

Line number five above was typed by BJ, but appeared on my screen preceded by "You say" to indicate that my "character" on the MUD said this. A long-term and experienced BlueSky participant, BJ objected to the new BlueSky rules requiring e-mail character registration and refused to register his usual character name. He and about three other similarly resistant regulars still frequently logged on to BlueSky and interacted with others, but always using the Guest character. Although I did not understand this historical context, nor the technical aspects of Guest usage, I had heard of "spoofing," in which one participant took control of another participant's character and made it do or say things "against its will." Thus, my initial interpretation of what happened on my first visit to BlueSky was that one or more of the other participants were deliberately and rudely making my character say things I did not want to say.

9. Spot went for an amazing ride last night.
10. Spot thinks you should all know this.
11. Elektra says "what type of ride was it, Spot?"
12. You say "did she scream a lot?"

The references to blowjobs and sexual innuendo, which increased my conviction that I was the victim of harassment, were in fact normal conversational gambits for BJ and accepted and acknowledged as such by other participants. Because I said little in my initial confusion, it took a few minutes for the others to notice that there was more than one guest. Thinking it might somehow disrupt the spoofer's ability to control my character, I logged off and logged on again. This time, my entrance was noticed.

13. You say "more guests!"
14. Guest grins at woozel. didja?
15. woozel sigh, no
16. Calvin says "2guest"
17. You say "well WHY NOT?"
18. You say "same guest, actually"
19. woozel beCAUSE no clothing was lost
20. You say "oh, my mom was going through old pictures today. There was one of me by my truck, in a Cat Diesel hat, with large belt buckle."
21. Guest 2 says hi; I'm going to try this again.
22. Spot too many Guests.

Lines 18 and 21 were typed by me. Guest utterances on lines 13, 14, 17, and 20 were BJ. Having recognized the existence of more than one Guest, the other participants found the confusion annoying and began to discuss technical ways to solve the multiple identity problem. (All of the Guest utterances in the following are BJ.)

23. Spot says "BJ: Why don't you bind your "and : keys to @emit BJ says," and BJ?"
24. You say "cause guests can't emit"
25. Spot swears
26. L-Train says "Besides, the binding would work for the other guest, too."
27. Spot says "But it was a good working idea. =P"
28. Spot says "No it wouldn't"
29. Spot says "The binding would be at the client end."
30. L-Train says "Oh, client end."
31. Spot says "My solution would be to filter Guest and replace it with BJ, but it relies on nobody else using the Guest account."
32. Guest cackles
33. You say "shorthop uses guest early and often"

I next clumsily attempt to understand the reasons for the treatment I think I'm receiving. Lines 34, 35, 39, and 41 below are me, and lines 36 and 37 are BJ. At the end of this segment, Spot explains BlueSky's reaction to new and anonymous participants.

34. You say "why the objection to guests. Surely you don't want scads of people registering and not using their characters."
35. You say "Isn't the guest character available for people to "check things out"?"
36. Guest nods.
37. You say "that, and to annoy people with."
38. Spot says "This isn't the point, Guest 2"
39. You say "I don't know the history of guest use here, but I have no intention to annoy."
40. Spot says "We don't like Guests, Guest 2."
41. You say "why?"
42. Spot says "Cause they are weenies."

I have edited out some of the interaction during this first visit, but very little else of note occurred. I logged on, found myself in the middle of a conversation that included habitual friendly insults, discussions of sexual activity, sexual innuendo, and technical discussions (all features that emerged as frequent aspects of BlueSky conversation), and, perhaps rather self-centeredly, misunderstood the interaction as a direct attack. Fortunately, this encounter did teach me two key aspects of BlueSky culture: newcomers are often treated with indifference or suspicion, and anonymous newcomers can encounter outright hostility, especially if they seek to maintain that anonymity.

In comparing the two stories, my "party story" emerges as a not-quite-accurate rendering of a complex situation. In part, the inaccuracies result from the need to tell the story as a brief, amusing anecdote. However, in part, the different tone and meaning of Story Three results from my understanding of likely audience knowledge about online interaction and my anticipation of audience reaction to my story. My story relies on (and in some tellings specifically mentions) the existence of numerous popular press stories about rudeness and harassment, especially of women, online. I know that even if they have heard nothing else about people who socialize online, my audience will likely have heard these stories. Story Three also represents the ethnographer in a more positive light than Story Four. Rather than blundering, clumsy, and clueless, the ethnographer in Story Three is a courageous and intrepid researcher. The ironic and self-deprecating tone I generally use during that portion of Story Three acknowledges to the audience my interest in appearing courageous, but this functions more as false modesty, since it does not decrease the overall impression that I overcame adversity for the sake of knowledge.

However, before I can appear as a competent researcher, I also must appear as a competent human being. Thus my account of why I returned to a MUD where I had arguably been the recipient of sexual harassment serves to deflect criticism of me personally, and specifically criticism of me as a woman or as a feminist (depending on the audience). A competent person, a reasonable woman, or a "good feminist" presumably would not willingly tolerate (or invite) abuse, so my account must provide a reason for returning to a hostile setting (especially since other information presented in stories about BlueSky nearly always exposes aspects of BlueSky culture, which could be interpreted as hostile or sexist). My identity before my audience, and my understanding of how I might appear—as a willing participant in sexist discourse—motivates my particular presentation of self, which also necessarily affects my presentation of BlueSky.

On BlueSky itself, I tell a different version of my "first contact" story. There, I need only mention that my first experience on BlueSky was "sharing Guest with BJ," and the other participants laugh, sometimes exchanging stories of their own first encounters. BlueSky regulars interpret the instance of two people sharing the Guest character as something akin to being stuck in a sleeping bag with another person. They find it amusing to think of one of the quieter participants (myself) being in such close quarters with one of the more obstreperous group members (BJ). On BlueSky, my first encounter story becomes a story of my initiation (by quasi-ritual hazing) into the group.

Story Five: The Ethnographer

When I finished my dissertation about BlueSky, I sent copies out to BlueSky participants who wanted to read it. Some sent me minor corrections and comments, and two sent lengthy critiques. But most of the reaction concerned names. First, participants began comparing the pseudonyms in the book to quotes they could identify and started figuring out who was who. Two participants even wrote a small program on the MUD to enable people to access a list matching "real" MUD names with the pseudonyms I had given them. After considerable discussion, and after all BlueSky participants had had a chance to review it, I convinced them to remove this object from the MUD. I had never held out hope for protecting their identities from each other (with a couple of exceptions where I split single participants into multiple participants to protect some who made sensitive revelations), but I wanted to keep outsiders from connecting the "real" BlueSky participants to my study.

Many participants objected to the pseudonyms I had used for them. Although I attempted to use names that retained some of the flavor and source material of BlueSky participants' actual MUD names, the names did not always match how participants saw themselves. For subsequent published material, I solicited substitutions from anyone unhappy with the name I gave them, and received many changes. In a medium in which faces are hidden, names take on greater importance as identity hooks. Most MUD names are somewhat fanciful (although several BlueSky MUDders use their real names as MUD names), but they nevertheless form an important part of participants' presentation of self.

The other name that caused comment on BlueSky was the name of the dissertation itself. Most found "Hanging Out in the Virtual Pub: Identity, Masculinities, and Relationships Online" somewhat silly, especially because of the standard academic construction of phrase-colon-list. Two participants found this amusing enough to program an automatic thesis title generator that uses a simple command to generate academic-sounding titles from a list of terms that participants continually supplement. The participant types a short command, and the program spits back a random string of phrases that sometimes form a coherent title. Some examples from a log of the generator in action follow. I have highlighted output from the thesis title generator in bold print. Only the nonbolded lines were actually typed by participants. (I am Copperhead in the excerpt below.)

1. *Copperhead's thesis title is "Laughing at a Male Space: Automated Conversation, A Bucket of Steaming Lard, and Displaced Hate"*
2. Mike Adams says "This may come in handy. I've been wondering what to do for thesis"
3. Copperhead says "hee"

4. *Mike Adams' thesis title is "An Overview Of South Park: Disassociation, Going to Church, and Gay Pride"*
5. *Copperhead's thesis title is "Ignoring Foucault: Class Distinctions, Gay Pride, and Fetishism"*

Participants quickly made a game of generating titles until one came up that was either sexually suggestive, mentioned someone on the MUD in a humorous way, or constituted a plausible title for a real thesis, at which point the person generating that title was declared the winner.

By making fun of academic conventions, the thesis title generator constitutes a mild critique of my research project. Although it criticizes my identity as an ethnographer, this critique extends also to my audience. It expresses the fact that most of what I have to say about BlueSky participants is more or less irrelevant to how they see themselves and to what they find important about their online experience. My translation of their culture into terms that are meaningful to me as an ethnographer, and then again into terms that are meaningful to various audiences results in stories that are often no longer particularly meaningful to the participants whom those stories purport to be about.

Coda: The Return of the Narrator

The issues involved in online ethnography are thus much the same as those involved in any ethnographic project. As recent critiques of anthropological research have pointed out, stories from the field reveal as much about ethnographers as they do about the groups studied. Furthermore, in writing to a particular audience, the ethnographer to some extent also writes about that audience, albeit in an oblique way. This chapter itself, as a story about stories, makes certain assumptions about the audience and strives to make particular assertions about the author (hence my labeling of the introduction and conclusion of this chapter with a fifth identity).

The ways these different groups—author, audience, research subjects—are intertwined suggest some important considerations for online ethnographers. First, for both ethical and practical reasons, any ethnographer must consider their own relationship to the people they study. Who has power, and in what ways? Similarly, researchers also need to keep in mind their audience(s). Increasingly—for all ethnographers, not just those online—these two groups may overlap, and the ethnographer may consider him or herself a member of both.

In addition, despite increased participation in and media coverage of the Internet, online researchers will find that they must explain what it is they study and how they study it, and they may need to justify their reasons for studying online interaction at all.[3] This requires giving some thought to the cultural context of the audience and the meanings that computers and the Internet have within that context.

While these aspects of online ethnography constitute some of the difficulties with ethnography as a method of online research, they are also strengths. Content analysis could not uncover the depths of meaning in these textual online interactions. The involvement of the researcher in online interaction and the length of time spent in participation provide additional sources of information and add depth to descriptions of the online culture. Ethnography entangles the different identities involved in research. This entanglement leaves these identities more vulnerable than is the case in other methods of research, but it also can provide more powerful bridges of understanding and analysis between subjects, observers, and audiences.

Notes

1 BlueSky is my own pseudonym, as are all participant names herein.

2 My intention here is not to parody my reviewers, most of whom have been very helpful to me in strengthening both my writing and analysis. Rather, I wish to highlight some of the very pertinent issues which they have brought to my attention.

3 Ironically, I did not take my own advice with regard to this very chapter; in an earlier draft, I failed to provide an explanation of the site I studied and my methods for doing so.

Representation in
Online Ethnographies:
A Matter of Context Sensitivity

ॐ

Annette N. Markham

> Ethnographies join culture and fieldwork. In a sense, they sit between two worlds
> or systems of meaning—the world of the ethnography (and readers) and the world
> of cultural members.... [C]ulture is not strictly speaking a scientific object, but is
> created, as is the reader's view of it, by the active construction of a text. (Van
> Maanen 1988, 4)

> On the net...one begins with the text of the other, which is directly coupled only
> to text and exchange of texts—and out of this, one constructs a real, constructs a
> world which is projected onto the other. (Sondheim et al., 1997, 9)

THE ISSUE OF REPRESENTATION is an evolving theme in many
disciplines, particularly interpretive sociology. Fundamental to the
nature of ethnographic texts and therefore our understanding of culture are
the voices of the participants woven together with the voice of the author.
Because the intersection of participant, interpreter/author, and audience
shapes our knowledge of emerging cultural forms in technologically mediated environments, careful attention to our methods of representation is
warranted.

This is a crucial discussion point in the emerging field of Internet studies. New communication technologies privilege and highlight certain features of interaction while diminishing or obscuring others, which confounds
traditional methods of capturing and examining the formative elements of
relationships, organizations, communities, and cultures. Even as new media
continue to provide new means of interacting with others, most environments under ethnographic study are text-based and computer-mediated
(e.g., e-mail, chat, mailing list, BBS). A key to understanding these contexts
is careful attention to and analysis of the points of connection between people whose exchanges comprise the very foundations of these emerging
forms of culture. Without traditional physically grounded sensibilities such
as touch, smell, or in many cases, sight of the other, discursive interaction

points create meaning in context and, over time, provide the means by which cultural members can assume a shared sense of reality. Moreover, ethnographers of these cultural formulations must acknowledge that in almost every case, our own discursive activities help to shape the context and therefore cannot be ignored as irrelevant to the activities of others or their responses to us as researchers or participants.

Working within the frameworks of social construction, symbolic interaction, and interpretive ethnographic inquiry, this chapter focuses on some problematic aspects of conducting discursive analyses of text-based interviews in online ethnography. Not exclusive to the interview or text-based research environment, these issues should be acknowledged as part of any research involving interpreting the meaning of others' discursive practices. The challenges I address here may not be as evident but are clearly present (in variation) in other forms of research involving computer-mediated communication. Whether the researcher is using text-based online environments as an interviewing tool or studying virtual cultures constructed and sustained solely through online media, knowledge claims about the Other are essentially mediated by the other's presentation of self through any medium, the interaction between the self (researcher) and other (participant) during the data collection process, and the researcher's production and presentation of the words of the other in the interpretation and writing phases of the research project. Indeed, when we drill down to the basic epistemological assumptions undergirding any study of discursive practices in culture (physical or virtual), consideration of how the interaction among participants and researchers reflects and shapes identities, relationships, and social structures constitutes a useful, reflexive, and ethically essential practice.

At several junctures during the research project we have the opportunity and responsibility to reflexively interrogate our roles, methods, and interpretations. Virtual cultures intensify this need because the frames of reference we use to guide our premises and procedures are deeply rooted in physical foundations and modernist ontologies. Multiple dialectic tensions operate simultaneously and perhaps unconsciously to influence the researcher's methodological choices and actions throughout the ethnographic project, as well as the outcome of the project in the written research report. To what extent is the researcher a part of that which is researched? Is it possible or desirable to isolate oneself as an observer in cultures formed solely through textual participation? Is the field more adequately defined and bound by notions of location or interaction? How can the researcher balance the traditional scientific impulse to know what is real (read: physical, authentic, embodied) through meaningful but disembodied interactions among personae who may or may not correspond to their physical counterparts?

These undercurrents flow through the ethnographic research project from start to finish. This chapter presents four arbitrarily selected moments in the research process when some or all of these tensions disrupt the seemingly placid surface of inquiry. First, identifying the field of inquiry involves decisions that both presuppose and reveal underlying assumptions about the extent to which the researcher considers his or her own textual participation a meaningful constituting feature of the field. Second, decisions about how to gain entry, establish rapport and collect information, often dismissed as simple matters of logistics, constitute essential processes of negotiating self, other, and context. All of the researcher's behaviors actively co-construct the participant's identity as known to the researcher or eventual readers, the researcher's identity as known to the participant, and the actual context of interaction; that is, the actual field of inquiry. How the researcher attends to these issues influences the stance taken toward the subject and the extent to which the researcher is treated as a part of the object being studied. Third, how the researcher resolves the questions of participant versus observer and real versus virtual will profoundly influence the delineation of data from nondata, among other things. Assumptions about the nature of the relationships between self, other, text, and reality guide our analysis of the textual performance of participants. Examining basic definitions operating both within the framework of the specific study and social scientific traditions will aid the researcher in identifying how and which data are defined as meaningful, whether or not physical presence is necessary to fully grasp the authentic reality of these cultures, and the extent to which bodies are used to make sense of these cultural contexts. Finally, as researchers write up their findings for publication, the representation of self and other becomes a reflexive juncture in the project. Great potential for restructuring culture and revising identities exists within the decisions made by the researcher to reach his or her readership with particular writing conventions.

The four junctures discussed in this chapter should not be considered mutually exclusive or exhaustive. Rigorous interpretive inquiry involves a constant and reflexive shifting between various elements and stages of the research project; marking these as discrete or linear stages provides heuristic evaluation of methodological assumptions and practices but does not reflect the actual process of inquiry.[1]

The Field

The question "How do we represent 'the Other' in our research reports?" cannot be separated from the related question of "Where is the field?" Our responses to the second question influence greatly the choices we make in

(1) what we consider important in the collection of information about the Other, (2) how we interpret their actions and discourse, and (3) how we represent them in the research reports. In this latter question, I mean to convey a vague sense of "field," because both the field as research site and field as disciplinary boundary guide and limit a researcher's choices and practices.

"In the field" hardly begins to describe the localities we study in cyberspaces. The shifting of ground from geographic to computer-mediated spaces constitutes an equally significant shifting of focus from place to interaction, from location to movement (Clifford and Marcus, 1986; Eichhorn, 2001; Hine, 2000; Markham, 1998).

If one seeks to investigate social practices in context, asking ethnographically grounded questions about identities, relationships, and social structures therein, several essential methodological questions arise. What criteria do we use to create the boundary around the field and separate meaningful from nonessential data? Should we participate in this social structure or simply observe? Answers to these questions are not simple, and the subsequent choices have significant practical, ethical, and epistemological consequences. Compounding this, the researcher's response will inevitably be entwined with his or her research paradigm, making the answers less universal or standardized than might make the methods choices easier.

The first question regarding the boundaries of the field has been addressed in depth elsewhere (Hine, 2000). Communities and culture are not neatly mapped before entering the field but instead are created as part of the ethnographic process. The ethnographer must read the texts and interactions of interest, much like trail signs, and make ethical and defensible decisions about which paths to follow and thereby which boundaries to draw. If one's decisions remain sensitive to the context, the boundaries will be derived from the culture rather than from a priori guides and criteria.

The second quandary of whether or not to participate or simply observe in whatever we conclude is "the field" warrants closer discussion here, as it directly influences our knowledge of and representation of the context and particularly the participants.

Talking with anyone formally or informally marks a significant shift from observer to participant or, more crucially, accomplice. Online, as interviewers, we co-construct the spaces we study. This is not a minor point. Our interactions with participants are not simple events in these online spaces, but are constitutive and organizing elements of these spaces.

In other words, we participate in constructing the very phenomena we label as the object of analysis. This includes the Other with whom we are interacting. In a place where the imagined boundaries of self, other, community, or culture are constituted and sustained solely by the exchange of information, participation in this exchange is the fundamental and necessary means through which recognition and response is possible (MacKinnon, 1995). As MacKinnon keenly notes in 1995, the common phrase "I think, therefore I am" is woefully inadequate. The more appropriate phrase in cyberspace contexts is "I am perceived, therefore I am" (MacKinnon, 1995, 119). Applying this logic to the issue of research procedures yields the conclusion that each time a researcher responds to another in these contexts, the researcher contributes directly and actively to the development of the other's identity and by extension, the field in which the study occurs.

Participation in the context is not only necessary to any inquiry that seeks to understand in depth these cultural forms but also inevitable. What we consider "the field," then, is both enabled and constrained by the technological possibilities, the ideological markers established by the participants, and the negotiation of self operating within, through, and outside these contexts.

The second notion of "field" as disciplinary boundary is worth mentioning as a reminder that research choices are never free from the constraints of academic traditions. To think about the question of participation or observation within the sphere of social science, I would begin with the premise—along with many in contemporary anthropology and interpretive sociology—that understanding what it means to be a part of any culture necessitates participation; to remain an observer is to remain distant from the experience of being-in-culture (Geertz, 1973; Clifford and Marcus, 1986; Jackson, 1989). This would imply that I must participate versus observe.

To what end do I either participate or observe? Thinking ahead to the outcome of inquiry—the research report—I consider the idea that our interpretation of culture will change depending on the form of the telling (Bochner and Ellis, 1996; Goodall, 2000; Wolf, 1992). Interpretative focus and the nature of the "findings" also shift with the passage of time, the venue for publication, the credibility of the author or notoriety of the subject, and innumerable other factors.[2] Frankly, whether or not the researcher participates or simply observes, the construction of the research report will present a particular reality of the object of analysis that is influenced by the identity and participation of the researcher. Thus, the effort or unconscious decision to absent oneself from the field will not remove the researcher from the process and product.

Having laid some epistemological assumptions out on this page, simple reasoning presses the conclusion that lurking online to collect data without participating in the culture may not just be less desirable but perhaps not possible if the goal is to explore sense-making practices in context. After all, an interpretive qualitative research stance compels me to talk with people.

The conventions for conducting research vary depending on where one is coming from, scholastically speaking. As a result, a researcher may or may not be allowed to acknowledge his or her presence in the study, either by formulating research questions that imply the co-constructed nature of online spaces or by writing research reports that address openly the notion that the researcher's choices influence the outcome of the study from start to finish. If we consider Internet Studies an emerging field of inquiry, critical attention to the way we are delineating acceptable from unacceptable research practices may allow more creative conceptualizations of the ways we demarcate the spaces we study.

Take, for example, the procedural question, "Should the researcher interview participants both online and offline?" The rationale for doing so might be to add authenticity to the participant's descriptions of self, to validate the researcher's assessment of the subject's identity, or to simply add another dimension to their personae. Yet, what are the foundations behind this rationale?

As more studies of online interaction emerge, I am more convinced that the primary criteria guiding a researcher's answers to this question are deceptively simple: Context sensitivity, flexible adaptation, internal consistency, and reflexivity. These criteria are simple, because they are acutely fundamental; they are deceptive because they are not easily negotiated.

Kate Eichhorn's (2001) dilemma of deciding whether or not to include the offline presence of her participants in her study of women and 'zines is instructive. Through constant attention to the context rather than the rules of inquiry, as well as reflection on contemporary ethnographic sensibilities, Eichhorn realized that interviewing participants in person was not appropriate because "it was precisely the absence of a proper locus that seemed to provide my research participants with a space in which to explore the aspects of their experiences and identities that otherwise remained interable" (Eichhorn, 2001, 572). Based on this discovery in the midst of her study, Eichhorn changed her conceptualization of the context and the operationalization of her approach. Her sensitivity to the context compelled her to flexibly adapt her methodology to achieve a stronger degree of internal consistency among her research questions and procedures.

Negotiating the Space, the Self, and the Other

The social reality of online culture is an ongoing accomplishment of conversation. We begin to exist as personae when others respond to us; being, in this sense, is relational and dialogic. Scholars such as Mikhail Bakhtin (1981), Martin Buber (1958), Herbert Blumer (1969), and R. D. Laing (1969) usefully remind us that this is not restricted to computer-mediated communication, noting that our identity cannot be completely abstracted from our identity-for-others, our identity-for-ourselves, the identities we attribute to others, the identities we think they attribute to us, what we think they think we think they think, and so on (Laing, 1969, 86). In text-based computer-mediated social spaces, Self and Other are constructed through interaction more obviously. The borders we draw are textual but also imagined; the liminal space of information exchange becomes the negotiation table for culture as well as the medium we use to collect texts we later consider as data.

The words we use both reflect and shape our understanding of our world, but this process never occurs in a vacuum. The process is thoroughly dialogic; cultural forms exist only through the exchange of messages and the subsequent adoption and reproduction of textual artifacts. As we sit in front of our computers, we type and send messages, composing ourselves through word choices, sentence structures, graphic accents, and typos. Exchanging pics, URLs, jokes, urban legends, and viruses, we give others a glimpse of the frames we use to view the world and reveal some of the masks we consciously or unconsciously think are important in the presentation of self. Responding to responses, we weave dialogic understandings of each other, sometimes connecting meaningfully, other times realizing it's best to just move on. All of this, which we might call the flotsam and jetsam of being, gets passed around and, at some discernable (or not) level, contributes to what is eventually bound into what can only be encapsulated as a static-for-the-moment form we call culture.

Methodologically, one should not ignore this feature because as interaction constructs and reflects the shape of the phenomena being studied, interaction also delineates the being doing the research in the field. Ethnography that ignores this remains at the surface and, more important, remains stuck in the modern notion that researcher observes but does not interfere or influence that which she or he studies.

Analysis of the Subject: Texts

As the researcher engages in analysis of visual, verbal, and interactive presentations of self online, certain elements become evident, highlighted, or passed over. Obviously, we cannot pay attention to everything, so the analytical lens is limited by what researchers attend to, collect, and consider as data. Reflexive attention to what we are looking at, looking for, or looking through can help us make more ethical and sensible choices, as well as inform our abilities to express our limitations in fully describing or explaining the phenomena under study.

When the participant, researcher, and context are nothing but text yet everything beyond mere language, our perceptual filters must be adjusted to accommodate the complexities of human expression. Discursive practices in these contexts provide multiple and sometimes strange clues that merit close attention in our interpretation.

A brief example may help begin the discussion of the complexity of analyzing a simple interview text and illustrate the real paradoxes of conducting ethnographies in virtual spaces. Sheol is a self-described "heavy user" of the Internet and a "budding hacker" interviewed in an anonymous text-based synchronous chatroom (Markham, 1998). Sheol (a pseudonym, which foregrounds a problematic issue even now) uses a lot of emoticons (pictographs created from punctuation marks or other keyboard characters used to indicate emotional responses in computer-mediated text) and punctuation, speaks in short sentences, and seems to always be laughing or smiling. Scattered throughout every part of the utterances, *LOL*, !!, :-) and other interjections send multiple messages from the moment our interactions begin.

The following excerpt is typical of interaction with Sheol, shown here as it appeared online:

> <Sheol>   *LOL* This is way cool!! I have never been asked for an interview before:)
> <Sheol>   I am intrested in talking to:) Could you be more spesific about what questions you will ask? Just let me know when you want to talk, and I will try to accomidate! :)
> <Sheol>   On the net you can be who or what ever you want to be. That is the trap! when you want your cyberlife to be your real life. That's what hapened to me.
> <Sheol>   I became a very popular (I know that sounds conseeded) figuar on the line I called home. I am ruled by the right side of my brain so I liked the diea of being that personality.
> <Sheol>   My cyberfriends and I liked to roleplay...we went on fantastic adventurs over the net. The only limit was our imagineations. Not anything like in the real world!! I am shy by nature...I am also a big fan of Shahspear langue. I can use that style of speaking, and not be shy about on the net:)

Problem: One of the first problems that will impede the interpretation of this interview is that the researcher does not know Sheol in culture but is interviewing from the outside. It is difficult to assess adequately the intention of Sheol's use of these graphic accents or the meaning of them because they are abstracted from the typical context of Sheol's online existence. More directly, Sheol is not participating in online culture, Sheol is participating in an online interview. Interpretation of Sheol's identity as marked by grammar might be more clear if (1) the interaction were taking place in the cultural context, (2) the interactions took place over a longer period of time than the four hours we spent in conversation, or even (3) if the researcher asked Sheol about Sheol's own use of language.

Throughout our interactions, Sheol appeared unconcerned with how the writing appeared and unaware of how the construction of text might mediate identity for others. Although Sheol mentions spelling once, Sheol never tried to change it or correct errors. Sheol did not seem to link identity to the text, but to the interactions allowed by the medium. For Sheol, conceptualizing text as a place afforded vital experiences not possible elsewhere.

I, by contrast, could not ignore Sheol's presentation of self through the text, both content and form. The number of social labels I attached to Sheol during our interviews probably came close to the number of spelling errors, which were considerable. This is not a tangential point. It might illustrate the researcher's tendencies to leap to conclusions or make hasty judgments about people; this is precisely the issue. The interpretive lens is not separable from the context. Alternately through the course of a single interview, Sheol was viewed as a female (stereotypical gendered language style was very evident in tags, qualifiers, expressions of emotion, and heavy use of graphic accents), young (spelling was phonetic, attention to language misuse was not at all evident), not highly intelligent (multiple spelling errors, unreadable messages, apparent lack of ability to be a real hacker), and white (default characteristic because of mainstream cultural assumptions about use of the Internet (Watson, 1997, 107-108) as well as the tendency to make the online other look more like the self).

Problem: How much does or should Sheol's typing influence the researcher's interpretation?

Problem: To what extent does or should the researcher include spelling or typing ability as meaningful information in the understanding of identity or culture?

Problem: How much of the identity of the participant is based on the tendencies, inclinations, and cultural filters of the researcher, rather than on what the participant desires, intends, or says?

These issues cannot be dismissed as unimportant to the ethnographer, even as much as we understand that the role of the ethnographer may indeed be to write culture, not simply reflect it (Clifford and Marcus, 1986). Yes, we make interpretive choices. But when the existence of the person we're studying is for all intents and purposes located solely in the pixels on a computer screen, the choices we make to attend to, ignore, or edit these pixels has real consequences for the persons whose manifestations are being altered beyond and outside their control. Hence, if someone types solely in lowercase and uses peculiar spelling, the researcher's correction of grammar may inappropriately ignore and thus misrepresent a participant's deliberate presentation of self. If someone spells atroshiously or uniQueLY, and the researcher corrects it in the research report to make it more readable, a person's creation of identity may be the price of smooth reading.

By contrast, a participant's exclusive use of lowercase may be simply a time-saving device. A new keyboard, carpel tunnel syndrome, or a project due tomorrow for the boss may prompt typographic errors in a person otherwise (at other times) fully capable of rendering accurate and precise words and sentences. Our interpretation of meaning or dismissal of data as irrelevant may be well founded or absolutely unwarranted depending on any number of things, only some of which are comprehensible. The methodological dilemma is to figure out what is the best interpretive path and to remain consistent.

Analysis of the Subject: Embodiment

Embodiment continues to be a problematic concept for researchers of virtual spaces. Preoccupation with the body—or absence of it—emerged in part as a response to both utopian and dystopian suggestions that humans in postmodern culture would soon experience the death of the flesh, transcend the social capsules of embodiment, merge with technology and live as cyborgs in an era of posthumanism (Benedict, 1991; Rheingold, 2000). Discussions of embodiment also are embedded in our continuing struggle with how we define reality, particularly in relation to virtuality.

These debates regarding embodiment directly influence ethnographic research of online culture as researchers make decisions about the nature of the space they study, the composition of the inhabitants, and the methods used to sense, interpret, and ultimately know the subject. The topic merits mention here because most contemporary research on cyberculture continues to privilege the researcher's body as the site of experience, the reliant gauge of authenticity, and the residence of knowledge.

How much of our information about the members of online communities should include the embodied presence of the participants? Why do we need the body? To make certain our respondents are expressively consistent? To find the authentic as opposed to the merely apparent? Naturalist Diane Ackerman would tell us that we only know the world through our body and our senses; that's what it means to be sentient. "We live on the leash of our senses. Although they enlarge us, they also limit and restrain us, but how beautifully.... To understand, we have to 'use our heads,' meaning our minds. Most people think of the mind as being located in the head, but findings suggest that the mind doesn't really dwell in the brain but travels the whole body on caravans of hormone and enzyme, busily making sense of the compound wonders we catalogue as touch, taste, smell, hearing, vision" (Ackerman, 1991, 2–5 *passim*). Researching online restricts many of the senses that would traditionally help the scientist make sense of place, Other, and context. Yet, in cultural spaces negotiated by information exchange, the ethnographer might be wise to go native; that is, to trust information as representation rather than use traditional senses as the most authentic filters for understanding and analysis. We still use our conglomeration of stereotypes and presuppositions and experiences to filter their textual representation into something we recognize but, because we chose this field, online ethnographic research entails choosing the context of intertextuality and information exchange as a way of knowing.

The impulse to discover the "real" meaning of the real people we are interviewing or observing in these online spaces is deeply rooted in modernist epistemologies. Real, in this sense, is equated with authentic; both are considered embodied knowledge, even as much as contemporary conceptualizations of mind and body provide a way out of this kind of thinking. Participants in thousands of studies of online life pronounce through their experiences and communities that life online is multifaceted, wildly idiosyncratic, and not encapsulated into easy classifications or worse, a monolithic cultural form called Cyberculture.

We know from both popular press and scholarly studies that the reasons for spending time with others online include the perceived ability to escape the confines of embodied social markers to engage in what many refer to as a "meeting of the minds." Whether or not this is truly possible, a user's desire to present and be perceived as a confluence of texts without body might best be read by researchers as a request to acknowledge text as ample and sufficient evidence of being and to study it as such.

Yet, social scientists persist in seeking the authentic by privileging the concept of the body. The desire to add validity to findings often results in efforts to hold up the textual representation of the participants next to their physical personae and measure the extent to which the images match. Researchers deciding to interview participants both online and f2f (face to face) may claim that their efforts will add authenticity to their interpretation (by adding paralinguistic or nonverbal cues to the words people speak) and thereby add more credibility to their findings. For many researchers this is an ingrained, if unconscious, part of sense making. We trust our traditional senses of sight, smell, touch, taste, and hearing to provide verification of concrete reality. In essentially disembodied relationships and cultures, however, this fallback bleeds integrity from the project of ethnographic knowing.

Centering the participant's experience in embodiment is ironically juxtaposed with the marked absence of the researcher's own embodiment in the research project. Although we seem willing to focus on the researcher's general role as either present (participating) or absent/invisible (lurking) in the group, there is little reflection on how the researcher's embodied being is or is not perceived and responded to by the participant. Perhaps this is simply overlooked as not meaningful in the context of the interaction between researcher and researched. Yet, considerable privilege is afforded the researcher to make his or her own embodiment a choice or even a nonissue while simultaneously questioning the authenticity of the participants' choices regarding their own embodiment. Ethically as well as epistemologically, it is vital to reflect carefully on the extent to which the research design privileges the researcher at the expense of both understanding the other and operating with a keen awareness of the context.

Bottom line, rigorously questioning the premises and goals of the study can help identify research design flaws. Asking constantly, "How will the method answer the research question?" will compel critical reflection.

(Re)presenting the Space, the Other, and the Self

The process of studying virtual culture with purposes ranging from exploration, description, interpretation, interrogation, critique, explanation, to prediction is one of comprehension, encapsulation, and control. To say otherwise is to deny our impulses as scholars and our roles as scientists. At a very basic level, we scholars go there to learn something about Other and—when we believe we know something—strive to figure out how to tell others what we think we know. To accomplish this goal, we must stop for a moment the flood of experience, extract a sample of it for inspection, and re-present it in academic terms with no small degree of abstraction. Accordingly, we are afforded a tremendous degree of control in representing the realities of the people and contexts we study.

In text-based computer-mediated communication, text is the means by which embodiment is constructed, disavowed, or reconfigured, a process that differs from traditional sense making wherein there are embodied research experiences that are studied and written in text later. van Manen (1990, 127) tells us that "writing gives appearance and body to thought." Revising his sentence slightly gives us the approximation of what happens online: Writing gives appearance *to* body and thought. While we are taught to think of language as an abstraction, online, language is the reality. Online, discursive practices create place, self, and embodiment.

This notion becomes even more important when we consider the way our research reports present, frame, and embody the cultural members. We literally reconfigure these people when we edit their sentences, because for many of them, these messages are a deliberate presentation of self. Even when they are not deliberate, texts construct the essence and meaning of the participant, as perceived and responded to by others.

The process of configuring texts for publication includes such taken-for-granted editing activities as transforming the participant's utterances from disjunctive nonsentence structures to smooth paragraphs; correcting grammar, spelling, and punctuation; or transforming the appearance of their fonts to reflect standardized typefaces acceptable for the venue and audience. Whether for purposes of interpretive clarity or readability, these transformations can have significant consequences. Introducing artificial linearity to certain interactions may not alter the meaning of the utterances, interaction, or identity of the textual being embodied through these utterances. By contrast, if a participant splits his or her utterances into fragments with the intention of conveying a sense of fragmented identity, our editing has not only devalued but also negated elemental aspects of this persona.

Rewriting disjunctive asynchronous text conversations into the form of spoken dialogue may be disingenuous and inaccurate. It presents a version of reality wherein we talk and think in a hyperorganized way. Organizing interactions into retrospective linearity may be a natural way of making sense of what happened, but it does not allow us to view, investigate, and build our knowledge base of how fragmented and disorganized interactions construct identities and relationships.

As soon as an interaction occurs, the study of it becomes an abstraction. Even so, simplification or dismissal of the challenge of representation is not warranted. Temporality is not problematized in many of our research reports, even though computer-mediated contexts highlight the phenomenological concern that "lived experience can never be grasped in its immediate manifestation but only reflectively as past presence" (van Manen, 1990, 36).

It is far too easy to rely on standard conventions in editing and presenting the participant's voices or to simply leave their texts-in-context out of the final report. Finding the processes and means for giving voice to participants is a difficult challenge worth pursuing; one that requires creative reconsideration of traditional writing conventions. How one accomplishes this might vary by discipline, but the ethnographically sensitive task remains to allow participants to retain their intentionally or unintentionally constructed spatial and temporal uniqueness.

It is important to note the epistemological principles that are the foundations of this discussion: the research questions and methods of collection and analysis must be a good fit; the research methods should reflect a considerable sensitivity to the specifics of the context; and rigor in qualitative interpretation relies on the researcher's ability to be reflexive about choices and, concurrently, flexible in practices.

Our sense-making practices, whether honed in the hypothetico-deductive, interpretive, or postmodern traditions, compel us in certain interpretive directions. Our understanding comes in moments, fragments, glimpses. We may shift our interpretation based on any number of things that happen outside the context we study or long after we have collected our data—conversations that spark new ideas, scents on the wind that provoke particular memories, dreams. The fields we live in as we interpret and write our research overlap with the fields of inquiry in meaningful ways, a fact that we should neither ignore nor deny. We make choices, consciously or unconsciously, throughout the research process. Simply stated, these choices matter. In text-based social structures, every act of creating and negotiating identity, other, and culture is begun by the formation and sharing of words, sentences, fragments of meaning that are pastiched by individuals into patterns, woven into an ongoing tapestry we call social life. If we do not grapple with natural and necessary changes (in both the social structures we live in and study and the research norms we practice) wrought by our growing connections with communication technologies in an epoch of decentered authority and multiauthored realities, our research will not reflect the complexities we strive to understand. Everywhere we turn in Western culture, we are bombarded with a cacophony of information: chaotic, multilayered, decentered, un- or deauthorized, fragmentary, and nonlinear. These comprise the shapeshifting format of contemporary culture. The study of these warrants our critical attention to methods of inquiry, which must be suited to the complexity of the contexts we study. Concrete answers are few, but as researchers we must continue to raise the questions.

The challenge for cyber ethnographers is to develop research sensibilities that enact reflexive adaptation to the context, or as Kenneth Gergen remarks, "If we are to survive, improvisation will become our way of life" (2002, xxiii).

Notes

1 For excellent detail on the art/science of qualitative inquiry, see Harry Wolcott (1994).

2 Margery Wolf (1992) presents three versions of ethnographic research to illustrate this point. More recently, the capacity to publish various versions of one's work on the

Internet allows us to see this process of interpretive changes as authors become better known or as their findings appear in various venues.

References

Ackerman, D. *The Natural History of the Senses*. New York: Random House, 1991.

Bakhtin, M. *The Dialogic Imagination*. Austin, TX: University of Texas Press, 1981.

Benedict, M. *Cyberspace: First Steps*. Cambridge: MIT Press, 1991.

Blumer, H. *Symbolic Interactionism*. Engelwood Cliffs, NJ: Prentice-Hall, Inc., 1969.

Bochner, A. and C. Ellis. "Introduction: Talking Over Ethnography." In *Composing Ethnography: Alternative Forms of Qualitative Writing*, ed. A. Bochner and C. Ellis. Walnut Creek, CA: AltaMira Press, 1996.

Buber, M. *I and Thou*. 2nd ed. Translated by R. G. Smith. New York: Scribner, 1958.

Clifford, J. and G. Marcus. *Writing Culture*. Berkeley: University of California Press, 1986.

Eichhorn, K. "Sites Unseen: Ethnographic Research in a Textual Community." *International Journal of Qualitative Studies in Education 14*, no. 4 (2001): 565–578.

Geertz, C. *The Interpretation of Cultures*. New York: Basic Books, 1973.

Gergen, K. "The Challenge of Absent Presence." In *Perpetual Contact: Mobile Communication, Private Talk, Public Performance*, ed. J. E. Katz and M. A. Aakhus. Cambridge, UK: Cambridge University Press, 2002.

Goodall, H. L. *Writing the New Ethnography*. Lanham, MD: AltaMira Press, 2000.

Hine, C. *Virtual Ethnography*. London: Sage Publications, 2000.

Jackson, M. *Paths Toward a Clearing: Radical Empiricism and Ethnographic Inquiry*. Bloomington, IN: Indiana University Press, 1989.

Laing, R. D. *Self and Others*. London: Tavistock Publications, 1969.

MacKinnon, R. C. "Searching for the Leviathan in Usenet." In *Cybersociety: Computer-mediated Communication and Community*, ed. S. Jones. Thousand Oaks, CA: Sage, 1995.

Markham, A. *Life Online: Researching Real Experience in Virtual Space*. Walnut Creek, CA: AltaMira Press, 1998.

Rheingold, H. *The Virtual Community*. Cambridge, MA: The MIT Press, 2000.

Sondheim, A., M. Avillez, S. Ostrow, and C. Ashley, eds. *Being Online, Net Subjectivity*. New York: Lusitania, 1997.

Van Maanen, J. *Tales of the Field*. Chicago: University of Chicago Press, 1988.

van Manen, M. *Researching Lived Experience: Human Science for an Action Sensitive Pedagogy*. Albany, NY: State University of New York Press, 1990.

Watson, N. "Why We Argue about Virtual Community: a Case Study of the phish.net Fan Community." In *Virtual Culture*, ed. S. Jones. Thousand Oaks, CA: Sage, 1997.

Wolcott, H. *Transforming Qualitative Data: Description, Analysis, and Interpretation*. Thousand Oaks, CA: Sage, 1994.

Wolf, M. *A Thrice Told Tale: Feminism, Postmodernism, and Ethnographic Responsibility*. Stanford: Stanford University Press, 1992.

Research Paparazzi in Cyberspace:
The Voices of the Researched

࿊

Shing-Ling Sarina Chen
G. Jon Hall
Mark D. Johns

O NLINE TECHNOLOGIES PRESENT researchers with an array of alternative arenas for data collection. Newsgroups, mailing lists (list-servs), online chatrooms, multiuser domains (MUDs) and object-oriented domains (MOOs), and more recently, Web logs (or "blogs") are all points of interaction through various computer-mediated communication technologies. All are also attractive environments for social research, providing easy access and identifiable location of research participants, low cost of access, easy data collection with transcripts of conversations effortlessly supplied, and a wide variety of topics of conversation and types of interaction from which to choose. However, what constitutes appropriate research conduct in online environments has been a topic of heated debates, as social researchers quickly come to the realization that applying traditional offline research methods in online environments has posed numerous problems. These discussions and debates have occurred among online researchers almost from the moment online technologies became available as research venues, with many offering insightful comments and propositions about ethical guidelines for online research (King, 1996; Reid, 1996; Sharf, 1999; Thomas, 1996a, 1996b). However, to develop a comprehensive understanding of appropriate conduct for online research, regardless of discipline or method, the concerns and views of the participants need to be taken into consideration; after all, it is they who are being researched.

To provide an understanding of the views of online participants, the authors conducted surveys of mailing list owners and newsgroup moderators. It is believed that the mailing list owners and the newsgroup moderators understand the culture of their respective groups, are sensitive to the perspectives of their members/participants, and by virtue of their role as custodians of their sites can provide meaningful insights to propriety in their groups. This chapter reports the views of these online proprietors regarding the use of their respective groups or lists by information gatherers.[1] Discussions of ethical conducts and perspectives of ethics approaches are provided later in the report.

To study the mailing lists, the authors utilized the 3,147 mailing lists available from the Publicly Accessible Mailing Lists, which was compiled by Stephanie da Silva (2001) as the population, and selected 34 mailing lists as the sample of this study. The selection criteria were lists that dealt with sensitive and controversial topics. In addition, of the 4,200 newsgroups available from the server of the University of Northern Iowa, the authors selected 94 newsgroups to be studied. The same selection criteria were used for selecting the mailing lists. It is the authors' contention that the concern for ethical protocols is generally more urgent in lists or groups that deal with sensitive and controversial topics (such as depression and abortion) than in lists or groups that deal with public and general topics (such as football teams or gardening). When selecting the mailing lists and newsgroups, the authors tried to include a wide variety of lists and groups that meet the selection criteria.

The authors constructed two survey questionnaires, one for the mailing list owners, and the other for newsgroup moderators, with nearly identical questions addressed in each questionnaire. In the questionnaires, list owners and group moderators were asked to describe their respective list or group, the characteristics of the list or group membership and culture, but most importantly, they were asked to describe their experiences of dealing with information gatherers, their reservations concerning these people using their lists or groups for research, as well as their recommendations for such research activity. At the beginning of the questionnaires is a lengthy introduction describing the nature and the purpose of the survey, and other general research concerns such as the protection of anonymity provided, and how the results of the survey will be shared.

Based on the information provided by da Silva (2001), the authors located the names and e-mail addresses of the owners of the 32 mailing lists selected, and sent each one of them a copy of the questionnaire. Within two weeks, nine list owners returned the questionnaire with their responses. To send out the questionnaires to group moderators is more complicated. As most of the groups selected are not moderated, that is, they do not have a central figure serving as a moderator or custodian for the group, the authors sent out calls in the 94 newsgroups for moderators or members who had a long standing in the group. A total of 110 individuals responded to the call, either self-identified or identified others as the moderators or long-time members of the groups. The authors then sent out around one hundred questionnaires to these moderators or long-time group members. Within two weeks, the authors received 38 usable questionnaires. The survey was conducted in the summer of 1998. When analyzing the data received, the authors found different patterns of responses to questions regarding the experiences of dealing with information gatherers, as well as reservations and recommendations for using their lists/groups for research.

Using Mailing Lists and Newsgroups for Research

Diverse responses were received regarding whether or not information gatherers should use lists or groups for research. The wide spectrum of positions regarding this question can be divided into three categories: (1) Animosity, (2) Conditional, and (3) Welcome.

Animosity

Many list owners and newsgroup members deeply resent the presence of researchers and journalists in their groups. One long-time member of a depression support newsgroup provided the following account[2]:

> All I can really tell you far more informally is what my personal experience has been since I first came online at Thanksgiving. The animosity toward researchers is so fierce that I got called "bitch" in a depression chat room over the issue—although I do not do formal research but simply collect mental health info for myself and now for other folks that I have placed on a help website. I have left the term Researcher-Writer in my AOL membership profile, even though it still gets me occasional hostile inquiries. I have also witnessed others being attacked in chats who were only doing personal research in regard to their own illness—that's how strong the "hate" mode is toward researchers.

> When I started my own chat room to help provide folks with practical info on like how to get college or job accommodations when experiencing a mental health crisis, I actually got asked because "researcher" was in my profile—if I started my chat room in order to spy on people! I am sure I still have that E-Mail inquiry in my filing cabinet—if you care to take your study beyond the framework of your project questions. I do not believe the individuals who ask such questions are technically paranoid. They are influenced by the myth (or reality?) of the evil researcher who exploits mental health peer support groups online. I still do not know what kind of exploitation this is supposed to be.

> Another thing I have seen is when researchers do leave messages on the newsgroups to recruit volunteers to answer a questionnaire--they are almost always insulted. A few weeks ago I witnessed a hostile exchange between newsgroup members and a college student. She came away with a very negative view of the mentally ill to say the least, and I had to write and explain to her something

about this hostility thing—so that she would not think that all of us are rude and crude folks. It beats me why college professors or whoever are telling their students to use newsgroups. And just let them try a chat room to recruit volunteers—then stand back for the fierce and often obscene verbal fireworks!

When responding to the question, "What is your attitude toward researchers using your group for research?" a newsgroup member wrote, "The groupmind grumbled 'Mmmmm! Fresh meat!'" To the question, "What are some of the objections or concerns group members might have toward researchers?" The person wrote, "How can we fuck with this guy's data?"

One list owner provided the legitimacy for this kind of animosity, as he wrote:

Our code of conduct explicitly prohibits information gathering from SPALS (Subsequent Pregnancy After a Loss Support) for other than immediate personal use. Any solicitations made to SPALS must be first cleared with list administrators. This includes researchers, journalists, research for books, solicitations for web sites, anything.

The reason for this is that the list participants are there for self-help and mutual support in a confidential and safe environment—while the size of our list may provide a niche group, we feel we must moderate the extent to which the list is solicited.

Some forms of research and solicitations would be entirely unacceptable—experimental designs, for example, where the support group is compared with a control group. In general, *acceptable* forms of solicitation are those where we simply make available contact information for a specific project.

We are bereaved, frequently openly grieving, and therefore fragile. Just asking questions about our current situation or experience can reopen wounds to a significant extent.

Privacy and confidentiality are also concerns. We don't want to attract the "research-papparazzi"...

One member from a newsgroup for sex addicts echoed the support, as he wrote:

People with compulsive sexual behaviors are like any other addicts. The tradition of anonymity is very important. Researchers and journalists are not welcomed. As mentioned previously, research is counter to the objectives and traditions of this group and the addiction community in general (at least those in 12 step programs). Researchers are not welcome.

A "devilbunnies" newsgroup member reported the general attitude toward researchers is "*Very* negative," as he wrote:

Such endeavors are almost universally seen as an intrusion into the world we've created and a burden to the sustained suspension of disbelief necessary to interact effectively and enjoyably.

There is also a widely held perception that such posters are trying to "get someone to do their work for them." Or trying to sell something.

Journalists are more tolerated, because we like to have our egos stroked by being referenced outside the newsgroup. But even then, a posted request will be perceived negatively and often ignored.

A member from a graffiti newsgroup wrote:

As graffiti/writing is being heavily persecuted any disclosure and correct answers may endanger survival of people so you cannot expect too many "openness" here. A difference may be in reporters from graffiti-fanzines... Since even police (undercover-stories) try to invade these groups you may imagine the general attitude to questions... If any, trust must be established before you get real answers and not fake information.

A moderator from a sexual abuse recovery newsgroup indicated that research is generally discouraged and the researchers are likely to get flamed in the newsgroup. He wrote, "Generally speaking they feel that the researchers are 'using' them."

Not only are university researchers are not welcomed, journalists had a even more difficult time being accepted in some newsgroups. One member of a "military brats" newsgroup wrote, "In the groups I hang out in, a journalist will receive short shrift, no matter what he does, by virtue of his despised profession." A list owner supported such a negative reception of journalists, and wrote, "Journalists would probably make most of the list members feel upset, so we won't encourage them at all."

Conditional

Some groups are more receptive to information gatherers with the conditions that such persons provide assurance of confidentiality and privacy, appropriate attribution of sources, and indicate sympathetic standpoints.

One list owner expressed the concern over the issue of privacy, as he wrote, "Research lurkers are positively encouraged in the list 'charter'; the posting of optional surveys, too, is fine, but we would prefer researchers not to publish information from the list elsewhere unless appropriate measures are taken to ensure privacy. In other words, statistical analysis is fine, but we'd rather researchers asked people before using them as case studies."

The commitment to confidentiality is so critical that it often is closely tied to the legal interest of these list/group members. The owner of a mailing list for grandparents who are raising grandchildren wrote that he has a positive but cautious attitude toward researchers, and his major concern is with privacy issues, as he stated, "as many people are involved in ongoing court activity." The owner of a mailing list for people with chemical injury echoed the same concern for privacy, as she wrote, "Some people on the list are involved in lawsuits against the companies (or government agency) that caused them chemical injury."

On the issue of privacy, again, support seems to be easier to get for researchers than for journalists. "I have allowed this in the past, but I feel that they should get permission first. I support researchers because I know how hard it can be to get the survey numbers needed for a statistically significant result. Journalists—We have some bad feelings because a particular magazine is printing some articles that are exactly what the list has just discussed and it happens too often to be chance. They are not directly quoting, so we can't prove anything, but the list feels bad about this and I think it is sneaky!"

Another member of a bondage subculture newsgroup reported a similar event, as he wrote:

> We had a case recently where a magazine publisher generated material for a free, electronically-produced 'zine by posting questions and then taking the replies as fodder. The majority of users considered this to be an infringement of copyright, as we were not asked about the redistribution of our words through the 'zine. A great deal of pressure was applied, and the practice stopped. Similarly, because of the nature of what it is that we do, few posters would like to see details of their personal lives redistributed.

In addition, unsympathetic and argumentative information gatherers are generally not welcomed. One member from the Satanism newsgroup wrote, "That they often have an anti-satanic agenda, and we simply don't want to play their game. My attitude is mixed, since such researchers and journalists have often come not looking for information or to do honest research, but instead with an agenda for which they were hunting ammunition. Though this attitude is not universal within the newsgroup, it is commonly held. Researchers and journalists tend to get very little useful response from this group."

Another person from a newsgroup discussing the conspiracy of JFK assassination concurred and wrote, "Indeed, the large proportion of university historians, have shown themselves to be merely puppets and spokespersons for the 'official' history, with no hint of original or independent thought. We have total disdain for such people, and they will find no hearty welcome in our group." A member from a JFK newsgroup indicated his frustration in dealing with university researchers who have predisposition on issues, and pointed out a condition that would allow the researchers to gather information in the newsgroup, as he wrote:

> Mainly, i.e. in the case of university researchers, that they bring an artificial orthodoxy and prejudiced perspective to bear—colored by the pseudo-history of the Warren Report. To our way of thinking, a genuine researcher must be skeptical enough to question that Report, and the official version of events surrounding the JFK assassination.

> He must be prepared to delve outside the official documents and boundaries, not merely confining or restricting legitimacy to sources that have been rubber-stamped by 'authorities', academic or other.

Several list owners concurred and pointed out that a sympathetic standpoint is important for researchers or journalists to gain their support. The owner of a chemical-injury mailing list wrote, "Many researchers in the fields covered by this list do research solely to 'prove' that our illness are faked or psychological. Most of us do not care to cooperate with people like that. Any truly unbiased research is fine." The owner of a grandparent mailing list echoed this view, as he indicated that he would appreciate researchers who have a working knowledge of grandparent issues, but would object to those who give a negative portrayal of grandparent issues.

Another condition that newsgroup members indicated would be more likely to persuade them to get involved in research activities is that the research be a legitimate and substantial study. One member from an anxiety support newsgroup wrote, "The group prefers to be involved in substantial studies, as opposed to brief student research projects that yield little feedback." A member of a philosophy newsgroup indicated a similar experience, as he wrote, "Legitimate research is OK, but we have had so many instances of 'studies' that were a college student's unauthorized attempt to gather factoids that we are a bit jaded by now. Most of these are merely rather transparent attempts to garner jerk-off material, and the answers are much more likely to be posted as fluff (humor) rather than to be serious answers."

Welcome

Some newsgroups provide a much more welcoming environment for information gatherers. The owner of a mailing list for women who are second wives wrote, "I have a positive feeling toward researchers and journalists—I believe the second wife/second family situation is a serious one and needs as much support/exposure as it can get."

One newsgroup member wrote, "We would welcome more people who want to know about what we are doing here. We wish more journalists would stop by. They might learn a lot about the topic here that they will not get anywhere else. And maybe they'll start reporting the facts of the case rather the many erroneous myths they keep repeating. One of our issues is how the media treats the information we generate on all sides of the issues. Journalists are not highly regarded, here."

Some wrote that as long as the information gatherers adopt a polite manner, they are willing to participate in the research. One wrote, "Personally, I don't mind as long as they're up front about what they're doing." Another wrote, "That is basically okay, provided (1) the subject of the article (thus, of the survey) is 'on-topic' for the newsgroup; (2) readers are offered fair means to verify that the survey is serious, honest and genuine."

Lurking as a Research Act

Lurking is the practice of reading posts to a newsgroup or list in order to understand the topics and tone of the exchanges in the group before the user offers his/her input. Many respondents indicated their positions on the act of lurking. Most of them believe that lurking is a requirement in learning about the groups or lists in which one is about to interact. However, some object to using lurking as a prime means of data collection.

Lurking as Socialization

Many newsgroup members pointed out the importance of lurking for researchers. One wrote, "We are amiable to anyone who drops in to ask questions about the case. But, we expect people to get up to speed quickly. Just know what you are talking about when you join." Another person indicated, "First, download the FAQ [Frequently Asked Questions document] and read it thoroughly. Perhaps read it several times, so its elements sink in. Second, if you have done your homework, and still have questions, then post a query or more to the newsgroup."

Many newsgroup members pointed out the negative consequences of researchers who failed to lurk. One wrote, "IMHO [In My Humble

Opinion], failure to lurk and get to know the newsgroup before asking any-thing. That, for me, is the cardinal failure of most clueless newbies' and all researchers and journalists. While I can be tolerant of clueless newbies', I take great offense at researchers and journalists who insult me that way." Another concurred and wrote:

> That they should do preliminary research (read the FAQs, the _Satanic Bible_, available web sites easily found through web searches, etc.), before attempting to do research in the newsgroup. The purpose of published material is to provide the first level of information. Those who have knowledge within the newsgroup don't mind sharing that knowledge with those who've done the first level of research, and they look upon those who come to the newsgroup without having done that first level of research as lazy fools.

Some pointed out that lurking is an indispensable element in the social-ization process in the newsgroup. Lurking assists building trust and mem-bership. One newsgroup member wrote, "Slowly and respectfully interact with the group to first become familiar with its character, and let the group get to know you. Only after some mutual basis of trust and understanding has been established should research data be asked for and collected. And research results should be freely presented to the group." Another voiced the support and wrote, "It appears that when it comes to research the par-ticipants are more willing to take part if it is a person who has posted with-in the group for a while."

Others pointed out the importance of using lurking to learn about the culture and common practice of the list or group. One list owner wrote about the information of the group's culture one can gather while lurking, as she wrote:

> Accepting of others little quirks, but only to a certain point. For example, most people are willing to use a lower-case "L" when talking about louise, but not to refer to bracketpeople (those submissives who follow a username with a Dominant's initials in brackets to indicate that they have been collared and have a partner) with their brackets (eg "sweetsub{JR}" would become "Sweetsub") nor to use honorifics to persons other than their own partner (eg someone who signs off as "Lady Brandy" would be called "Brandy"). Gender ambiguous pronouns like "sie and hir" may be used at times by some posters who don't think a particular person's sex is relevant, or who are adding a layer of anonymity to a discussion.

Lurking as Data Collection

Even though lurking is highly regarded as a prerequisite for any research, list moderators and group leaders generally agree that it should not be used as a method of data collection. That is, observation without participation, which is a legitimate field observation method, is generally considered unethical in the virtual environment. One list owner wrote, "These folks [list members] do not want their privacy invaded by lurkers. It is ok to read, but not ok to archive the lists for any purpose." The list owner indicated that if the information gatherers simply want to lurk and gather data that way, she would need to get permission for the list members, as she wrote, "I usually ask the list to vote if the person wants to just listen and gather data that way."

Identity Disclosure and the Informed Consent

When respondents were asked if the information gatherers should disclose their identity and research intent in the groups, there is an unanimous "yes." One newsgroup member in responding to the question, wrote, "YGTBSM!!!!!!!!!!!!!!!!!!!!! I am actually at a total loss for words. Do you actually expect *anyone* to say no? Aside from being ethically questionable, failure to disclose identity and purpose is just plain stupid." Another newsgroup member indicated the same position, as he wrote, "Be honest and explain what you're doing...don't try to suck us in by being vague. If you read our newsgroup after the request for someone to answer these questions was posted you will see how cynical people are to someone who is unclear in their motives."

A list owner pointed out that identity disclosure is a requirement in the lists, as he wrote:

> A mailing list, unlike a sidewalk, has a membership list—and only members are part of that list. Many lists have few restrictions on their membership rolls—so they seem public—Others have tight restrictions and their very existence is secret. But in all of these cases the mailing list retains an identity as a PRIVATE forum. With that in mind, no individual or entity should be using it for research without explicit permission from both the people who writes the message as well as the people/group who runs the mailing list. Any researcher that joins a mailing list should identify themselves as such as soon as they have joined—Or, better yet, before they have joined and ask permission of the list owner. As a person I have a right to know I am being experimented on or studied. Just because my physical realness is hidden by a computer connection, that doesn't make my rights any less valid. A mailing list should get the same respect a private home gets.

Another list owner voiced his support for this view, as he wrote, "Discussions we have are sometimes private and emotional—the last thing we need is anyone deciding our emotions are 'research' and publish that without our permission. A certain level of respect, privacy is expected from the list members—a researcher or a journalist can destroy that feeling of respect and privacy if they don't identify themselves and ask permission. In addition, the community that a list-owner has worked so hard to build up can be destroyed."

Some pointed out the benefits of identity disclosure by information gatherers. One wrote:

> Yes. It helps frame the importance/legitimacy of the undertaking and helps the potential information source feel they are contributing to something useful. It also helps reassure them your are a legitimate researcher or journalist—not some marketing goof trying to profit from our time and effort. Remember, we get a lot of spam...from people hawking trinkets to announcements of sleazy adult sites. You are one voice among all of that riff raff, from our perspectives. That is what you must differentiate yourself from.

One member from a newsgroup that advocates changes in drug laws concurred. "Yes, because we can be a paranoid lot (with good reason), and disclosing the identity of the researchers and the purpose of the research would do a lot to improve trust. Without trust, you will probably get skewed research, because a lot of the posters who are fearful for their safety will refrain from responding for fears that you are involved in law enforcement."

When researchers disclose their identity and research intent, it is advised that the identity provided should be verifiable to increase the credibility of the claimed identity. One newsgroup member wrote, "Yes. And in a checkable way. For example, with your address, it was easy enough to verify that you really are faculty at UNI. If you had posted from, say, compuserve, I would have dismissed it as another person who didn't really have a university's approval. If you hadn't been staff, I would probably have ignored it as an undergrad's ill-thought project."

One member of a JFK conspiracy newsgroup indicated the difficulty in building trust even when the researcher's identity is disclosed. "It helps, but the truly paranoid among us will label you as a CIA spy anyway :-) ."

In addition, identity disclosure will not ensure the acceptance of the newsgroup members. When responding to the question, "In your judgment, should a researcher/journalist disclose identity and purpose when using your group for research?" one newsgroup member wrote, "Oh, yes, of course! He should also walk around with a sign saying 'Throw cream pies at me!'"

The following response from a newsgroup member sums up the dilemma of identity disclosure by researchers, as he wrote:

> It is generally believed that without disclose of identity the researchers data could very easily be skewed. Also there is a tendency to feel that it would be unethical on

the part of the researcher. On the other hand, if a research were to disclose their intent, they would likely get flamed.

I believe your approach was one of the best that I've seen when you entered the group. They do generally like to know who the person is and what specifically they want the research for. However, even with your approach, if others came into the group seeking research material too often it is most likely to irritate [people] within the group.

Feedback

Many of the respondents indicated that they would like to hear from the information gatherers again when the information gathering is completed. The respect and feedback from the researchers will deter the group members' experience of "feeling used." One newsgroup member wrote, "Researchers and journalists are welcome, so long as they respect the group's sensitivities, give appropriate credit and provide feedback. The group does not appreciate being used and forgotten."

Online Research Processes

Based on the above report, several observations can be made regarding processes for information gathering. These observations are provided to guide information gatherers toward success in online environments.

The Selection of a Research Site

It would seem logical to assume that participants in a newsgroup, blog, or other online forum that is readily accessible without seeking permissions or membership would have a lesser expectation of privacy than those posting messages in a moderated listserv or MUD, where registration and at least some level of vetting is required. Users, however, do not always appear to make such distinctions. Whether the technology utilized leaves the postings completely open or keeps them restricted to a private list of members, participants generally express the view that the texts on the screen, and the interactions these texts represent, belong exclusively to those who have created them. This attitude pervades whether posts are relatively anonymous or identities are somewhat apparent.

The key factor that differentiates the categories of animosity, conditional and welcome appears to be the level of perceived "risk." That is, the level of risk involved in the members' participation in the list or group seems to dictate their willingness to allow researchers or journalists to use their groups for information gathering. The level of risk can generally be assessed from the topic discussed in the group. High-risk topic groups generally include groups that deal with traumatic, problematic, and/or depressing personal experiences. Support groups are the prototype of high-risk topic groups. For instance, in support groups for depression sufferers, transgender individuals, or drug or sex addicts, the discussions often center on the sharing of personal experiences that involve a high level of self-disclosure of personal problems or trauma. Often the disclosure of this information in the face-to-face social environment may jeopardize the personal well-being of individual participants, which may be why they gather and share this potentially risky information in the virtual environment. In such an environment group members generally have a great concern for their own safety, even if they remain essentially anonymous. Facing an information gatherer who has not participated in the group with the same level of self-disclosure, but who has acted, rather, as an "examiner" from the outside, is troubling. Therefore, these participants are highly suspicious about the "outsiders" such as researchers and journalists.

When using these high-risk topic groups for information gathering, the concern for disclosure, trust, and confidentiality should be brought to the forefront. To act effectively in high-risk topic groups, researchers and journalists need to self-disclose to a greater extent, devote more effort in building the trust with the group members, and provide more assurance of confidentiality for the group members, than they would generally do in low-risk topic groups. Without investing more effort in these groups, information gatherers are generally not welcomed. Therefore, there is a high level of animosity toward information gatherers in these environments.

Medium-risk topic groups generally include groups that deal with personal experiences which are not as traumatic or stigmatized as those in the high-risk topic groups. These are lists or groups that deal with personal experiences such as growing up in the military, grandparents raising grandchildren, beliefs concerning JFK assassination conspiracies, or Satanism. In these groups, the discussions often involve disclosures of personal experiences such as involvement in graffiti or revenge, or expression of passionate feelings over controversial issues such as the death penalty or assisted suicide. The disclosure of information concerning these beliefs in the face-to-face social environment could potentially damage reputations of participants at least among persons with strongly held opposing views. Group members generally have a concern for their own well-being, facing an information gatherer in the groups. However, as long as the information gatherers can provide group members the assurance of confidentiality, and indicate their sympathetic standpoint toward the group members' experiences or beliefs, group members are generally supportive of the information gathering process. Group members do not mind the "outsiders" as long as it is safe to interact with them; they do not mind having supportive and understanding strangers in their midst.

When using these medium-risk topic groups for information gathering, group members' concerns for disclosure, trust, and confidentiality are not as strong as in the high-risk topic groups. However, to act effectively in these groups still requires information gatherers to disclose their identities and standpoints on the issues discussed in the groups, and to provide assurance of confidentiality for the group members. Therefore, the use of these medium-risk topic groups for information gathering is conditional, based on the satisfactory fulfillment of the above-mentioned basic rules.

Low-risk topic groups generally include groups that deal with personal experiences or beliefs on general matters. Social groups that deal with personal experiences such as adoption or body art, or personal beliefs on issues such as politics or sports, are prototypical of the low-risk groups. In these groups, the discussions often involve disclosures of personal experiences with issues such as infertility, or heated debates over issues which generally do not include personal involvement such as commenting on political issues or sporting events. The disclosure of this information in the face-to-face social environment usually does not jeopardize the reputations or personal well-being of participants. Group members thus have little or no concern for their own safety when facing a researcher or journalist gathering information in the groups. Generally, members of these groups are satisfied that protection afforded by the pseudonyms or server addresses they have devised themselves is sufficient to guarantee their privacy and confidentiality. Group members generally welcome information gatherers in their midst. Such a research activity provides exposure for their groups, legitimatizes the validity of their arguments, and enhances the ego of the group members. Group members often do not mind educating uninformed information gatherers. Even so, basic manners and attention to common "netiquette" are required when using these low-risk topic groups for information gathering.

Online Acclimation

Many list owners and group members stressed the importance of lurking as a preparation for participation in their mailing list or newsgroup. Lurking is essential to avoid many uninformed mistakes made by newcomers. In addition, information gatherers need to gradually build themselves into the community of the list/group by lurking over time and participating in the ongoing discussions, before posting questions of their own. Constructing a membership identity and rapport is crucial to one's success in online information gathering.

This practice is not new to researchers. Ethnographic researchers exercise such practice in the field when engaging in participant observation. This kind of acclimation over time needs to be established in the practice of online information gatherers, as well, whether they are conducting quantitative or qualitative studies (Babbie, 1992). The kind of "one-point-in-time," or "hit-and-run" type of practice, utilized in some online survey research, may not be suitable for effective online information gathering. While doing online research, the distinctions between quantitative and qualitative research are not viable. Effective online research, quantitative or qualitative, requires relationship building with the participants.

The Sharing of Results

Another aspect of online research that is parallel to traditional field research is the requirement to share the outcome of the research with the participants. Traditional survey or experimental research does not require the researchers to consult or share the outcome of the research activities with the participants when the research is completed. In the virtual environment, researchers, regardless of quantitative or qualitative methodology, are strongly recommended to bring back to the online community what they have gathered from that community.

The sharing of research results alters the relationship between the researcher and the researched from an authoritative mode to an egalitarian mode. In traditional surveys and experiments, the researchers give the participants instructions, and the participants are only allowed to respond or react to a predetermined research instrument/environment. The researchers are in control, and the communication between the researchers and the participants is a form of vertical, top-down communication.

Conducting online social research requires researchers to become a member of the list/group they study, and to share with the list/group the information gathered. The researcher is thus operating in an egalitarian mode when researching the participants. It is likely that the participants will not only provide responses to the research questions posted but also will contribute to the formulation of the research questions, and will certainly provide correctives to the researcher's analysis and interpretation of the data. In this environment, both the researchers and participants are in control, and the communication between them is a form of horizontal communication.

The sharing of the research outcome is necessary to repel the feeling of being used by the researchers for selfish gains. The sharing of information gathered also completes the cycle of give-and-take that occurs among individuals in an egalitarian relationship. This give-and-take is the compensation the researcher pays for the easy and inexpensive access to information that the group provides.

Several considerations for effective online research are pointed out in the discussion above. Without noticing the levels of risk involved in the group/list that one studies, the researcher cannot function effectively online. Without an acclimation process and a sharing mentality, online researchers are likely to be labeled as paparazzi.[3]

Ethical Rationalism Versus Feminist Communitarian Ethics

The above discussion represents the views of some online participants, which are shared by some online researchers who believe that the online environment where the research is conducted is a private space. Other online researchers, who do not share these views of the participants, tend to see the online environments as a public space. The different views among online researchers regarding whether the online environment is a public or private space represent a fundamental difference in the approaches toward what constitutes ethical research conduct online. The disagreement is a reason why ethical guidelines for online research are difficult to formulate.

Growing out of these different views of public or private cyberspaces are disagreements on other, related issues, including whether informed consent is needed, and how to attribute sources when citing texts posted by participants in online research. Online researchers who believe that the online environment is a public space tend to operate with an assumption that informed consent is not needed, and disclosing participants' screen name or e-mail addresses is permissible because the information is already publicly available. Those who believe that the online environment is a private space would normally secure informed consent when conducting online research, and remove identifiable information of the participants to provide privacy for and protection of the participants. To perceive the online environment as a public or private space seems to be an individual choice on the part of the researcher. However, behind these two seemingly individual choices lies two drastically different philosophies of ethics.

The perceptions that the online environment is a public place is supported by the presumptions of utilitarian rationalism (Denzin, 1997). Ethical rationalism presumes that rationality defines all legitimate acts, and claims about moral obligations can be settled by a rational examination of their logical structure. Utilitarian rationalism is an ethical philosophy based on the logic of providing the greatest good to the greatest number of people. It thus privileges the benefits of increasing general knowledge over the rights of individual research subjects. One of the presumptions of this viewpoint is individual autonomy. Based on this presumption, some online researchers would consider online participants to be competent and autonomous individuals who make rational decisions when communicating online. Therefore, no form of protection is needed, as most online participants have sought measures to protect themselves, for instance, using pseudonyms. In addition, these researchers are confident that online participants should be responsible for their own safety—they should know that the Internet is a public place where anyone can access/view their correspondence (in the case of public newsgroups), or when their correspondence is stored in public archives. Online researchers of this type tend to perceive themselves as external to the online groups that they study. Instead of forming a "solidary" relationship with participants, they tend to operate with a "you versus me" mode of acting with respect to the participants (Couch, 1989). Their goals are the generation and transmission of plentiful data, and not community facilitation or civil transformation. This approach centralizes the research project, decisions regarding research conducts are made by the researcher based on this concern.

Researchers who see the online environment as a private place abide by an ethic enriched by feminism. Feminist research ethics is participant-oriented rather than researcher-centered. Based on this consideration, researchers seek measures to respect—gaining permission for access, and consent for participation—and to protect—creating pseudonyms and composite characterizations—the online participants. In addition, informed by feminism, researchers would share the research outcome with the online participants as a measure to give back to the community that has informed the research. Researchers of this type do not see themselves as external to the groups that they research, rather, they seek to be involved as group members. They seek to foster a solidary relationship with the group, and operate using a "we" mode, acting with the participants (Couch, 1989). Their goals are not to generate or transmit plentiful data but to inform the community, as well as to interpret the community to others outside.

Norman Denzin (1997), who develops feminist communitarian ethics, further articulates feminist relational ethics within communitarian democratic theory. He maintains that the aim of social research should go beyond simply informing the community. He argues that social research is a tool for community transformation. Denzin believes that social researchers' reciprocal care and understanding of the community should extend beyond informing the participants, and that the central question that guides social researchers should be what they need to improve the community, and how such transformation can be accomplished.

Denzin's articulation of feminist communitarian ethics poses a great challenge for online researchers to go beyond the relatively passive act of interpreting and informing the community, and to seek measures to enrich particular cultures and citizen groups. It is true that a genuine sense of solidarity is characterized by acts of altruism—voluntary acts on behalf of others for the welfare of others (Couch, 1989). An altruistic attitude would require researchers to commit themselves to conduct that would enable community life to prosper. It is the altruistic attitude and not simply a sharing participation that enables social researchers to conduct "research that makes a difference in the lives of the real people" (Denzin, 1997, 268) in the virtual world.

This chapter provides an understanding of the views of some potential research participants regarding researchers utilizing their respective groups and lists for online information gathering. This understanding is helpful for online researchers to get to know the views of the people on the other side of the research table. From these views, we also know how they are tied to the existing debates among researchers regarding appropriate research conduct. From these debates, we are better able to understand the diverse ethical approaches that have been adopted by researchers. These understandings of participants' views, researchers' conduct, and ethical philosophies, hopefully, will aid in the formulation of ethical guidelines for online research.

Notes

1 Because this research was conducted in the context of academic journalism, no distinction was made in the survey questions between the work of information gathering done by academic researchers and that done by working journalists in the course of developing stories. However, as is evident from the responses, some of the respondents drew sharp distinctions between these two types of online information gathering (see note 3). Except in instances in which journalists and academic researchers are specifically differentiated, the more general term "information gatherer" is used in reference to both groups.

2 All responses are presented here as they were received from the respondents, with no effort made to correct errors in spelling, grammar, punctuation, or capitalization errors. The authors wish to think those who responded to the online survey for the information they provided. Their eagerness to share shows the need to address these issues.

3 The differing reactions some respondents have toward journalists may stem from the perception that journalists are more likely than academic researchers to act as paparazzi in online research. Because of the nature of their profession, journalists are required to write objectively, which may give the impression of a less than sympathetic account of an online group. Also, the pressure to meet deadlines may preclude them from spending the time

necessary to establish rapport with online participants. Furthermore, journalistic ethics would not normally encourage a journalist to share a story with a source prior to publication, thus preventing an opportunity for participant input or correctives. Add to this the fact that a journalist's report, by definition, generates publicity for the online group which may not always be entirely welcome. Therefore, we speculate that it is for these reasons that some respondents indicated that they regard journalism as "a despised profession," and reported that journalists would receive "short shrift" compared to academic researchers.

References

Babbie, E. *The Practice of Social Research.* Belmont, CA: Wadsworth, Inc., 1992.

Couch, C. *Social Processes and Relationships.* New York: General Hall, 1989.

da Silva, S. "Publicly Accessible Mailing Lists, 2001." http://paml.net/

Denzin, N. *Interpretive Ethnography: Ethnographic Practices for the 21st Century.* Thousand Oaks, CA: Sage, 1997.

King, S. "Researching Internet Communities: Proposed Ethical Guidelines for the Reporting of Results," *The Information Society, 12*(2) (Spring 1996):119–128.

Reid, E. "Informed Consent in the Study of Online Communities: A Reflection on the Effects of Computer-Mediated Social Research," *The Information Society, 12*(2) (Spring 1996):169–174.

Sharf, B. "Beyond Netiquette: The Ethics of Doing Naturalistic Discourse Research on the Internet," in *Doing Internet Research,* ed. S. Jones, pp. 243–256. Thousand Oaks, CA: Sage, 1999.

Thomas, J. "When Cyber-research Goes Awry: The Ethics of the Rimm 'Cyberporn' Study," *The Information Society, 12*(2) (Spring 1996):189–197. (1996a).

———. "Introduction: A Debate About the Ethics of Fair Practices for Collecting Data in Cyberspace," *The Information Society, 12*(2) (Spring 1996):107–117. (1996b).

Part III

Ethics of Online Social Research

Introduction: Ethics and Internet Studies

≈≈

Steve Jones

CLIFFORD GEERTZ ENDS his landmark book *The Interpretation of Cultures* with the statement that to study interpretations in a culture, "one has only to learn how to gain access to them" (1973, 453). Although Geertz was (at least at the time of that book's writing) not "wired," there is something almost cyberpunk or hackerlike about the attitude he expresses. At present for most Internet researchers it is likely that gaining access (be it to newsgroups, listservs, what have you) is the least difficult aspect of the research process. As Katherine Clegg Smith points out in her chapter in this volume, one can routinely "stumble across a goldmine." What has become more difficult is determining how to ensure ethical use is made of the texts, sounds, and pictures that are accessed for study. More difficult still is jumping through the hurdles that Institutional Review Boards (IRBs) at academic institutions place in front of virtually every scholar, researcher, artist, teacher, and student.

The authors represented in this section of *Online Social Research* share their experiences as Internet researchers and their thinking about online research ethics. Their contributions encourage those engaged in Internet research and those overseeing research to think about what we need to think about when it comes to Internet research ethics. For all intents and purposes, doing so amounts to a form of agenda setting. When it comes to research ethics, an agenda is needed. It is particularly easy among those who do not know very much about the kinds of interactions that take place online to be alarmist. And make no mistake—there are plenty of people who still have little experience online, even among those at universities. (I have known a few members of human subjects research review boards who were of the opinion that Internet research should be summarily denied approval, because the Internet is a domain of liars, thieves, pornographers, and hackers.)

Why that would make the Internet a worse place to do research than, say, a gang-infested neighborhood, I have no idea.

But my usual response when confronted with someone who is fearful of the Internet as a medium in which one may do research is to point out that, in general terms, there is little that is "new" in "new media." Not that we have seen it all, or that we do not find that the Internet has brought about new forms of communication. But for scholars the advent of *every* new medium has typically required some renewed thought about methods and ethics, and the Internet ought not cause alarm among institutional review board members.

The numerous issues Internet researchers have already begun to study, such as gender, access, identity, and community, have implicit within them ethical and political dimensions. Yet, the discussion of these ethical dimensions has been unfortunately taking place at a time when research ethics are becoming increasingly confused and mixed up. Jim Thomas notes in his chapter that there are important "ideological influences on ethical thinking" that should be brought to the fore, and should we fail to do so we will likely not understand both the high degree of ethical scrutiny of research and the basis on which we may argue for appropriately normative ethical guidelines.

Some researchers wonder why ethics is such an important matter. Some are historians, artists, journalists, or independent scholars, and have not been bound by the rules established by IRBs that govern human subjects research. If I may respond to them for a moment and sound like the *Star Wars* character Yoda: You will be.

In September 1999, the U.S. Office for Protection from Research Risks blocked my university from beginning new research projects involving human subjects. *The Chronicle of Higher Education* noted that "the action marks the continuation of what some university officials see as a trend of tougher enforcement of research protocols by the federal watchdog agency" (Brainard, 1999, A44). In short, much as a university undertakes its own self-study when the NCAA finds possible rule infractions and then goes well beyond the NCAA's sanctions in hopes that self-flagellation counts for something, my university suspended all human subjects research—for months. All human subjects research was first put on hold, then re-reviewed under new guidelines. All researchers on campus had to undergo research ethics training, and, here is the rub, most of that training focused almost entirely on medical research. Such training is ongoing and requires annual recertification.

One can imagine the consequences for those holding research grants, or near the point of tenure and promotion, or making progress toward earning a degree, whose work was summarily stopped.

My point in using my own university as an example is not to continue any self-flagellation. I should point out that ours was not the only institution to come under scrutiny. In the spring of 2001, historians at Illinois State

University were featured prominently in a *Chronicle of Higher Education* article concerning the federal mandate designed to oversee research involving human subjects. A history student's thesis, which explored how social science curricula evolved in the Pekin, Illinois School District, came into question, as his research included interviews with school officials and oral histories from teachers—that had not received prior IRB approval. Fortunately for the student, the board eventually approved his research, thanks in large part to the efforts of his adviser, who convinced the IRB that his student's questions posed minimal risk to the persons interviewed. Oral histories, database research, even journalistic and creative work have, at some universities, come under scrutiny. Given the heightened interest in policing human subjects research, we are all likely to come under some form of scrutiny, for better or worse, when it comes to research ethics. But the scrutiny is likely to be driven, improperly, I believe, from the perspective of the medical sciences (as those cases involving medical ethics are the most high-profile ones in this day and age) and from the perspective of institutional self-preservation (or at least reduction of liability). And when it comes to Internet research, my desire in this climate is to point out that Internet research ought not be singled out for special treatment as compared to other types of research.

And yet I am not convinced that the procedures and, more important, the conceptual frameworks we have for reviewing research protocols are up to the task when it comes to Internet research. During the past few years I have had, for example, several graduate students spend a good deal of time and effort convincing human subjects review boards that the Internet research they wished to pursue should be approved. In two cases, neither the review board nor the student were easily able to determine the risk to the human subjects to be studied, appropriate methods for obtaining consent, and appropriate ways to ensure anonymity. In one case, it was difficult to determine whether human subjects were in fact being studied, since the research involved explorations of online interactions that may have involved bots [computer programs written to simulate human interaction on the Internet].

What has proven most difficult is that the IRBs have treated these researchers as guilty until proven innocent, and have required them to give evidentiary proof in cases when it is not possible to obtain it. To provide but one example, a student was told she would have to provide a signed informed consent form for each subject in an online chat room, no matter that the participants were perfectly anonymous and were likely, in fact, using multiple identities. The IRB believed that she needed a signed informed consent form for each identity.

It will be confusing for IRBs and researchers alike to confront some of the issues that Internet research brings to the fore. But the issues must first be assessed independently of the current institutional climate and the uniqueness of the Internet as a social space must be considered. For example, in a 1998 report titled *Fostering Research on the Economic and Social Impacts of Information Technology*, it was noted that:

> "Informed consent" in surveys and experiments is a dimension of privacy that strikes close to home for social scientists. Quite strong safeguards are in place for social science work involving human subjects, but in some ways it is difficult to apply some of these practices to the Internet. For example, the fact that data is being collected can easily be concealed from subjects. One source of useful data comes from retrospective examination of existing records such as server logs or "Usenet" postings where a social science experiment was not the original intent of the data collection. Just as in the case of private data, cross-tabulation of innocuous data sets can identify seemingly anonymous subjects. Certainly, social scientists must develop a code of practices, ethics, and perhaps regulations that will help deal with these issues. (National Research Council, 1998)

Similarly, the American Association for the Advancement of Science published a report in 1999 titled *Ethical and Legal Aspects of Human Subjects Research on the Internet*. Its authors note that:

> The ability of both researchers and their subjects to assume anonymous or pseudonymous identities online, the complexities of obtaining informed consent, the often exaggerated expectations, if not the illusion, of privacy in cyberspace, and the blurred distinction between public and private domains fuel questions about the interpretation and applicability of current policies governing the conduct of social and behavioral research involving human subjects. (Frankel and Siang, 1999)

Yet these are all possibilities with research offline, and therefore I cannot understand why the report's recommendations make the Internet seem so in need of special attention.

> At a meeting in California in the spring of 2002, I had the opportunity to discuss and debate the AAAS report with one of its authors, Sanyin Siang. One of her responses to my queries made me think again about something I brought up a few years ago in a collection of essays I edited entitled *Doing Internet Research*. In one essay I wrote, "it is possible that when it comes to Internet research, our methods are not *scalable*. Or, perhaps, that our methods do not scale is a failure of our epistemology rather than our methods: Comprehension is always less than (perfectly) efficient." (Jones, 1999, 25)

Yet, I have found some who are arguing that, *a priori*, our ethical considerations, which are to no small degree a forecast of the *potential* consequences of our research, must now be premised on an assumed nature of the online individual. Never mind that the Internet is increasingly a medium of person-to-machine, and even machine-to-machine, communication. Who we are online, the reasoning of most IRBs seems to go, is not only identical to who we are offline, but it is also a one-to-one correspondence, and all interaction online is with singular individuals.

You might think I am now going to take a postmodern turn and talk about multiple selves online, but I am not. What I want to stress is that concomitant with the above the degree to which the researcher's integrity is assumed by the IRB has dwindled to less than a minimum. The researcher is practically a Machiavellian figure, a manipulator of behavior, the embodiment of the Hawthorne effect, and then some.

But it is important to keep in mind what actually happens online. Most online research (and interaction) is concerned with participation, rather than experimentation or treatments that would make us consider online actors "human subjects." It is important that we understand that those online are participants in cultures of their own making. Those we study are no more "subjects" than the online texts they create are "mere messages." And as Internet use continues to increasingly incorporate images we should not lull ourselves into the sense that textual communication is the last word (pun intended) in online communication.

One risk, then, to be avoided, is the diminishing of the human element online and the diminishment of human agency as we assume risk for others. Participants in online communication, virtual worlds, cyberspace, and so on, are not to be subsumed by the texts they create, they are not to be rendered wholly disembodied, they should not be considered somehow not human, powerless or valueless, they should not be presumed victims of their utterances. The issues regarding attribution and identification that Susan Barnes brings up in her chapter concern precisely the need for an awareness of Internet users' subjectivities.

Another level of subjectivity of which one needs to be aware is the difference in experience that Internet users may have. Jon Hall, Douglas Frederick, and Mark Johns note in their chapter, by way of a newsgroup member's comment, that if a scholar recruits volunteers online, "verbal fireworks" are likely to be greater in a chatroom than a newsgroup. Researchers must take care to note that there is no such thing as "the Internet," no single, common experience of its use. Indeed, there is little that is convergent about the Internet as a medium. While interaction with television, radio, and the telephone does not greatly differ from one model to another, unlike media before it, the experience of the Internet, as a medium tied (for now, at least) to the computer, is as malleable and changeable as the computer is itself.

There is, of course, an Internet of computers, wires (albeit increasingly wireless), routers, servers, and so on. But researchers in general tend to play fast and loose with the term "Internet." It is important to be specific about what the term means in context. Online research takes place in a range of venues (e-mail, chatrooms, web pages, various forms of "instant messaging," MUDs and MOOs, USENET newsgroups, audio/video exchanges, etc.). In addition, both the great variety of human behaviors observable online and the clear need to study these behaviors in interdisciplinary ways have thus engaged researchers and scholars in disciplines beyond those traditionally involved in human subjects research: for example, researching the multiple uses of texts and graphics images in diverse Internet venues often benefits from approaches drawn from art history, literary studies, and so on, approaches not considered forms of "human subjects" research.

Are there Internet-specific ethical concerns? Probably, among them: anonymity, consent, privacy, confidentiality, and others. Ethics are not our only concern but also legal matters. One admittedly vulgar way to draw a line between ethical and legal concerns is to determine whether one is concerned with values or value, that is, with human or financial issues. The law alone, however, is insufficient. If we have only the law to guide us, our work as scholars will ever be subject to what James Carey (in another context) described as "a nest of juridically derived meanings, an instrument to adjust and avoid disputes, to advance and promote interests, to protect and enhance rights" (1997, 208).

And that is precisely, and unfortunately, what our IRBs are driving us toward. As Mark Devenney noted in a recent article: "Identification with an ultimate contingency implies that the ethical, as an impossible ideal, should be contrasted with any particular normative order which attempts to achieve that ideal" (2001, 224). The politics of IRBs has radically veered away from the normative, and now seeks to avoid "a constant contestation of all those rules which demarcate *demos*, a constant reinvention of the laws which also means their constant amelioration" (Devenny, 2001, 224). While we must acknowledge the consequential and political dimension of Internet studies, be that in relation to ethics, policy, censorship, access, privacy, or any number of other important issues, we also must acknowledge that the Internet does not exist apart from life offline, and therefore the sensitivities we bring to our research offline also should guide our efforts at study of new and emergent cultures, be they real or virtual. Raymond Williams reminds us in the title of one of his essays that "Culture is Ordinary" (1997). Our ethics, to truly counter the extraordinary demands of forces external to the academy, must, in the same sense as Williams applies the term to culture, be ordinary.

References

Brainard, J. "Research Blocked in Illinois." *The Chronicle of Higher Education 46*, no. 3 (September 10, 1999): A44.

Carey, J.W. *James Carey: A Critical Reader*, eds. E. S. Munson and C. A. Warren. Minneapolis: University of Minnesota Press, 1997.

Devenney, M. "Toward an Ethics of Incommensurability." *Strategies: Journal of Theory, Culture & Politics 14*, no. 2 (November 2001): 209–224.

Frankel, M.S. and S. Siang. "Ethical and Legal Aspects of Human Subjects Research on the Internet." Washington, DC: American Association for the Advancement of Science (AAAS), 1999.

Geertz, C. *The Interpretation of Cultures*. New York: Basic Books, 1973.

Jones, S. (Ed.) *Doing Internet Research*. Thousand Oaks, CA: Sage, 1999.

National Research Council. Fostering Research on the Economic and Social Impacts of Information Technology (1998). Washington, DC: National Academy Press. Available at http://www.nap.edu

Williams, R. "Culture is Ordinary." In *Studies in Culture: An Introductory Reader*, eds. A. Gray and J. McGuigan, 5–14. London: Arnold, 1997 (Original Work Published in 1958).

Reexamining the Ethics of Internet Research: Facing the Challenge of Overzealous Oversight

Jim Thomas

INSTITUTIONAL WATCHDOGS and moral entrepreneurs continually remind us, and often require, that we demonstrate prior to, during, and after our research that our practices conform to established ethical codes. Especially with the recent federally imposed oversight of human subjects review and enforcement by Institutional Review Boards (IRBs) (Thomas, 2002a, 2002b), the ethics of research, especially Internet research, has become an increasingly contentious issue. But, while it's generally nicer to be nice than not nice, sometimes we perhaps try to be too nice and take ethics far too seriously. As a consequence, discussions of Internet research are part of a larger debate over what constitutes ethical conduct, who "owns" accountability, and how we construct a shared community of responsibility while not simultaneously creating a chilling effect that hampers inquiry.

There has been no lack of commentary on computer ethics and Internet behavior in general (e.g., Forester and Morrison, 1990; Stoll, 1995) or Net research ethics in particular (King, 1996; Thomas, 1996a, 1996b; Waskul, 1996). Yet, debates over what constitutes "ethical" Net research continue as if the Internet poses a dramatically new venue for which we must find new ethical principles and establish and enforce explicit rules for restricting conduct. This problem has become especially acute for those of us who have presented our research proposals for IRB approval or who develop educational programs for federally mandated Responsible Conduct of Research (RCR) initiatives (Thomas, 2002a).

In this chapter, I argue that ethical precepts, while a cornerstone of research, risk being reified by moral entrepreneurs who advocate drafting explicit and immutable prescriptions and proscriptions for Net research. I argue that we need not invent new ethical rules for online research or try to reduce ethical behavior in Internet research—or any other—to an immutable set of prescriptions and proscriptions. We need only increase our awareness of and commitment to established ethical principles. At stake in this discussion is not only why we should continually examine the possible ethical quandaries that arise in Net research. We must also—even before we begin—satisfy our IRBs and familiarize the more recent RCR committees about the problems we may face and how they might be resolved.

Who Cares?

I strongly support ethical oversight and attention to ethical issues in our scholarship. There is obviously a need to be vigilant when using the Net for scholarship activities, which include research, teaching, and interacting with others in our capacity as professionals or students. Yet, many of us forget that ethics extend beyond formal research, and encompass all levels of life. Why should social scientists or anybody else take an aggressive stand in supporting ethical scholarly activity? One reason is that, as methodologists, teachers, journal editors, reviewers, commentators, and policy makers, we continue to confront ethical dilemmas in our respective fields. There are a number of other reasons, some ethical, others in our self-interest, why we all should take aggressive measures to reflect on scholarly ethics in all situations beyond the Net.

First, ethical behavior is inherent in, and essential to, scholarship. Second, awareness and practices of Net ethics enhance the credibility of research and contribute to a climate of trust and integrity. A single egregious violation by one researcher poisons the credibility of others as well. Third, members of the academic community, even those not directly involved in research, identify and reaffirm the principles of responsible scholarship in manuscript review, teaching, advising, classroom activities, and discussions with peers. Awareness of potential problems raises red flags that enable peers to proactively screen for potential problems. Fourth, promoting ethical standards complies with Federal and institutional requirements and helps ensure a positive professional image internally and externally.

Fifth, promoting ethical scholarship increases familiarity with potential issues in one's one field as well as in other fields, illustrating the complexity of seemingly simple potential problems. Such cross-fertilization helps to bind researchers across disciplines. Sixth, promoting human subjects protections creates an awareness of the rationale that guides identifying and resolving problems. As Thomas and Marquart (1988) have argued, formal ethical rules or the ethical codes of professional organizations are not always helpful, and sometimes sharing principles, instead of rigid precepts, helps resolve some problems. Seventh, ethical awareness increases recognition of the investigator's own social location in the process of scholarship and can highlight our obligations to the public we served by our scholarship.

Sometimes, the researcher owes conflicting allegiances to subjects (Thomas and Marquart, 1988), which requires us to identify where our ethical loyalties lie and who we are bound to protect. Eighth, an awareness of ethical issues contributes to shared awareness of the diversity and complexity of issues facing practitioners involved in human subjects research, and promotes an environment of collegial recognition and discussion.

In Internet research, these issues are compounded by the dilemmas of privacy, protection of human subjects, the blurry line between public and private spaces, the ease of archiving data, and the increased possibility that our fieldnotes can be accessed or inadvertently released to others.

Dilemmas of Internet Ethics

The complexity of Net ethics was illustrated a few years ago when a study of online pornography (Rimm, 1995) became the cover story in *Time Magazine* (Elmer-Dewit, 1995). Riddled with ethical lapses, the research passed through at least 10 levels of potential gatekeeping, including attorneys, journalists, researchers, media editorial staff, and even the U.S. Congress, without a single question being raised (Thomas, 1996a). The lesson? Discussions of ethical issues in online research should be addressed to the general public as well as academics and students.

I emphasize that I am neither an ethical zealot nor a moralist, and there is some irony in my continued research in and writing on research ethics. Perhaps my own lapses in field research and elsewhere have sensitized me to the complexity of "right" behavior and made me more aware of the lapses of others. As a teacher of research ethics in methodology classes, I emphasize to students the importance of reflecting on the consequences of their research for themselves, their subjects, and society. As an ethnographer who studies culture from the participants' point of view through participant observation, I study the prisoner culture created and maintained by "bad guys." I also have studied online conventional and underground computer culture, including hackers and software pirates. From my background as a would-be philosopher in graduate school, I retain a bit from the ethical and moral writings we plowed through. However, while philosophical writings are useful for academic conferences and esoteric papers, they too often provide too little substantive direction for researchers and others in the trenches. Distinctions between ethical systems based on invariant rules or on the consequences of our ethical decisions are not always useful for solving the nitty-gritty dilemmas that occur without warning.

When Is Net Behavior an Ethical Transgression?

Most people want to "do the right thing," even on the Net. But, several incidents in the past two years illustrate how "doing the right thing" may not always mean the same thing to all of us. The incidents suggested that, while people may generally prefer doing right, the Net may be like bars and other social settings where a "time out" ethos exists, excusing participants from many conventional social obligations (Cavan, 1966). The issues raised here are not so much whether the behaviors are wrong, but where the line lies between right and wrong, and how the line is defended.

In the first incident, a persistent hacker broke into several of our university computer systems. The UNIX server of about two hundred users that I maintain was among them. There was no evidence that users' files were compromised or that file systems were damaged. Doing so, of course, would be an egregious violation of the "hacker ethic" (Levy, 1984). However, over a seven-day period, I invested over 30 hours of increased system monitoring and tightening security. Two of my colleagues, who did the bulk of the technical work, invested more. The incident dramatically ate into the time required for grading student work and meeting deadlines. Evidence suggested that the intruder was participating in a popular hacker game, and likely saw nothing unethical about the conduct. To me and my colleagues, the intrusion was an unethical violation of trust that was demonstrably unfair to our students who needed our time and attention. It also unjustly added to an already heavy and uncompensated work burden.

In a second incident, students in my large (250-person) introductory sociology course were required to write book critiques. Among the final batch of about two hundred papers, I verified at least 20 lifted nearly verbatim, or substantially drawn from, Internet sites. Among these, five used the same paper submitted for a class assignment at a different university. I found the original paper on a site specializing in term papers; students had to upload a paper in order to download a paper. I discovered a sixth paper in my class, and a wordprocessor comparison indicated that it was identical with the paper from the second university, including punctuation. When I confronted the author of the sixth paper, the student informed me:

> I did not plagiarize! I wrote the paper the other woman submitted to that site and uploaded it so that I could obtain information. What's wrong with that? It's not my fault that other people cheat. I can't help what they do. As long as it's my own work, what's the problem with me uploading it?

The student saw nothing wrong with uploading a paper to an online "term paper mill," even knowing that it would be downloaded and submitted by others as their own, as long as the student did the actual work. When confronted with what I considered an egregious ethical violation, the other students acknowledged that they knew they were violating a rule, but none saw it as a significant ethical lapse. In their view, they knowingly violated university policies, but each felt that their need to excel absolved them of ethical culpability, because they were capable of doing quality work. Cruising the Net for papers, they felt, was not an ethical violation, because they were good students who could do superior work on their own. Were the students being unethical? Or, were they engaging in what Matza and Sykes (1961) called "techniques of neutralization" to redefine challenged behaviors as acceptable?

A third incident involved a university home page competition in which the winning page would be determined by tallying the electronic votes of university computer users. The intent of the competition was to encourage the university community to browse each homepage and vote on the merits of the pages. The competitions' nominees represented individual users, small staff units, academic departments, and one large student computer research laboratory. Representatives from the large computer laboratory staged a "vote-in" by mobilizing hundreds of students who used the lab to vote directly for the lab's page without viewing the others. There was heated debate within the offending department over whether this constituted an ethical violation. However, the more interesting issue was that few of the department's faculty or lab personnel considered that stacking the electronic vote might constitute an ethical lapse. It did not occur to those involved that it might be unfair to those web page authors without a large constituency, or unjust to web page authors who chose to adhere to the spirit of the competition and not solicit votes. The special relevance here is that the participants, from the home page author to the lab's director and the technological committee ultimately responsible for lab oversight, initially saw nothing to question about vote-stacking behavior. The point is it was not even seen as a relevant question worth addressing.

The final incident involved a senior professor, respected for his integrity and sense of justice, who posted a long copyright-protected article from a national newspaper on a publicly accessible university discussion group. He included a three-paragraph justification offering four reasons for the full repost. First, the work had been published two weeks previously; hence it was "old news." Second, the repost was intended for "scholars" in a university forum; hence, it was fair use, and therefore not subject to copyright law. Third, the work was a small portion of the entire newspaper; hence, it was a negligible infraction. Fourth, old newspapers have no value, "fit only for wrapping fish"; hence, there was no commercial loss to the paper. Did the professor stray over the thin boundary of ethical behavior? As one who runs online discussion groups for students, I often admonish them for reposting copyright-protected articles. As a consequence, while I find no reason for ethical outrage against my colleague, I do find the questions raised to be of specific relevance to the issues of Net ethics.

Each of these incidents arguably subverted core social values such as trust and honesty, respect for privacy, principles of fairness and justice, and protection of intellectual property. However, what I find most interesting about these incidents is that there is no consensus on whether there was an ethical violation or, if there was, that it constitutes "any big deal." The reason for the disparity in judgment likely reflects not so much a decline of concern with ethical issues as it illustrates the degree to which ethical precepts and appropriate social responses to them are, at root, a social construct. As a consequence, we cannot examine Net research ethics independently from the larger settings in which they arise.

The Ideological Dimension of Ethics

To the extent that ethics are a social construct, all ethical systems reflect an ideological component that supports an underlying cultural value system. Ideology refers to those shared beliefs, attitudes, and basic assumptions about the world that justify, shape, and organize how we perceive and interpret the world. As a set of the most-basic collective assumptions and rationalizations about our social world, ideology provides the basic framework for decisions and policies pertaining to social and political activity. More specifically, ideologies are the relatively invisible conceptual machineries for maintaining social order.

Examples of ideological preferences include belief in "due process for all," which guides our criminal justice system; "my country right or wrong," which underlies such corresponding beliefs as "flag burning is wrong" and "it's unethical to avoid military conscription"; or adherence to the principle of free enterprise, which guides our economic system and generates ethical criticisms of people who advocate political alternatives such as socialism. Because ideologies are preconscious, emotionally charged, and pervasive, their substance tends to be less visible than other beliefs and shared tenets. Because ideologies function to preserve and justify the status quo by reproducing basic cultural conceptions of social order, right and wrong, and who does (or does not) have the right to enforce or be protected by ethical precepts, the ideological basis of research ethics cannot be ignored. The point, of course, is that we can use ethics to justify a variety of behaviors on which there might be room for honest intellectual disagreement. In this sense, ethical positions often contain a contextual ideological component in which issues of "right and wrong" are based on political expediency, preferred norms, or self-interest.

Each of the four incidents above reflects competing ideologically based value systems that generate ethical precepts justifying or opposing the behaviors in question. They can be examined within the context of two basic ethical positions. The intent here is neither to defend nor attack the ethics of those involved in the incidents, or to map out a detailed ethical position for making judgments. Rather, with acknowledged oversimplification, the goal is to illustrate some of the ideological influences on ethical thinking as a way to underscore the relationship between each.

Mapping out the broad brush strokes of competing ethical perspectives helps us more easily understand the principles by which ethical problems are identified and solutions to them sought. It also helps us understand the fundamental premises of our own and others' positions. Parenthetically, although many of us tend to use the terms "ethics" and "morality" as synonyms, they are not the same. The concept of ethics refers to the character or conscience of a person in relation to a group, and morality refers to the value system of a group in relation to the individual. Stanage (1995) summarizes ethics as person-in-culture, and morality as culture-in-person to remind us that the two may not always coincide. Here, I maintain the distinction.

One basic foundation of ethics is based on absolute "rule following" and proceeds from formally specified precepts that guide how we ought to behave. An example would be professional codes of ethics in the social sciences, which codify researchers' obligations and responsibilities to research subjects. These formal systems generally guide IRB judgments. This position adheres to the premise that we follow the rules, even if seemingly inappropriate or irrational, an ethical outcome will follow.

Second is what is called a teleological, or ends-driven perspective, associated with, but not exclusive to, utilitarianism. Ends-driven perspectives operate from the premise that ethical behavior is determined by the consequences of an act. The goal or end of an act should be weighed with a calculus that, on balance, will result in the greatest social good or the least social harm. Here, the consequences for a collective beneficial outcome drive our decisions, and we should constantly be aware of the consequences of our actions, not just the rules we follow. Unfortunately, these two positions often conflict.

The Ethics of Hacking

In the first example of Net misconduct, a tension exists between the professed hacker philosophy of freedom of exploration and system administrators' goal of protecting the integrity of the system for users. Hacking behavior has been justified as ethical by defining it as a knowledge-producing activity that confers on intruders the right to explore systems to see how things work. A corollary to this view is that hackers actually enhance Net ethics by ultimately requiring tighter security to protect users. A second rationale for hacking is the adage that "information wants to be free." In this view, hackers are a type of freedom fighter intent on liberating knowledge and preventing it from becoming monopolized by potentially malevolent corporate or governmental forces. Hacking is justified by a narrow utilitarian rationale that takes two forms. The first derives from a primitive utilitarian view in which the exploration underlying computer intrusion contributes to the stock of public knowledge. In a less noble and more primitive variant, hacking is simply a form of Nietzschean ethical egoism in which individuals pursue the course of action most likely to fulfill individual self-interests. Both views can be justified by an appeal to a social context in which hacking, on balance, provides greater long-term good than harm.

For system administrators, by contrast, hackers are a malevolent force whose behaviors unfairly sap their limited time and other resources. System administrators are charged with assuring that users' private files are secure. Even if intruders do not target private files, once the potential for compromise exists, user trust in the integrity of the system dissolves. Opposition to intrusions and other disruptions also can be based either on rules-based or on ends-driven theories. For ends-based utilitarians, uninvited explorations cause short-term harm by draining system and personnel resources, and result in long-term harm by subverting user trust. Worse, they lead to decreased system openness by restricting users' rights and privileges in the name of security. An alternative rationale by which hacking would be judged unethical is based on a rule-based perspective. This view, Kantian in nature, establishes as a type of categorical imperative the principle that would be held by any reasonable person similarly situated: Intrusions are a fundamental violation regardless of context or perceived utility.

The Ethics of Intellection Property Violation

Using the example of the professor's copyright transgression, both defense of and opposition to reposting the intellectual property of another can be made on utilitarian grounds. For the professor, the context of the situation and motive for the act trumped the laws protecting intellectual property. As with hackers who publicly distribute information about the security holes of computer systems or make available proprietary information in the belief that "knowledge wants to be free," the professor, too, argued that the utilitarian ends (contributions to knowledge) outweighed the normative and legal prohibitions protecting others' intellectual property.

Conversely, utilitarianism also provides two reasons why, on balance, reposting causes more harm than good. First, reposting may reduce the commercial or other value of the work. Second, the professor's action, on balance, subverts principles of fairness and long-range respect for ethical Net behavior by symbolizing the wrong ethical message to students and others.

Although cursory, this overview should nonetheless be sufficient to illustrate that the Net behaviors described do not necessarily reflect an inattention to ethics. It also suggests that, at root, ethical arguments tend to be used to provide an account for justifying a preferred ideological outcome rather than an attempt to determine a universalistic guide to "what's right."

Ethics or Pragmatism: Where to from Here?

One dominant theme of existential literature centers on the delicate balance required when navigating between personal preferences and the broader issues of ethical, normative, and institutional obligations. Typified by Camus's Sisyphus (1955) and his view that the human condition is necessarily an indelicate balance between uncertain alternatives, or Gide's (1958) immoralist, who rebels against conventional norms of appropriate conduct, we are reminded of the often irreconcilable choices when weighing what we prefer to do against what we ought to do. The lesson, of course, is that rigid adherence to scripted ethical or moral precepts may be neither a virtue nor a beneficence.

Those of us involved in the type of research that may skirt the edge of ethical propriety often come away with muddy shoes resulting from unsuccessful balancing attempts. When this happens, two consequences ideally follow. First, it provides the opportunity to constantly reassess the relationship between the goals of scholarship and the means of gathering and processing data. Second, it reinforces the need to constantly raise ethical issues with colleagues, students, the media, and the general public. But, we ought also take care to avoid self-righteousness by presuming that ethical standards are absolute and can be applied to every situation. Several caveats arise when discussing implementation of research ethics through policy or legislation.

First, reification of ethical principles tends to do more harm than good. Reification gives primacy to rules, which relegates their context to secondary status. Even if consensus on ethical prescriptions and proscriptions could be attained, elevating absolute principles to some standard of immutable "realness" risks several consequences that, ironically, could subvert ethical awareness in at least two ways. Not only could research become subject to the religiosity of puritanical gatekeepers, but excessive control invites existential rebellion (Milovanovic and Thomas, 1989).

Second, we should remember that ethics are distinct from other forms of socially preferred behavioral guidelines. Conflating ethical principles with private morality, legislation, institutional policies, or basic courtesy norms as if the same obligations were owed to each dilutes the power of ethical principles by making "thou shalt nots" equivalent to "don't wear grunge to the opera." This results in a weakening of the foundation of fundamental standards for all behavior, including computer-centered research and related Net activity.

Third, there is a danger of confusing ideological predilections with ethical predications. It is helpful to remember that, while most of us agree that we ought not do that which is ethically wrong, we often disagree on what counts as "ethically right." The principles by which we assess value judgments are normative and socially contingent. They are rarely as clearly defined as they seem. We can agree that it is wrong to take a life without cause, but we may not agree that it is also wrong to copy a commercial software program or never to observe research subjects without permission. Often enough, our views of personal privacy, our definitions of public/private spaces, and our conception of social or personal harm are based not so much on ethical principles as on ideological, or even idiosyncratic, preferences.

Fourth, it is useful to distinguish between "pseudo ethics" and legitimate ethical imperatives. An ethical imperative is, very broadly, an "ought statement" (distinguished from convention and value judgments) that, if not followed, would cause significant demonstrable harm. A "pseudo ethic" is a behavioral dictate mandated by the norms of a particular group that, if not followed, potentially challenges the interests of that group. Many of our institutional policies on research ethics derive from the latter. Organizational self-interest and liability concerns become translated into ethical discourse, and the ethical discourse becomes translated into the rhetoric of self-interest—based policy formulation, legislation, and enforcement. IRBs are an example. Too often, their decisions seem driven not so much by protecting research subjects, but by following federally mandated bureaucratic procedures that will protect the institution from sanctions in the event of a federal audit. This leads to seemingly irrational hoopjumping by scholars seeking IRB approval who are required to engage in processes where common sense often seems trumped by extreme, often ignorant, nit-picking.

Does this all mean that ethical decisions are relative and that discussions of research ethics are of little use? Not at all. The intent here has been to describe the complexity of Net behaviors as well as to illustrate some of the ambiguities underlying any set of definitive rules. I have always followed three broad principles in my own research and teaching. First, always protect informants. This precept includes keeping promises and never putting them at risk. Second, always protect the integrity of research inquiry. This means that we cannot sacrifice the methodological rigor or norms of empirical science by skirting issues or ignoring sensitive data. Although this precept is complex in the abstract, in practice it simply means that, for example, if the researcher cannot protect informants without sacrificing scientific principles, then stop the project. Third, in the classroom and professional life, I try, albeit imperfectly, to reinforce the norms and practices of ethical behavior. Plagiarism is wrong not only because it violates a rule, but because it leads to an unacceptable result: it deprives students of a learning experience and erodes academic trust. Hacking is wrong, not simply because it's against the rules, but because it subverts higher ends of computer system integrity, user resources, and administrator energy. Violation of copyright material may or may not be unethical, but we should carefully assess our act and at least be able to make an informed judgment before acting.

There are two broad courses we can pursue in implementing research ethics. The first, a rather Sartrean approach in which we identify explicit ethical rules and commit ourselves completely to their realization and accept responsibility for the consequences, seems a bit dogmatic, even dangerous. At best, it entails little latitude for discretion, and offers too little recognition of the world of greys that blur boundaries of right and wrong in many social situations.

A second course seems more beneficial, or certainly more viable. In this view, we recognize the potential ambiguity of social situations in which most value decisions are made and commit ourselves not to rules, but to broad principles of justice and beneficence. Although this view makes establishing formal rules impractical, if not impossible, it does allow an ends-driven and somewhat pragmatic set of guidelines to steer us through the murky situations we often encounter. The policy implications for this view do not lie in establishing more stringent IRB review policies or in creating and enforcing new rules. Instead, we could adopt a number of strategies, including the following.

First, educational institutions at all levels could expand discussions of ethics across the curriculum. Second, professional organizations should build ethics sessions into their annual conferences. Third, journal editors should assure that editorial boards and peer reviewers are attuned to the subtle ways that ethical issues creep into research, and publish periodic special journal issues on ethics. Fourth, professional associations should increase the visibility of ethical issues by systematically and aggressively sharing with media, politicians, and others the results of ethical deliberations and critiques, as well as by monitoring governmental and media lapses in reporting or using research. Fifth, professionals should more rigorously police themselves, not by punitive responses, but by open challenge and remedial debate when perceived lapses occur. Sixth, we should aggressively educate IRBs on the nuances of Net research and resist their attempts to impose special restrictions in areas of human subjects protection, the distinction between public and private areas of social action, or privacy that do not apply to other topics or methods. Finally, we must recognize that Net research ethics cannot be separated from broader social milieu. Hence, we should take a global, rather than parochial, view of the problems.

Conclusion

Once, when invited to participate in a forum addressing the presumptively new challenges of Internet technology to ethical precepts, I recalled an exercise many of us experienced as children. We are first asked to look around the room and silently identify and remember as many blue items as we can. Next, we are asked to close our eyes tightly. No peeking! Then, with our eyes still closed, we are asked to name anything we recall that was colored red. Most of us either could not identify a red object, or named one only after considerable cognitive and mnemonic strain. The exercise illustrated the manner in which perception, cognition, and memory are often prepatterned by assumptions, suggestions, and preformed conceptions that channel our gaze and corresponding responses in narrow directions that cloud our perceptions, understandings, and actions. When applied to assessing guidelines for Net behavior, it suggests that we should "think outside the ethical box" while not losing sight of the contents.

The fundamental ethical questions posed by new technology are not new. Basic beliefs in the precept that it is better to do good than ill do not change. What changes is that the relationship between behaviors and the ethical conceptions by which we judge them shift and become ambiguous, vague, and perceived through a sometimes foggy prism. The problem for those involved in Net activity, then, is not one of deriving new ethical principles or imposing more policy-based rules. Our task instead is one of understanding the social bases of the complex relationship between technology and conflicts over the meaning of familiar concepts, and how changes in one affect the images and language by which we define and act upon the other. We can summarize with five simple points.

First, we ought not assume that all researcher peccadillos are ethical transgressions. Accidents, errors in judgment, or misreading of a situation may account for seeming lapses. A safe adage is, "Never attribute malice to that for which stupidity will suffice."

Second, we ought take special care when considering what we want policies to prescribe in the new electronic age, and we ought recognize the reciprocal relationship between individual responsibility and the legal and organizational power utilized to enforce it.

Third, we should remember that we are living during a time of dramatic social changes. Although fundamental ethical principals remain reasonably constant, the context in which we apply them shifts. Rather than resort to comfortable but not always appropriate rules, we ought more aggressively confront the shifting new contexts in which we are required to act and then more aggressively debate these issues as a society. It seems unwise to relinquish the terrain of discourse primarily to those with a vested interest in maintaining their preferred (but limited) view of ethical boundaries.

Fourth, as participatory researchers remind us, our view of ethics may reflect the class, race, or ethnocentric biases of our own location in the social hierarchy. This is, of course, not necessarily bad. But, it does mean that we ought not accept our own value preferences as necessarily universal.

Finally, we ought remember that the ethics of cyberspace do not begin in cyberspace. They begin—among other places—in the homes, the classrooms, the workplace, boardrooms, legislatures, and on playgrounds.

Like the social world of youngsters in Golding's novel *Lord of the Flies*, too many areas of cyberspace are populated by intellectually, emotionally, and existentially immature colonizers (of all ages) who discover freedom without having developed a corresponding sense of responsibility. Issues such as privacy, sexual harassment, racism, or courtesy are, for some, esoteric irrelevancies. I do not think that the ethical standards of social scientists are weakening. Nor do I see ethical depravity among Net or other scholars. What I do see is ignorance and unreflective pursuit of egocentric goals, often without corresponding consideration of the ethics underlying the means toward those goals. As a society, we need a more systematic and unifying system of integrating—at the societal level—our ethical expectations within the rapidly changing technology that clouds the current system.

A final afterthought illustrates the complexity of making ethical decisions. In illustrating student use of the Net in plagiarizing above, I quoted a student's justification. The student is unaware the comment is being made public, I have no signed consent form, and I certainly do not have IRB approval to include the comment as part of this article. Yet, the comment is arguably part of the scholarship process. Because the information was obtained from a living human being through direct interaction, the student could be classified as a human subject. Although the comment was given in a semipublic forum, some might argue that, because I lack IRB approval to include the information here, I have acted unethically, both by failing to obtain the student's consent and by failing to obtain, let alone seek, IRB approval.

Has an ethical lapse occurred? On what ethical grounds can we defend or criticize the inclusion? Does failure to consult the IRB anytime we use information from human subjects, whether from the Net or otherwise, itself constitute unethical behavior? Now, imagine that this quote came from private e-mail or from a public Internet discussion group. Would this change our ethical assessment? Others can answer these questions for themselves, but one conclusion seems inevitable: ethical conundrums are never easily resolved, and dialogue, critique, constant vigilance, and accountability seem far preferable to more rules and increased oversight.

References

Camus, A. *The Myth of Sisyphus and Other Essays.* New York: Vintage, 1955.

———. *The Rebel: An Essay on Man in Revolt.* New York: Vintage Books, 1956.

Cavan, S. *Liquor License: An Ethnography of Bar Behavior.* Chicago: Aldine, 1966.

Elmer-Dewit, P. "On a Screen Near You: Cyberporn." *Time Magazine* (3 July 1995): 38–43.

Forester, T. and P. Morrison. *Computer Ethics: Cautionary Tales and Ethical Dilemmas in Computing.* Oxford, UK: Basil Blackwell, 1990.

Gide, A. *The Immoralist.* New York: Vintage Books, 1958.

King, S. A. "Researching Internet Communities: Proposed Ethical Guidelines for the Reporting of Results." *The Information Society 12*, no. 2 (1996): 119–128.

Levy, S. *Hackers: Heroes of the Computer Revolution.* Garden City, NJ: Doubleday, 1984.

Matza, D. and G. M. Sykes. "Juvenile Delinquency and Subterranean Values." *American Sociological Review 26*, no. 5 (1961): 712–19.

Milovanovic, D. and J. Thomas. "Overcoming the Absurd: Prisoner Litigation as Primitive Rebellion." *Social Problems 36* (February 1989): 48–60.

Rimm, M. "Marketing Pornography on the Information Highway: A Survey of 917,410 Images, Descriptions, Short Stories, and Animations Downloaded 8.5 Million Times by Consumers in Over 2000 Cities and Territories." *Georgetown Law Journal 83* (1995): 189–194).

Stanage, S. "Adult Education as Ethical and Moral Meaning Through Action." Unpublished paper, Department of Philosophy, Northern Illinois University, DeKalb, 1995.

Stoll, C. *Silicon Snake Oil: Second Thoughts on the Information Highway.* New York: Doubleday, 1995.

Thomas, J. "When Cyber-Research Goes Awry: The Ethics of the Rimm 'Cyberporn' Study." *The Information Society 12*, no. 2 (1996a): 189–197.

————. "Introduction: A Debate about the Ethics of Fair Practices for Collecting Data in Cyberspace." *The Information Society 12*, no. 2 (1996b): 107–117.

————. "Big Brother, or Allies? In Defense of IRBs and RCR." *SSSI Notes 29* (March, 2002a): 4–6.

————. "Re-examining Human Subjects Protections in Ethnographic Research: Unpacking the Memes of Over-Zealous Oversight." Paper presented at the Annual Meeting of the Midwest Sociological Society, Milwaukee, April, 2002b.

Thomas, J. and J. B. Marquart. "Dirty Knowledge and Clean Conscience: The Dilemmas of Ethnographic Research." *In Information, Communication and Social Structure*, eds. D. Maines and C. Couch, 81–96. Springfield, IL: Charles C. Thomas, 1988.

Waskul, D. "Ethics of Online Research: Considerations for the Study of Computer Mediated Forms of Interaction." *The Information Society 12*, no. 2 (1996): 129–140.

Issues of Attribution and Identification in Online Social Research

కోత

Susan B. Barnes

DO INTERNET MESSAGES OCCUR in public or private space? The public versus private nature of Internet communication has significant consequences for the ways in which research is conducted and participants are protected or cited. For instance, in some cases, researchers who collect data through the Internet need to receive human subjects clearance from their universities. In contrast, researchers who observe public Internet discussions should properly cite messages. But, not all public groups want their messages to be attributed. For instance, members of online support groups often want to remain anonymous. Members of discussion groups engage in both public and private conversations, which researchers need to report about in different ways.

To complicate matters, participants in some public discussion groups perceive their messages to be privately exchanged. These people are often outraged by the idea of researchers using their messages in studies. Internet users do not clearly understand that they are exchanging messages in a public space and they often reveal private information. The Internet should be considered a public space because messages are often distributed to numerous people. Moreover, system administrators, Internet service providers, and organizations providing e-mail addresses can monitor and access any message sent through their system. Although the Internet should be considered a public space, people often use it as a private space. As a result, researchers must develop a set of strategies for attributing or protecting individuals who create the messages that are used in Internet studies.

Public Versus Private Communication in the Media

Since the introduction of mass media, there has been an expanded blurring of the boundaries between public and private messages. Beniger (1987) argues that increasingly mass-distributed messages attempt to appear personal. Publishers, editors, and marketers know that mass media are not as influential as interpersonal communication. Consequently, they try to personalize mass messages through specialized magazines, neighborhood-edition newspapers, talk-radio programs, and targeted mass mailings. Mass marketers use computer technology to personalize their mailings by individually addressing each consumer by name: "With even modest computing power and straightforward programming, laser printer letters might include any amount of individually targeted boilerplate and personalized insertion" (Beniger, 1987, 355). These messages are designed to disguise the large audience receiving them by appearing to be personal. The Internet continues this trend because mass-distributed commercial spam arrives alongside personal e-mail messages from friends. The Internet can be used to send one message or a thousand. At times, it is difficult to distinguish personal from mass-distributed messages because spam is designed to look friendly and personal. On the Internet, mass-distributed messages often appear to be personal. Additionally, private information is often made public.

Journalists blur the distinctions between what is considered public and private information. Sabato, Stencel, and Lichter (2000) describe why journalists report about the private lives of politicians, including secret affairs, minor indiscretions, and family problems. Frequently, these reports are based on rumors instead of carefully checked facts. Rumors will sometimes first appear on Internet scandal sheets, such as the *Drudge Report*, before they are printed or broadcast in mainstream media. The Internet combined with increased competition between news media have led to the reporting of highly personal and private information, such as the highly publicized affair between former President Clinton and Monica Lewinsky. Private information about politicians that was once considered inappropriate to report is now mass distributed through numerous media channels.

In addition to erasing the distinctions between public and private messages and information, mass media also erase the boundaries between public and private space. This phenomenon was first described by Meyrowitz (1985). He contends that electronic media destroy the specialness of time and place. Television images invade our bedrooms, living rooms, and family rooms by bringing public settings into private homes. Thus, television blurs the boundaries between public and private space. The Internet further blurs these spatial boundaries because individuals can now broadcast images from their bedrooms across the Internet, which makes an individual's personal behavior public. People can sit home alone with their computers and visually and verbally communicate with others from around the world. The Internet erases the spatial boundaries between the private bedroom and the public chatroom, newsgroup, or discussion list.

Because the Internet has the ability to bridge geographic space, it is often referred to as cyberspace. In addition to bridging physical space, the term cyberspace emphasizes the idea that computer networks create some type of data or imaginary space. It is the nonspace in which long distance communication occurs. In 1984, the science fiction writer William Gibson coined the term to describe a virtual world of computer data that his characters would enter. His inspiration for cyberspace came from watching kids playing video arcade games because the "kids clearly believed in the space games projected" (Gibson, cited in McCaffery, 1992, 272). Gibson observed that video game players and computer users appear "to develop a belief that there's some kind of actual space behind the screen, someplace you can't see but you know is there" (273). Cyberspace is the perceived experience of space created by computer networks.

Strate (1999) defines cyberspace as "the diverse experiences of space associated with computing and related technologies" (383). He identifies three different levels of cyberspace, including simulated space, conceptual/perceptual space, and social space. Computer screens simulate space by creating the visual illusion of an electronic workspace. Interface designers use perspective and overlapping windows to create depth and dimension. Perceptual space is established through user interaction and visual metaphors, such as cyberspace, the desktop, and chatroom. According to Strate, the perception of space in cyberspace is an amalgamation of the visual/perceptual space created by the computer's interface, the information space established by the network, and the social space experienced through computer-mediated communication. In sum, cyberspace is the construction of imaginary space that is developed by combining technological interactions and interpersonal communication.

Dery (1993) and Stone (1995) have written about conceptual cyberspace or the sense of space created by the mind when people interact with computers to engage in computer-mediated communication. People who participate in Internet communication often perceive their correspondence to occur in a social space. Viewing the Internet as a social space is important for the formation of interpersonal Internet relationships. As computer networks increasingly mediate communication, they enable people to correspond with each other in cyberspace instead of real space. Baym's (2000) research illustrates how personal relationships develop through Internet correspondence. Moreover, Cathcart and Gumpert (1986) have argued that for a "mediated exchange to work as interpersonal communication, there must be tacit agreement that the participants will proceed as though they are communicating face to face" (325). Similarly, Stone (1995) observed that people who converse through the Internet act as if they meet in a physical place. As a result, Bukatman contends that "there exists the pervasive recognition that a new and decentered spatiality has arisen that exists parallel to, but outside of, the geographic topography of experiential reality" (1993, 105).

The construction of social space through Internet communication is strengthened by language usage. For instance, the chatroom metaphor reinforces the idea that online communicators are going to a place to talk with others. According to Shirky (1995), Internet interactions are referred to as talking to someone instead of typing messages into a keyboard:

> Before I got on the net (note that I "got on" rather than "started using" the net), a programmer friend would tell me about the time he spend there (!), saying things like, "Oh, I went to that conference and I was talking to this guy, and what we were talking about was more interesting than the conference so we went into another room and finished our conversation." I was always dazzled by what seemed a startling metaphorical transition; to me, that language "I went," "I was talking," "another room," "conversation" seemed a fanciful way of describing an evening sitting alone at a computer and typing. (Shirky, 1995, 3)

The use of metaphorical face-to-face descriptions to describe Internet communication contributes to the perception that online messages are exchanged through private interpersonal exchanges rather than a public system that is accessible by others.

Misperceptions About Online Privacy

Social messages exchanged by individuals through computer networks can foster the illusion of privacy because correspondents do not see the other people reading online messages. Because individuals do not see the numerous people who are reading their messages, individuals often believe they are communicating with a small group rather than a large audience. Another reason why people perceive the Internet to be a private space is the personal nature of many online conversations. Computer-mediated communication researchers Rice and Love (1987) discovered that online messages generally include a percentage of socioemotional content. Socioemotional content is correspondence that shows solidarity, tension relief, agreement, disagreement, antagonism, and tension. This type of content demonstrates an emotional reaction to an e-mail message. Similarly, Walther's (1996) research revealed that in some instances levels of affection and emotion that develop through computer-mediated relationships can equal or surpass face-to-face ones. He refers to this experience as hyperpersonal computer-mediated communication. Furthermore, books such as those by Odzer (1997), Phleagar (1995), and Slouka (1995) describe intimate online conversations. Cybersex, the most private of all computer-mediated messages, is a topic that has been featured on national television programs, including HBO's *Real Sex* and *Dateline NBC*. Similar to webcams in the bedroom, these programs show intimate personal behavior on public media.

When individuals build close Internet relationships with others, they can forget that they are communicating in a public space. Internet users report that they often directly type their thoughts into the keyboard and immediately send messages through the Internet. One Internet user reports that "a friend once said to [her] that when she e-writes, she feels as if her brain is directly wired into the computer, with no 'interface' at all. She just THINKS and it appears there on the screen" (Barnes, 2001, 103). Similarly, Ullman (1996) says that the urge to immediately reply to an e-mail message is so great that she often responds without thinking about the message.

Often quick replies to e-mail messages will self-disclose personal information. When this occurs, computer-mediated communication can create a sense of anxiety in people because they sent unedited messages through the Internet. Whittle (1997) refers to this anxiety as postcyberdisclosure panic. A person reveals their inner thoughts and secrets and later becomes frightened by the idea of who might read the message. Public e-mail messages sometimes include private information that people disclose without thinking about the audience that will read them.

Ideas about message privacy are also reinforced by the small number of participants engaged in online conversation. The majority of public discussion list members usually lurk or only read messages. This can create the illusion of intimacy because it appears that only a small number of people are group members. In reality, messages are often sent to hundreds and sometimes thousands of people. In contrast to being private, many discussion lists state that they are public discussions and keep archives. Researchers can access these messages without the knowledge of group participants. The following is an excerpt from the welcome message from an online group called NetDynam:

> Archives of NetDynam mail items are kept in weekly files. You may obtain a list of files in the archives by sending either of the commands: INDEX NETDY-NAM or GET NETDYNAM FILELIST to the listserver. Archived messages are accessible only by current subscribers, but subscription to NetDynam is public (unrestricted). (NetDynam, 1997)

Individuals must be members of the discussion list to access the archives. However, membership is open to everyone. An Internet researcher could subscribe to the list, download the archives, and use the information in a study without asking for anyone's permission. Although this can be done, members of the group may consider this action to be an invasion of their privacy. NetDynam is a public discussion group; however, the private nature of member conversations creates the illusion of intimacy. Researchers should be aware that members of public discussion groups sometimes mistakenly believe that their messages are privately shared. Introductory welcome messages will often provide some information about the public or private nature of a group. For example, some academic discussion groups will provide a welcome statement that includes specific instructions on how to cite messages distributed through the list. Moderators of academic lists often consider electronic messages to be a form of publishing and they want the authors of e-mail messages to receive proper credit for their ideas.

In contrast, support groups want their messages to remain private. Support groups try to maintain some privacy standards because these groups are established to enable people to share their intimate feelings. However, private messages exchanged between support group members have been leaked to the press and published in major newspapers. For instance, when a member of an online support group confessed to a murder in an e-mail message, the e-mail was later published in *The New York Times* (see Harmon, 1998).

People mistakenly believe that their e-mail messages are private because they are sent directly to another individual. But, e-mail messages can be read by systems administrators or recovered from hard drives after they have been deleted. For example, the "Star Report" revealed that Monica Lewinsky's deleted e-mail messages had been recovered from her home and office computers. Additionally, e-mail messages can be saved or forwarded to other people who are not group members and e-mail can be distributed to others without permission. For instance, people have been fired from their jobs because e-mail messages were forwarded to their boss. Because private e-mail exchanges can be accessed and forwarded to others, all Internet correspondence could be considered to occur in a public space. But, when people write e-mail messages, they generally perceive their conversations to be interpersonal and private like a telephone call or written letter. In contrast to e-mail, which is often considered private, web pages are generally recognized as a public form of communication.

Collecting Online Data

Today, academic researchers, marketers, pollsters, and organizations use e-mail and the World Wide Web to collect information from individuals and consumers. Smith (1997) estimates that there are thousands of web sites collecting, polling, and gathering information. Most people consider the web to be an open and public information space. After the information is gathered, web surveys can become closely held proprietary information because they contain personal consumer data.

Marketers openly collect data through the Internet. If someone fills out an online form, there is an understanding that the consumer has consented or agreed to give this information. In some cases, marketers collect information by using a mechanism called a "cookie." Cookies quietly collect information when users are visiting web sites. Some users are concerned that software will be able to connect cookie data with e-mail addresses. As a result, the right to protect private information on the web has become a major privacy concern. According to Lin and Loui, "Because we currently do not have a reasonable expectation of privacy on the Web, informed consent is important: if we do not have enough knowledge to make an informed decision about revealing our personal information on the Web, we should be given that knowledge before making our decisions" (1998, 39). For this reason, a number of web sites now include privacy statements.

Web information can be accessed by anyone who can use a computer. As a result, the web is generally considered to be a new mass medium. As previously discussed, mass media erase the boundaries between public and private situations. For instance, one of my students examined the home pages of African-American women. In setting up her study, she encountered highly personal information placed on some of the web sites. Although the web is used to distribute information to large audiences, individuals also use it as a private medium to present personal information. Including personal information found on web sites in a research report could cause emotional harm to the people under observation. When the student attempted to ask one woman why she placed this type of information in a public space, the woman told the student to "mind her own business." The web site creator was not concerned about making personal information available to others. But, the student was concerned about using personal information in her Internet study.

Moreover, once the student shifted from analyzing the content of the web site to asking questions about the site, she had to have her study reviewed by the human subjects committee. Analyzing web content is similar to analyzing a television program because it is publicly available information. In contrast, sending e-mail messages to people involves the collection of data, which places the study into a different social science category. Whenever human subjects are involved in a project, researchers must obtain the subject's consent to participate in the study. After obtaining human subjects approval, researchers must protect the identity of the participants. E-mail is now being used as a research tool to conduct interviews and distribute surveys.

According to Sheehan (2001), the first e-mail survey was conducted in 1986. Since that time, e-mail has become a popular method for data collection. E-mail has several benefits over traditional mail, including response speed and cost efficiency. Although e-mail is less expensive than traditional mail for administering a survey, the response rate to e-mail surveys appears to be on the decline. To improve response rates, researchers need to select the proper target audiences and they should send out prenotifications about the survey. Sending random surveys to individuals and openly posting surveys on web sites can be problematic. First, e-mail surveys have become so popular that individuals will ignore them and not reply. Second, allowing individuals to voluntarily reply to web surveys creates problems because there is no way of knowing who is filling out the form. Additionally, researchers can forget to remove the survey from the web. As a result, individuals will attempt to participate in the survey after the data collection period is over. It is better to locate the right audience, send a pre-notification message, and provide a date in which to return the survey.

A major advantage of observing Internet behavior is the ability of computer software to keep a log of conversations. Journalists and researchers can automatically record online interactions without having to make transcripts of their observations. Additionally, researchers can record online interactions without telling the participants that they are being observed. This raises ethical concerns.

Ethical Issues and Journalists

From the very beginning of my online research experience, questions about the ethical reporting of online observations emerged. Journalists were the first major group to write about life on the Internet. Following the trend in political journalism, these accounts included all types of original e-mail messages with personal information. Books written by Howard Rheingold (1993), J. C. Herz (1995), and Jonathan Seabrook (1997) reveal names, publish e-mail messages verbatim, and generally report about online experiences without showing concern for the participants being observed. Similarly, Katie Hafner's (1997) account of Tom Mandel's obsessive and unethical behavior on the WELL is a "tell all" description that blatantly describes Mandel in highly negative ways. Furthermore, Tom Mandel (1995) wrote a negative account about himself that described his online addiction to the Internet.

The journalist Jullian Dibbell (1993) became aware of the ethical issues associated with reporting actual screen names and conversations when he developed his *Village Voice* (1998) article about a rape in cyberspace into a book. In the book, the MUD and the screen names of its characters were given pseudonyms. Dibbell changed the screen names of the individuals, which protected the online identities of people participating in a social MUD. In contrast to this approach, the majority of journalistic accounts depicted actual people, places, and events in ways that portrayed individual behavior as both positive and negative.

As a result of this type of journalistic reporting, online academic researchers began to follow the journalistic habit of openly reporting Internet experiences. For example, in 1995 I was working on an Internet book that wanted to reveal both the positive and negative aspects of online interaction. My coauthor, Gerald M. Phillips, was writing his chapters as a "tell-all" story that included long passages of e-mail messages written to him by numerous people from all over the world. We planned to publish these passages verbatim to illustrate some of the perils of online correspondence. The identity of authors was mixed because some messages included names and identifying information, while others did not. For instance, messages that included descriptions of abusive behavior had the names deleted, but, messages sent by Phillips's personal electronic friends included their names because these people were being treated as characters in the book.

At first, Phillips was not concerned about publishing the messages of his online friends. In his personal life, Phillips believed that "an unexamined life is not worth living," therefore, he did not always portray himself in a positive way when he wrote his own autobiographical account describing his Internet adventures (Phillips, 1995). However, after reading one of the chapters, a friend demanded a rewrite because she believed her description was not very flattering. The friend's negative interpretation of the text raised the question: How are Phillips's other online friends going to interpret our descriptions about them? At this point, I came to the realization that the names of individuals needed to be protected and I began to review the types of messages we had gathered.

Types of Online Messages and Their Ethical Implications

In my own research, I have encountered the following five types of Internet messages: (1) messages exchanged in online public discussion lists; (2) messages exchanged in private discussions between individuals and on private lists; (3) personal messages sent to me with the names and e-mail addresses deleted; (4) interesting messages that were reposted and passed around the Internet; and (5) messages generated by computer programs. Each of these categories presents a slightly different ethical concern for attribution.

Messages exchanged between members of public discussion lists were the first type of messages used in my research. There are thousands of discussion groups on subjects ranging from Apple Computers to zoology. People subscribe to these lists and receive all of the messages posted by group members. As previously stated, Internet users frequently forget that their messages can be accessed by others without their knowledge. For example, many of the discussion list messages utilized in my research came from a list called Interpersonal Computing and Technology (IPCT-L). It was a discussion list that talked about issues relating to computer- mediated communication and education.

To figure out how to treat IPCT-L messages in a printed book, I went back to the introductory welcome message and discovered a statement that gave specific instructions on how to cite messages distributed through the list. The moderator of IPCT-L clearly viewed this electronic list as a form of publishing and he wanted the authors of e-mail messages to receive proper citations. The moderator even provided an example of how messages should be cited. As a result, I had to follow the IPCT-L procedures and go back through the material to make sure all of the e-mail authors received proper acknowledgment. It should be noted that members of IPCT-L and other academic discussion lists generally use their real names. Occasionally, people join lists using a pseudonym and they develop a reputation using an online persona. In my research, the actual name or pseudonym attributed to the message being cited is given credit for the statement.

While participating on IPCT-L, I discovered that members had different perceptions about the public versus private nature of their conversations. For example, prior to checking the introductory message, I decided to post a message to IPCT-L asking if members considered their conversations to be public or private. Most people answered public. However, several members were surprised at my message and replied that they thought messages should be considered private. Obviously these members did not remember the welcoming message that described the list as a form of publishing. During the exchange that followed, it was revealed that an archive of IPCT-L messages was publicly available on the web and these messages could be read by anyone. Despite the introductory message that clearly states IPCT-L was a public space, some people believed it to be a private one. The fact that IPCT-L archives were available on the web reinforced my decision to treat messages exchanged on the list as a form of publishing. As an extra precaution, I decided not to cite any messages written by the individuals who argued that their messages should be considered private.

In order to respect the individuals who share their ideas on public lists, the names of these participants should be properly attributed. This is a practice that other researchers have utilized when citing public online discussions among scholars. For instance, Gumpert and Drucker (1998) have used this approach when they cite e-mail messages from the media ecology discussion list. Ideas are identified with specific authors, many of whom are published academics. Lists such as IPCT-L and media ecology are trying to protect the copyright of e-mail authors because they instruct people to cite messages from the list as if they were a printed text. This advice attempts to follow the guidelines of traditional copyright law. One perspective about citing e-mail messages is to treat them as you would any other form of published literature. Herring states: "Quoting a message or part of a message in another published work without giving full credit to the source (naming the message writer, the group it was posted to, the time and date, etc.) is a violation of copyright and legally actionable" (Herring, 1996, 154). There is no reason why traditional copyright rules should not apply to electronic messages. Underlying this perspective is the idea that messages exchanged on discussion lists are public forms of discourse and the web is a form of publishing. According to the public point of view, when using Internet messages, authors should receive credit for their ideas.

In another study, an online group was discussing whether to make their archives public. There was a heated debate because some members were concerned that too much personal information would be revealed if the messages became available in an archive. The discussion illustrated the difficulty in trying to make list archives publicly available after a group has been established. People do not realize that when information is distributed through the Internet it can become accessible through archives and the web. As a researcher observing this group, I made the decision to respect the privacy of the individuals.

The second message category is messages exchanged on private discussion lists. When describing my observations about private groups, the names of the lists and individuals involved are never revealed. However, I do maintain a private printed archive of the materials used in the study. To further protect the identities of individuals, messages are combined and behavior is described through general descriptions rather than specific messages.

Some groups consider their discussions to be private. Depending on whether the groups being observed consider themselves to be public or private, I treat them differently. Or if there is any question about the group's perception about being a public or private discussion, I treat the group as being private. King says: "Depending on the nature of the group under study, members may post extremely self-revealing information. Their text may be subject to analysis and later reporting [*sic*], with no knowledge on the part of the participants" (1996, 120). Participants can have a feeling of violation when they later find they were the subject of a study. "The sense of violation possible is proportional to the expectation of privacy that group members had prior to learning they were studied" (King, 1996, 120). Moreover, the publishing of private interpersonal exchanges can adversely impact the dynamics of the group under observation.

King's research explores support groups where anonymity can be an important aspect of the support process. Many of his concerns are ones that I share when observing private messages and groups. To solve some of these ethical issues, he proposes a list of suggestions for protecting participants by minimizing the ability to directly connect subjects to the data collected. King recommends the following procedures as guidelines for conducting online research in private groups:

1. Remove all headers and signatures.

2. Remove all references within the citation to any person's name or pseudoname.

3. Remove all references to the name and to the type (e-mail, BBS, etc.) of the group.

4. Do not make any specific reference to the location of or exact type of forum studied.

5. Store the original data in a safe manner and make it available to other qualified researchers who may wish to validate the findings. (King, 1996, 127)

These guidelines help to conceal the identity of individuals observed in online spaces that are considered private. Taking this advice one more step, I also will combine several people into a composite personality type to describe online behavior. Usually, I will observe more than one person behaving in a certain way and these people can be described in a manner that combines them into a personality type or profile that takes emphasis away from a single individual. For example, I observed more than one person develop a codependent online relationship. When I write about this topic, I have several people in mind to keep the description more generalized and to protect the individuals.

These are the guidelines that I follow for the first and second types of messages utilized in my research, public and private discussion groups. The third and fourth message categories, e-mail sent privately to individuals and reposted messages, introduce new factors. First, many of the private e-mail messages that I received while working with Phillips were written to him. When he forwarded messages on to me, the headers and signatures were removed. Therefore, I had no idea who wrote the messages and the authors were anonymous. When citing these messages, the author is noted as being anonymous and Phillips is cited as the source of the information. Because the real identities were unknown to me, I follow King's advice of further removing location names, nicknames, and any other features that would enable someone else to identify the author. This is a strategy that I also use when working with a research assistant. By removing the names and identifying information in a series of messages, the content can be analyzed anonymously. Thus, individual privacy can be protected.

The fourth message group is reposted e-mail. Reposted messages are ones that people forward on to other people and discussion lists because they think the messages are interesting. For example, a number of people repost or forward e-mail jokes to each other. There are two types of reposted messages on the Internet. These messages can be distributed as anonymous e-mail or they can contain the name of the original author. Recently, I discovered that creative web searches can reveal the identities of anonymous authors of popular reposted messages. For example, a web search located the author of the classic message titled the "Life Cycle of an Online Group," a message that has been anonymously circulating around the Internet for several years. The web now makes it possible to locate these authors and I believe it is worth the effort to try and find the original author to include proper credits in research reports. When using reposted messages that include names and e-mail addresses on them, I generally e-mail the individual and ask for permission to use all or part of the message in my research. When permission is granted, the message is cited with proper attributions.

However, receiving permission from individuals to publish their messages is not always the end of the ethical dilemma. For example, Reid (1996) encountered an entirely new set of ethical issues when she asked individuals for permission to use their messages exchanged during her observations of a support-group MUD. During her research, Reid states: "In the absence of clearly defined legal or cultural specifications regarding the use of material distributed via Usenet I felt it best to take the more cautious and courteous path of asking each author's individual permission to include their material in my thesis" (Reid, 1996, 170). But this decision created an unexpected ethical dilemma for Reid.

Participants in the support group that were "violently" and "sexually" attacked by other MUD players embraced the opportunity to be research subjects and eagerly gave their permission. However, reading the data made Reid uncomfortable because she had permission to publish very personal information about the participants' lives and experiences. Reid (1996) says: "I chose not to do so, and though I did write about the MUD I did not quote from the logs or e-mail sent to me by the users. It was not an intellectual discussion of research ethics that decided me against this. It was purely a personal decision" (Reid, 1996, 144).

Reid's experience really hit home for me. There are many people that I have observed behaving badly on the Internet. Although the most convincing way to tell the story or argue a point would be for me to use real names, places, and situations, for personal reasons, I don't want to hurt the people involved. Therefore, I look for other ways to describe the darker side of Internet behavior. For example, by using examples from published works combined with my own general observations and composite personalities. Creating composite examples is a method that protects the identity and privacy of the individuals under observations.

Composites are also used in the final message category, computer-generated messages. Weizenbaum (1976) described one of the first natural language programs called ELIZA. ELIZA was programmed to parody a Rogerian psychotherapist who interacts with patients by repeating their own statements back to them. For instance, if a patient types "I am sad" into the computer, the program would respond with "Why are you sad?" When describing messages generated by ELIZA, Weitzenbaum first explained the source of the messages and then provided examples. Other researchers, such as Foner (1999), follow this procedure. Foner first explains how software agents generate messages and then he describes social interactions with people by using generalized examples, rather than specific incidents. Programs, such as mailer deamons and chatter bots, also have been described in general ways, and it is always noted that the exchange is between a program and a person, not two people.

Informed Consent

Reid's experience, described earlier, illustrates how attempting to create a list of ethical guidelines that can be applied to all types of Internet research, appears to be an impossible task. However there is another way to approach this ethical dilemma. The Association of Computing Machinery (ACM) published an ethics statement in the Spring 1993 issue of *Communications of the ACM*. According to the article: "The ACM imperative clearly advises limiting the amount of information gathered, and seeking consent of individuals whose information a researcher is interested in using" (Boehlefeld, 1996, 144). This code of ethics attempts to protect the privacy of individuals involved in any type of Internet research report.

The ACM guidelines also raise the issue of "informed consent." Informed consent is another factor to be considered when engaging in

Internet research. As an active member of IPCT-L, Gerald M. Phillips pro-
voked a heated debate about this topic. The online debate started when
Phillips discovered that a number of students had joined the list as part of
a class assignment. Instead of joining the group as observers, 20 percent of
the student grading process was based on posting messages to the list.
Therefore, students had to actively interact with group members. Interaction
with group members raises the issue of human subjects approval. Members
of IPCT-L criticized the professor for not getting prior permission from
IPCT-L members to participate in the assignment. This raised the following
question: Should an instructor involve other people in a student assignment
without first receiving human subjects approval?

At the time, I had never heard of human subjects approval and neither
had many other people participating in the discussion. However, upon questioning Phillips about this issue and researching the topic further, I discovered that human subjects approval and informed consent have legal and ethical implications for both Internet researchers and the universities that host
the groups being observed. Individuals and universities receiving federal
grant money must follow human subjects guidelines when conducting
research projects.

Thomas (1996) describes the importance of federal and university policies toward protecting human subjects. According to Thomas, many universities derive their human subjects guidelines from the *Belmont Report* (1979)
and the *Federal Register* (1991). The *Belmont Report* identifies three broad principles for protecting human subjects participating in research projects,
which include respect for individuals, beneficence or "do no harm," and justice or fairness toward the subjects and social interests. The report also identifies informed consent as a way to implement these principles.

The informed consent process has three elements: information
(research procedure, their purposes, risks and anticipated benefits, and
opportunity for subjects to ask questions and withdraw from the research);
comprehension or making sure that the subjects comprehend the information and understand what they are consenting to; and voluntariness or making sure that consent is free of coercion. These rules should apply when
researchers are using human subjects for any systematic investigation.

The *Federal Register* defines a human subject as a living individual about
whom an investigator is conducting research to obtain data through interaction or through observation in a context in which an individual can reasonably expect no observation to take place. Here again the idea of public versus private space becomes an issue. Obviously when people are in public
spaces they can expect to be observed; conversely, in private spaces they do
not. But consent also can be required for public observations. For example,
one IPCT-L member argued that he was an involuntary subject in a college

experiment because students were interacting with him on the list. Another group member provided support for this position by sharing the following story:

> The issue raised [here] was addressed last week in my statistics class; the instructor, who also teaches organizational communication, gave her students an assignment to research "face behaviors" by observation. One of the students proposed that they all go out and confront people on campus, to see how those thus confronted would act. The instructor vetoed the proposal on the grounds that the assignment might then require human subjects approval. (Donovan, 1995)

Although the student observations were taking place in a public space, the act of involving people in the exercise could turn it into an experiment that requires human subjects approval. Publicly confronting people to observe a facial expression could cause harm or an accident. An analogy can be made here between confronting people face-to-face and interacting online. The professor should have gotten consent from group members prior to letting his class go online to interact with them. Students were participating for a grade rather than sharing a discussion topic. Because people were unknowingly involved in a classroom experiment, the student involvement in the group could fall under a category that requires informed consent. Moreover, the student participation could have unintended and negative consequences for members of IPCT-L. Choriki summarized the situation as follows:

> To sum:
> Individuals have a right to know when their resources are being used by others for purposes other than those initially intended... Intentionality is important to the sense of community of a discussion group.
> To conclude:
> If I were teaching a course and thought that the students could gain by joining, I would either not have made participation mandatory, or would have asked for permission first. (Choriki, 1995)

A central issue here is the mandatory involvement of the students. If students had just observed the group, then the issues of human subjects would have never come up. In defense of the professor, it does appear that he asked permission from IPCT's moderator before his students joined the group. In contrast to perceiving IPCT-L as a social space, the moderator views the Internet as a publishing medium. When describing the student involvement on the list, the moderator made an analogy between acquiring information through the Internet and going to the library. As a result, the moderator did not think that human subject approval was necessary. In contrast, other group members did think it was required because human interaction was involved. Comparing the Internet to a publishing medium raised another set of issues. The students involved with the experiment tended to believe that once information is distributed through the Internet, it is in "public domain" and can be freely used by anyone. But this is simply not the case. Most information distributed through the Internet has a copyright notice on it and must follow the "fair use" guidelines or else infringement could be claimed. Students and researchers need to check writing style guides for the proper citation of electronic messages (see Radford, Barnes, and Barr, 2002).

From the previous examples, it becomes clear that we do not have an agreed upon understanding about the public versus private nature of Internet communication. A key issue involving online research is whether individuals and group members consider their correspondence to be public or private. Newsgroups are compared to public bulletin boards and most people are aware that messages placed in a newsgroup are distributed to a large audience. Similarly, web pages are often considered to be published documents. In contrast, discussion lists are both public and private and it is important for researchers to respect the privacy guidelines of online groups. Many discussion groups will state their privacy or citation policy when you join them. For example, some social MUDs and support discussion groups post disclaimers stating that researchers must notify the group in advance of any research being conducted. Unfortunately, these groups have been subject to unethical research practices in the past and they no longer want to become the subjects of new studies. When researching any Internet group, it is a good idea to contact the group in advance and ask for permission to observe them.

Sensitivity is required in Internet research for legal, practical, and ethical reasons. Duncan (1996) provides an outline of the codes of ethics that should be used when conducting Internet research. First, researchers need to "respect the rights of individuals to privacy, confidentiality, and autonomy" (Duncan, 1996, 67). When observing private groups and social interactions, researchers should protect the individuals under observation and ensure confidentiality. Moreover, they need to follow the human subject guidelines outlined by their university. Second, researchers should not disrupt online groups or communities. Methods of data collection should be established by a research design that is credible by social science standards. Third, if participants are promised confidentiality, they should be protected by removing personal identifiers (including screen names or online pseudonyms) and techniques should be used to limit the risk of inferential disclosure. Finally, researchers need to obtain approval for their research from host institutions or organizations prior to conducting the research. Internet research needs to be conducted in accordance with proper research conventions.

Protecting the privacy of individuals under study is important in Internet research. Often people who are corresponding in public chatrooms or discussion groups perceive their conversations to take place in a private setting, which in social science research requires the researcher to get informed consent from the people under observation. In contrast, public lists, especially academic lists, request that proper citations be given to materials used from their discussions. Equally important to protecting privacy is providing proper attributions for works "published" on the Internet. Published works include web pages, newsgroup messages, and public discussion lists.

Conclusion

Prior to the introduction of the Internet, mass media blurred the boundaries between public and private messages, information, and space. The Internet contributes to the blurring of these boundaries. As a result, Internet researchers should be aware of the confusion that many Internet users have about the public versus private nature of online communication. Internet researchers should make sure that the individuals they study are aware of their role in the research process. When the Internet is utilized as a method for data collection, a researcher should contact their university's human subjects committee to clear their study. Spaces that a researcher may consider public, could be considered private by their university because the research may be interacting with others.

When engaging in Internet studies, researchers should pay particular attention to the confusion over the public versus private nature of e-mail messages. Check the welcoming messages of public discussion lists for guidelines on how to properly site e-mail messages. If list members are confused about the public versus private nature of the group, researchers need to protect the privacy of the individuals being observed. Conversely, proper citations should be included for all "published" materials collected from the Internet.

References

Barnes, S. B. *Online Connections: Internet Interpersonal Relationships.* Cresskill, NJ: Hampton Press, 2001.

Baym, N. *Tune In, Log On: Soaps, Fandom, and Online Community.* Thousand Oaks, CA: Sage Publications, Inc., 2000.

Belmont Report. Ethical Principles and Guidelines for the Protection of Human Subjects of Research. Washington, DC: Department of Health, Education, and Welfare, 1979.

Beniger, J. R. "Personalization of Mass Media and the Growth of Pseudo-Community." *Communication Research 14*, no. 3 (June 1987): 352–371.

Boehlefeld, S. P. "Doing the Right Thing: Ethical Cyberspace Research." *The Information Society 12*, no. 2, (1996, April–June): 141–152.

Bukatman, S. *Terminal Identity.* Durham, NC: Duke University Press, 1993.

Cathcart, R. and Gumpert, G. "The Person-computer Interaction: a Unique Source." In *Intermedia: Interpersonal Communication in a Media World,* eds. G. Gumpert and R. Cathcart, 323–332. New York: Oxford University Press, 1986.

Choriki, D. "Re: The Cox Controversy." Electronic message to Interpersonal Computing and Technology Discussion List. IPCT-L@GMUV. GEORGETOWN.EDU. April 13, 1995.

Dery, M. *Flame Wars: The Discourse of Cyberculture.* Durham, NC: Duke University Press, 1993.

Dibbell, J. "Rape in Cyberspace." *The Village Voice* (December 21, 1993): 38.

———. *My Tiny Life.* New York: Henry Holt, 1998.

Donovan, D. "Re: The Cox Controversy." Electronic Message to Interpersonal Computing and Technology Discussion List. IPCT-L@GMUV. GEORGETOWN.EDU. April 13, 1995.

Duncan, G. T. "Is My Research Ethical?" *Communications of the ACM 39*, no. 12 (December 1996): 67–68.

Federal Register. Part II: Federal Policy for the Protection of Human Subjects: Notices and Rules. Washington, DC: U.S. Government Printing Office, 1991.

Foner, L. N. (1999). "Are we having fun yet? Using social agents in social domains." In *Human Cognition and Social Agent Theory,* ed. K. Dautenhahn, 323–348. Amsterdam: John Benjamins Publishing Company, 1999.

Gibson, W. *Neuromancer.* New York: Ace Books, 1984.

Gumpert, G. and S. Drucker. "The Demise of Privacy in a Private World: From Front Porches to Chat Rooms." *Communication Theory 8*, no. 4 (1998, November): 408–425.

Hafner, K. "The Epic Saga of the Well." *Wired.* May 1997: 98–142.

Harmon, A. "On-Line Trail to an Off-Line Killing." *The New York Times,* April 30, 1998: A1, A30.

Herring, S. "Linguistic and Critical Analysis of Computer-Mediated-Communication: Some Ethical and Scholarly Considerations." *Information Society 12*, no. 2 (1996, April–June): 153–168.

Herz, J. C. *Surfing the Internet: A Nethead's Adventures On-line.* New York: Little, Brown and Company, 1995.

King, S. "Researching Internet Communities: Proposed Ethical Guidelines for the Reporting of Results." *The Information Society 12*, no. 2 (1996, April–June): 119–127.

Lin, D. and M. C. Loui. "Taking the Byte Out of Cookies." *Computers and Society 28*, no. 2 (1998, June): 39–51.

Mandel, T. "Confessions of a Cyberholic." *Time Magazine,* Spring 1995, 57.

McCaffery, L. *Storming the Reality Studio: A Casebook of Cyberpunk and Postmodern Fiction.* Durham, NC: Duke University Press, 1992.

Meyrowitz, J. *No Sense of Place.* New York: Oxford University Press, 1985.

NetDynam. "Usage Guidelines for NETDYNAM." April 6, 1997. (E-mail message).

Odzer, C. *Virtual Spaces: Sex and the Cyber Citizen.* New York: Berkeley Books, 1997.

Phillips, G. M. Personal correspondence. April 1, 1995.

Phleagar, P. *Love Online: a Practical Guide to Online Dating.* Reading, MA: Addison-Wesley Publishing Company, 1995.

Radford, M., S. B. Barnes, and L. R. Barr. *Web Research: Selecting, Evaluating and Citing.* Boston, MA: Allyn and Bacon, 2002.

Reid, E. M. "Informed Consent in the Study of On-line Communities: A Reflection on the Effects of Computer-mediated Social Research." *The Information Society 12*, no. 2 (1996, April–June): 169–174.

Rheingold, H. *The Virtual Community.* Reading, MA: Addison-Wesley Publishing Company, 1993.

Rice, R. E. and G. Love. "Electronic Emotion: Socioemotional Content in a Computer-Mediated Communication Network." *Communication Research 14*, no. 1 (1987): 85–108.

Sabato, L. J., M. Stencel, and S. R. Lichter. *Peepshow: Media and Politics in an Age of Scandal.* New York: Rowman and Littlefield Publishers, Inc., 2000.

Seabrook, J. *Deeper: My Two-Year Odyssey in Cyberspace.* New York: Simon and Schuster, 1997.

Sheehan, K. "E-mail Survey Response Rates: A Review." *Journal of Computer-Mediated Communication 6*, no. 2 (2001, January): 1–43 (Online). Available at http://www.ascusc.org/jcmc/vol6/issue2/sheehan.html (May 3, 2001).

Shirky, C. *Voices from the Net.* Emeryville, CA: Ziff-Davis Press, 1995.

Slouka, M. *War of the Worlds.* New York: Basic Books, 1995.

Smith, C. B. "Casting the Net: Surveying an Internet Population." *Journal of Computer-Mediated Communication 6,* no. 2 (1997, June): 1–19 (Online). Available at http://www.ascusc.org/jcmc/vol3/issue1/smith.html (September 4, 2001).

Strate, L. "The Varieties of Cyberspace: Problems in Definition and Delimitation." *Western Journal of Communication 63*, no. 3 (Summer, 1999): 382–412.

Stone, A. R. *The War of Desire and Technology at the Close of the Mechanical Age.* Cambridge, MA: The MIT Press, 1995.

Thomas, J. "Introduction: A Debate About the Ethics of Fair Practices for Collecting Social Science Data in Cyberspace." *The Information Society 12*, no. 2 (1996, April–June): 107–117.

Ullman, E. "Come In, CQ: The Body on the Wire." In *Wired Women*, eds. L. Cherney and E. R. Weise. Seattle, WA: Seal Press, 1996.

Walther, J. B. "Computer-Mediated Communication: Impersonal, Interpersonal, and Hyperpersonal Interaction." *Communication Research 23*, no. 1 (1996, February): 3–43.

Weizenbaum, J. *Computer Power and Human Reason.* San Francisco: W. H. Freeman, 1976.

Whittle, D. B. *Cyberspace: The Human Demension.* New York: Freeman, 1997.

"Electronic Eavesdropping": The Ethical Issues Involved in Conducting a Virtual Ethnography

ॐॐ

Katherine M. Clegg Smith

THIS CHAPTER OUTLINES the ethical issues faced when integrating a "virtual participant observation" into a more traditional ethnography. The research project set out to explore the reaction of British family doctors to recent health care reform measures. A professional listserv[1] set up by family doctors was one setting in which such reactions could be observed. The research was conducted between 1997 and 1998, before the establishment of common ethical guidelines for cyber research. This chapter recounts the author's ethical decision making in a relatively unknown territory, and in doing so, offers some reflections on the nature of the virtual realm as it pertains to social research.

Online Research as a Novel Endeavor

The Internet is now central to the way that many people communicate with others, with virtual interaction being woven into the way that they work and play. People have incorporated this medium into their existing social structures as well as having used it to create new ones. Alongside such advances, cyberspace has become an important focus for social researchers (Jones, 1994).

Early social research in this area, however, tended to focus on "creative" or "imaginative" interaction on the Internet, as set apart from "offline" interaction. Of most interest was the extent to which the Internet challenged our established forms of communication, rather than how it was integrated with them. The novelty of the setting, as well as the opportunities for unique interaction that it posed led to a flurry of studies of relatively "extreme" uses of the domain (Correll, 1995; Hamman, 1996). This focus has, however, led to a certain level of neglect for research into the extent to which more mundane applications challenge existing social structures.

In my research, I set out to incorporate a new electronic social setting and the novel data emerging from it, into ongoing "real-world" analysis. I soon learned that such an endeavor would present various challenges-both on methodological and theoretical levels. In this chapter, I illuminate the challenges posed by focusing on a new form of human interaction-particularly my attempts to resolve established ethical considerations. Ethical issues such as whether the Internet is a private or public space and how one goes about attaining informed consent have required careful consideration. Addressing such issues has been an important step in the process of incorporating the virtual data into my more traditional ethnographic research.

The Larger Project and the Virtual Setting: Stumbling Across a Goldmine?

Imagine, if you will, embarking on a piece of research about a substantive area of which you have only rudimentary background knowledge. Furthermore, your research interest is the impact of rapid change within the setting. Your intention is to conduct participant observations within key organizational structures. Unfortunately, the organizational form is modifying so quickly that it is impossible to know who to approach for access. You also plan to conduct in-depth interviews, but the nature of change within the setting is such that it is difficult to know both who to approach, as well as the important questions to ask. Imagine now that someone "in the field" tells you of a listserv where people working in your research area discuss important issues. An answer to your prayers? It would appear so.

The scenario that I have outlined reflects the circumstances in which I found myself during the early stages of my doctoral fieldwork. I was interested in organizational change and the role played by professionals in such events, but I knew little either about the substantive area of the British health care system (the National Health Service or NHS), nor of the realm of general practice (family medicine) on which my research would focus. Luckily, while planning my fieldwork, I learned of a listserv that was becoming popular with British general practitioners (GPs).[2] I therefore sought access to this list primarily as a means of gaining important background information and of following the changes that were so central to my research.

Although I registered with the listserv (which is open to nongeneral practitioners) with only the intention of "mapping the field" and preparing for my "real" fieldwork, I soon discovered that the discussion occurring therein was particularly relevant to the research questions that I was formulating. The participants used the list as a forum in which to discuss their feelings about the proposed reforms. They frequently outlined their opinions as to the likely effects that the reforms would have on their practice. For example, planning oppositional tactics to unpopular measures was a common focus of the list. Essentially, I had stumbled on a "setting" in which GPs were "talking" among themselves about the significance of the proposed health care reforms for them as individuals, for the wider profession and generally about the future of general practice in Britain.[3] It soon became clear that these messages might serve as data, as well as enhancing my background knowledge of British health care. With this realization came an acknowledgment that using listserv interaction as data would raise challenging ethical and methodological issues. The complexities of this "setting" and the interaction therein would need to be addressed in order to ensure that I did not contravene either personal or professional ethical standards, nor use data inappropriately within the overall structure of my research.

I will state at this point that I "participated" in ListX over 15 months (insofar as I received and read messages daily) without ever explicitly stating or explaining my presence on the list to the majority of the listserv members beyond describing myself as a research student in the members' file. During the early days of my research, I did informally discuss my presence on the list with one of the list owners (in person), and a few of the key members who also were engaged in discussion on a more restricted and moderated "spin off" list to which I also negotiated access. I am aware that in making the decision not expound my presence on the list, I may face considerable ethical critique. My research appears analogous with the notion of "covert" research so demonized in the usual discussions of research ethics. I therefore present the following discussion as a means of unpacking the access decisions that I took in relation to this research project. It is my assessment that the nature of the list itself, as well as the intended place for the data within my research, both present a scenario not adequately addressed within existing research, and provide a supportive context for the decisions that I came to take.

I resolved the methodological and ethical issues with little official guidance as to conducting research in this new cyber domain. This is not to say that I sought no such guidance, but rather that little existed at the time. I submit that my decisions were appropriate given the particular nature of the setting and the interaction being observed therein. I frequently called on adaptations of "real-world" guidelines to the extent that they were appropriate within cyberspace.

The Challenges Posed by Online Ethnography

Social science has held a long and continuous debate regarding issues arising from engaging in empirical social research. Topics as wide ranging as the existence of objectivity, reality, knowable phenomenon, the appropriate means of investigation, the value of research, and the rights of research participants have been the source of controversy for as long as research has been conducted. Although the social research community has not reached a consensus on many (or any) of these topics, when a researcher embarks on traditional forms of social research, there is a substantial literature to which they will be expected to refer for guidance in making sound research decisions.

Research on and with the Internet, however, raises issues that have not previously been subjected to such scrutiny. Essentially, it has taken some time to hammer out the legal and ethical issues in relation to online interaction (Ess and AoIR, 2002; Moursund, 1997). To this end, there have been large holes lying in wait for shortsighted or careless researchers. Researchers engaged with online research have had to determine which historical debates are relevant, and to carefully contemplate whether there are issues raised by their research that have not been previously considered in relation to research in more traditional settings.

It is perhaps a mistake to first consider virtual research from such a negative perspective. It is also the case that the existence of wide-ranging social interaction that can be accessed easily and with little disruption to participants offers incredible research potential. Selwyn and Robson (1998), for instance, note sizable advantages to be gained through conducting interviews by e-mail. E-mail interviews offer speed and immediacy to the researcher, and are potentially less invasive toward potential participants. A further, often cited, benefit of virtual research is the extent to which it provides one with the ability to conduct research with virtually no "observer effects." The mode of communication on listservs, for example, is established for generalized distribution of messages to participants who may or may not be present. In effect, on a listserv one is "speaking into cyberspace" to an invisible audience of a potentially indeterminate size. The researcher is not "seen" to be intruding, and thus may be less imposing on the interaction that is occurring. Thus, virtual settings may provide the opportunity for "naturalistic research" in the extreme.

Thus, the learning opportunities posed by this new domain have drawn researchers into the field with the idea of gaining greater understanding of newly emerging forms of social interaction, as well as with hopes of progressing existing research methodologies. Forging such new paths, however, requires that one engage with issues and questions that may have been settled within more traditional research domains.

What Has the Social Science Research Literature Had to Say About Interaction on the Internet?

In general, our daily lives are becoming ever more defined by interaction that is at least somewhat virtual. This transition is being mirrored in social research where the significance of research regarding "virtual interaction" is being increasingly recognized. Hammersley and Atkinson (1983) stated that, in literate societies, written accounts are important features of many settings. Following this logic, computer-mediated accounts will be important features of an increasingly computer-literate society. Indeed, such a sentiment is finding its way into the published literature (Jones, 1994).

As I posed earlier, early research on "virtual interaction" tended to focus on "fantasy interaction,"[4] where part (if not all) of the appeal of the mode is that one is able to become anonymous because of greatly restricted social cues (for example, people can neither see nor hear you). Correll's (1995) description of interaction in an "electronic bar" is one such study. The chapter describes in some detail the decision to assume a particular research position and the typology of participants that was constructed in this online project. Ultimately, however, the interaction occurring in virtual bars, hot tubs, and sex clubs is likely to be very different from that in which most people engage on a daily basis and which I encountered in relation to my research on a "professional" (work-focused) listserv.

I maintain that the issues faced in amalgamating such interaction occurring in fantasy settings into existing "real-world" projects will be quite different from those posed by research conducted in virtual settings that essentially mirror offline interaction (such as ListX). In fantasy settings, it would seem that part of the "fun" is locating oneself in a mutually constructed virtual setting and in describing the "virtual activities" taking place. Furthermore, anonymity is often important; participants in the Lesbian Café studied by Correll made themselves anonymous through the use of "handles," and on this basis engaged in a mixture of public and intimate interaction. In comparison, the interaction occurring on ListX all takes place in a seemingly more public virtual setting—more akin to a conference hall or boardroom table than to a bedroom or a bar. The nature of the setting calls on participants to use their real names and to refer primarily to events occurring within the "real world," rather than to create "fantasy" activity that exists only online.

In studies such as Correll's, attention is largely focused on the potential differences between the virtual and "real world."[5] Studies such as Correll's tend to conclude that participants in such online settings are taking the opportunity to engage in behavior with which they would not be comfortable engaging as part of their "real" lives. In relation to my research, however, the interaction is not presented as being based on any such fantasy.

In asserting that the interaction on ListX is not "fantastical" like many of the virtual settings already described in social research, I do not deny that the nature of virtual setting (in which participants communicate via printed words appearing on a computer monitor) is likely to have a significant impact on both the form and meaning of the interaction taking place therein. Previous social research has established the effects of reduced social cues on social interaction (Boshier, 1990; Dubrovsky, Keisler, and Sethna, 1991; Paccagnella, 1997). It has been theorized that the virtual realm may provide a setting in which features such as one's age, gender, ethnicity, and aesthetic appearance do not dominate social interaction. Boshier (1990) asserted that a setting with limited social cues held great potential for a democratization of interaction. In such a setting, people are more likely to respond to the content of other's interaction rather than their appearance or personality. Furthermore, Boshier suggests that such a potential might actually make an approximation of Habermas's (1987) "ideal speech situation."

It is possible that the participants on ListX were less structured by any difference in age, ethnicity or class than they might have been offline. This was not, however, a central focus of my research. Furthermore, recent research has challenged the notion that online interaction offers any particularly meaningful opportunity to displace fundamental hierarchies simply through reducing the effect of social cues. Kendall (1998) contends that norms created in the "real world" are usually simply carried over into the virtual setting, and that faced with greatly reduced social cues, participants rely upon stereotypes. In essence, there is a tendency to assume that participants are similar to oneself. In terms of the interaction on ListX, it seems quite unlikely that online interaction would challenge existing social hierarchies based on gender, class, and age (in the way that Boshier describes). It seems more plausible that the doctors interact on the assumption that the other participants are similar in terms of social position and outlook to themselves, or to their colleagues outside of cyberspace.

Willson-Quayle (1997, 235) contends, "Computer information systems, as with most communication technology, have the capacity to alter our sense of place and, more to the point, the public sphere. This configuration of the public sphere can affect individual and social behavior." The notion of how "cyberspace" might differ from "offline" space is potentially important.

Goffman (1963) emphasized the importance of space in terms of social gatherings, situations, and occasions. In order for any of these forms of social interaction to occur, participants need to be sharing a common "space" in which they can encounter and interact with one another. Kitchin (1997) also notes that space is essentially socially created, and that cyberspace is a new setting in which social interaction can occur. I maintain that such a space has not previously existed for British general practitioners; there is neither a place nor a time in the "real world" where large groups of GPs can gather on a regular basis. ListX provides at least some GPs with a novel opportunity to create professional networks and foster professional interaction. My interest in this setting was not one in which the "constraints" of the real world might be set aside but, rather, as one in which the geographically removed nature of the cybersetting itself offered new potential for significant interaction.

ListX

Providing certain details of both ListX and my research project has been important in order to frame the particular issues that I faced in conducting this research. I realize, however, that in doing so, certain identifiable features of the list may have become apparent. I have attempted, as far as possible, to protect the identity of this list and the contributors to it. The issue of whether cybersettings are "anonymous" places is one of the central dilemmas with which I have struggled, and was one of my key concerns in incorporating these data into the larger research project. I will preface further discussion of this issue through reference to the warning posted to each member on subscription to the list and again at monthly intervals, "MEMBERS ARE ADVISED TO CONSIDER COMMENTS POSTED TO LISTX TO BE IN THE PUBLIC DOMAIN" (ListX introduction file, capitalization as in original).

ListX is described by its list owners as being "the first listserv for UK general practice." Its stated aims are to, "facilitate discussion of new ideas, research, workshops...for the UK General Practice community. Non-UK views are also welcome. ListX intends to promote collaborative work, problem solving, and support" (ListX introduction file).

ListX is a very large, unmoderated[6] listserv—particularly in relation to its "professional" nature. When this research was conducted (January 1997 through April 1998), ListX had a growing and extremely active membership. In January 1997, the list had over five hundred members and an average of nearly 22 postings per day. At last count (February 1999), there were just under 650 members and an average of about 44 postings each day. Thus,

ListX certainly appeared to fill a niche within the GP "community" at this time. The size of the list was a significant factor in how I would come to conceptualize the setting in relation to ethical issues. A statement that is made to over five hundred potential listeners (as compared to a hypothetical listserv with only a handful of members) has a particular value that I took to shape how I, as a researcher, might take and apply such a posting as data.

The Ethics of "Electronic Eavesdropping" on "ListX"

With the development of the Internet as a significant site for social interaction, the social science literature has gradually turned its attention to the ethical issues pertaining to online research (such as gaining informed consent and the position of the researcher). Between 1993 and 1994, an international team of scholars known as the Project H Research Group embarked on a quantitative study of electronic discussions (Sudweeks and Rafaeli, 1995). The establishment of such a "think tank" is in itself an acknowledgment of the unique ethical issues posed by research in virtual settings. This group recorded their decisions regarding ethics and methodology for their online research, and I used their findings to guide many of my decisions.

The key Project H decision that I incorporated into my research design was that it is not necessary to explicitly seek permission for recording and analyzing publicly posted messages. In making this decision, Project H set an important precedent, and they justified their decision as follows, "We view public discourse on Computer Mediated Communication as just that: public. Analysis of such content, where individuals', institutions' and lists' identities are shielded, is not subject to human subject restraints. Such study is more akin to the study of tombstone epitaphs, graffiti, or letters to the editor. Personal? Yes. Private? No" (Rafaeli, as quoted in Sudweeks and Rafaeli, 1995).

These early "online" researchers deemed research on public listservs not to be delving into "private" space. Rather, the interaction on such lists was conceptualized as occurring within the public domain, and as such open to general scrutiny. Such online research was portrayed as being akin to conducting research in a marketplace, library or other public area, where observers are not necessarily expected to obtain informed consent from all present. By contrast, I still feel that the "virtuality" of online interaction poses some unresolved challenges regarding ethical concerns. For instance, unlike a marketplace, in cyberspace the researcher is not always clearly visible. While we seem willing to accept a researcher openly taking notes on interaction in a public park from a bench, we might have more concerns about them doing so while hidden in a bush. The nature of online interaction blurs the issue for researchers; "lurking"[7] is somewhere between hiding in a bush and sitting on a bench.

For the purposes of this chapter, I have essentially treated the notion that my research position in relation to ListX is that of a participant observer as unproblematic. This is not, however, a completely accurate portrayal. The novelty of this method of data collection as well as the data themselves meant that even such a seemingly basic issue as defining in which type of research I was engaged required considerable contemplation. One reason that this was important was because the issue of whether my research was more akin to participant observation or to documentary analysis raised competing ethical considerations.

I concluded that my methodology was more aligned with participant observation than with documentary research on the basis that I faced access issues (although these were not particularly challenging ones), the research involved active participants, and I had a "role" within the setting (although it was not a particularly active one). Furthermore, the action of "reading" a record of postings to the list (which had led me to consider whether my research was most similar to documentary analysis) directly reflected the form of interaction with which the participants themselves were engaged. Thus, in reading ListX messages, I was engaging in ListX interaction. Finally, the ethical issues raised seemed to closely resemble those addressed in previous participant observational research. The template of ethical concerns for this project was therefore taken from existing nonvirtual participant observation studies. Such a template, however, posed considerable ethical ambiguities.

The Issues of Whether and How to Seek Informed Consent for Research Conducted in a Public Cyberspace

In social research, the general convention has become that one's research should be as overt as possible; people have a right to know what one is doing with regard to research if it in some way involves them. Usually, the key factor is gaining informed consent from those individuals who you seek to include in the research in any way. In other instances, if one does not set out to fully inform those whom they wish to involve and provide an opportunity for refusal, then the research is likely to be rejected by the research community on the basis that it is invasive "covert" research. However, one instance in which such explicit consent may not be required is when the research is being conducted openly in a public place.

In actuality, the traditional dichotomy between overt and covert methods rests on simplified notions of public and private space, the position of the researcher, and the nature of the interaction itself. This is certainly only of limited direct application to the virtual realm. In line with conventional research norms, I initially planned to explain my research personally and individually to participants on ListX. This plan did not, however, account for the complexity of the online setting to which I sought access.

I did not take the decision to "observe" the interaction on ListX without specifically informing the participants of my presence either lightly or hastily. My preferred approach would have been similar to that of Jacobson (1999), whereby I would have posted messages requesting voluntary participation in the research. Unlike Jacobson (who conducted online interviews), however, I wished to "observe" ongoing conversations. From my experience on ListX, I anticipated difficulties in informing participants about my research without intruding in the ongoing interaction to an unacceptable extent.

The dichotomy between public and private space, particularly in relation to the Internet, shaped my consideration of this issue. Research conventions prohibit intrusion into the private domain without explicit, informed consent of those inhabiting it. Such requirements are not, however, placed on those who are conducting research in a public space. From another perspective, the private has been defined as contexts in which an individual can reasonably expect that no observation or recording is taking place (Jones, 1994). Common examples of such settings might be one's home or workplace. Jones (1994) poses the question of whether we can and should "reasonably expect" no observation or recording to be taking place on the Internet.

Although the interaction on ListX may seem like a private conversation occurring in cyberspace, the introductory message sent to every member when they join establishes the list as a public setting and clearly warns that comments posted should be considered to be in the public domain. All messages posted to the list are archived and become matters of record. "ListX is an open list. This means that any opinion you express will be read by members who are not of the medical professions" (ListX introduction message, emphasis in the original).

Moreover, the "owners" of ListX forwarded guidelines on the copyright implications of e-mail messages to all list members. These guidelines state that messages posted to public lists are considered to be comparable to sending letters to a newspaper editor. There is an implied intention of publication in sending messages to such a list. In addition, the guidelines also establish that messages sent to public discussion lists may be copied, archived, forwarded, and quoted in discussion.

I considered time and again posting to the list to inform members of my existence and to ask permission to continue to read daily postings. I had, however, been advised on several occasions that it is polite (and advisable) to "lurk" on a listserv for some time before "joining in" in order to learn acceptable practice. After only a few days as a member of ListX, I became acutely aware that sending "spam" messages (unsolicited messages deemed to be inappropriate by active members) was considered to be the ultimate online transgression. ListX participants sent angry messages to GPs who advertised job vacancies, to anyone trying to sell a product, as well as to "newcomers" who veered from the focus of conversation. I felt that a message outlining my intention to "observe" interaction on the list was highly likely to be badly received. I also judged that hostility would not necessarily reflect concern over the research itself (in fact, none of the members with whom I spoke individually about my research raised any issues about my presence on the list) but, rather, the contravention would be in "spamming" the list.

My decision not to post a research request to the list was not based solely on the problems raised by offensive "spam." The nature of the list and its membership also raised questions regarding the validity of any such request. In the first instance, it was both unclear from whom I should seek access, and who would have the right to deny me access to the list. The list was not "moderated," thus there was no gatekeeper from whom I might seek permission (list owners do not generally involve themselves in mediating the content of list messages or list membership). If one thinks of a listserv as a virtual "room" in which interaction may occur, then on an unmoderated list there is nobody monitoring who enters and leaves the room. The only control is through collective response to behavior displayed on the list (or in the room).

The situation was made more complex by the fact that the membership of ListX was in a state of constant flux, and any "one time" posting of my existence and purpose on the list would have been essentially useless in terms of gaining "informed consent" for my observations from members. This factor was key. I embraced the idea that it was the populace of the list who had the right to grant or deny my access to it. Following this logic and noting the fluidity of membership, the only appropriate way to gain informed consent would be to repeatedly post requests to the entire list. Through my previous exposure to the list, however, I knew that such behavior was clearly out of line with accepted practice in this domain.

In sum, I made the decision not to post a request for permission to observe on ListX based on several factors. The stance adopted by Project H in which it was maintained that the Internet is a public domain with regard to research was persuasive. In addition, the owners of ListX established a similar perspective in their initial welcome message to list members and regular warning updates. Furthermore, members expressed hostility toward any use of any kind of "spam" (unsolicited) messages. I judged there to be a higher risk of offence from repeated requests (which would have been necessary given the membership flux) than from unobtrusive "observation" in this public domain. Thus, I suppose that I did, in some way, engage in conducting a covert virtual ethnography.

Traditionally, when one conceptualizes covert research, the idea of hiding one's identity and frequently "running to the restroom" to make notes comes to mind. The nature of cyberspace, however, changes the way in which observations are conducted. Although my research was covert in that I never stated explicitly to list members that I was "out there" taking more than an idle interest in what is being said, neither was I ever deceptive in my identity, nor did I try to hide my fieldwork. I was given access to the list through an open application, the same way that the other members would have been. My details, including my position as a graduate student, existed on the list members' file that is stored electronically and available to all members. Thus, in terms of the structure of the list, I was out in the open. My details were fully visible. However, the disembodied nature of both the setting and the interaction therein mean that I could be both visible and hidden at the same time.

The Ethics of Incorporating Observational Data from a Public Virtual Setting into Analysis

Given that I chose to adopt a stance in which I approached ListX as a public space, I was left with the dilemma of whether I should anonymize the data, or attribute the messages to the members who posted them. At first, I simply assumed that I should protect the identity of the participants when reporting my findings (just as one would if the research was being conducted in an "offline" public setting). However, with time and exposure to ListX, I became aware that the participants might wish to be "credited" for their postings, rather than to have their identity protected. This was made most clear through a stream of postings to the listserv in which several members expressed unhappiness about the use of list messages by the medical press without any acknowledgment being given to the members who had made the postings. The members were fairly disgruntled about the fact that they did not receive the appropriate "credit" for the ideas that they posted to the list that were subsequently either quoted, or even incorporated into journalists' musings about the state of the profession.

I determined, however, that the most defensible position for research purposes would be to make all data anonymous. I felt that this was particularly pertinent, since I had not specifically sought informed consent from all of the list members. I maintain that my treatment of the postings as "data" rather than making attempts to incorporate ideas into my own theoretical work avoids potential plagiarism conflicts. My decision to anonymize the messages is linked to my decision not to reveal the name of the list. The existence of a message archive would enable individual messages to be traced too easily, thus destroying my attempts to protect participants' identities.

Virtual Ethnography: A Summation of the Strengths and Challenges Posed by Online Participant Observation

The dilemmas involved in engaging in the "virtual ethnography" described in this chapter have made me wonder at times—was it worth it? I certainly gained the valuable background information for which I set out. In conducting this research, I faced various new iterations of long-standing research issues, which was, in itself, a valuable academic endeavor. My hope is that in working these through, I perhaps stretched the boundaries of knowledge a little further.

The core issue, as I see it, has been one of defining the nature of the setting itself. The Project H Research Group asserted that the Internet is a public domain, and that interaction therein should be treated as public. This position was supported on ListX by the repeated warnings posted by the list owners to the general membership. Yet, I am aware that the physical setting and mindset in which the actual participants frame their interaction may seem far from public. One can assume that members will often be alone in their home or place of work (neither of which is public) when they post to the list. Furthermore, the active participation (actual postings rather than just receiving) of a somewhat limited number of other members may create a false sense of intimacy. This created a somewhat disturbing discrepancy that has structured my ethical deliberations.

I am comfortable with the decisions that I made in relation to the ethics of using this list as a setting for social research. I feel that the use that I made of the messages is in keeping with the academic spirit of the list. The public nature of the Internet and the fluidity of participation are both a strength and a challenge when utilizing it in social research. Jones (1994) asserts that an uncritical translation of ethical guidelines from their more traditional application to cyberspace tends to negate the difference in the nature of the settings—often the very focus of the study. Rigid definitions between public and private, for example, are contrary to the trajectory of Internet interaction.

On the most basic level, I feel that following the discussion on ListX has served its primary function. It proved to be a useful way of keeping up with the fast pace of change in the world of British health care reform. Reading the messages on a daily basis effectively served to inform my "real-world" research. I was made aware of new initiatives and their impact within different settings throughout the country.

The ListX data provided a context or comparison group for my main body of research. Hearing different interpretations of government proposals often shed light on particular perspectives adopted within my case setting. The existence of ListX provided access to ongoing and developing professional dialogue regarding the reform measures, whereas my more traditional data often provided only "snapshots." I was aware that the offline dialogue to which I was privy was preceded and followed by interaction to which I had no access, and that ListX sometimes seemed to serve as a proxy for such inaccessible interaction. However, the context in which messages were posted was ultimately quite different from the settings that make up the bulk of my research.

Early on in this discussion, I described how I moved from seeing my participation on ListX as an educational exercise to that of data collection. With such a transition various methodological and ethical dilemmas became apparent, which I have outlined here. The process of engaging in this "virtual" ethnography drove me to consider the nature of participant observation, the ethical issues raised by such a research design, and the nature of the resulting data as it may pertain to any resulting analysis. These deliberations have been insightful not only in relation to conducting this and future virtual research but also they have provided an important opportunity for comparative insight into the process of traditional ethnographic research.

Notes

1 By listserv, I am referring to a program that automatically redistributes e-mail to names on a mailing list. Users subscribe to a mailing list by sending an e-mail note to the mailing list and then receive copies of all future e-mail postings to every subscriber.

2 For the purposes of this chapter, I will refer to this mailing list as ListX. I wish to avoid identifying the particular list in order to protect the anonymity of the participants on it and the messages that they posted. I recognize, however, that the details that I provided as background to this chapter may have the unfortunate consequence of making the list more identifiable than I would like.

3 I place the terms "setting" and "talking" in speech marks because the listserv did not provide an actual physical setting, nor did the members actually talk to one another. Rather, these are the closest offline approximations to the virtual conditions and interaction.

4 I am using this term to refer to settings in which it is considered appropriate (essential) to assume new identities for the purposes of the interaction. Such new identities might

involve assuming a different name, gender, social position or a whole host of other personal characteristics.

5 By "real world," I mean noncomputerized interaction.

6 This means that there is no one person (or group of people) who controls who posts to the list, nor what is posted.

7 "Lurking" is defined as receiving messages from the list on an ongoing basis without posting any yourself.

References

Boshier, R. "Social-psychological factors in electronic networking." *International Journal of Lifelong Communication 9* (1990): 49–64.

Correll, S. "The ethnography of an electronic bar: The Lesbian Café." *Journal of Contemporary Ethnography 24* (1995): 270–298.

Dubrovsky V., S. Keisler, and B. Sethna. "The Equalization Phenomenon: Status Effects in Computer-mediated and Face-to-face Decision Making Groups." *Human Computer Interaction 6* (1991): 119–146.

Ess, C. and the Association of Internet Researchers (AoIR). "Ethical Decision Making and Internet Research: Recommendations from the AoIR Ethics Working Committee." 2002. Available from World Wide Web at http://www.aoir.org/reports/ethics.pdf

Goffman, E. *Stigma.* Englewood Cliffs, NJ: Prentice Hall, 1963.

Habermas, J. *The Theory of Communicative Action. Volume II.* Boston: Beacon Press, 1987.

Hamman, R. One Hour in the eWorld Hot Tub: A Brief Ethnographic Project in Cyberspace. http://www.socio.demon.co.uk/project.html, 1996.

Hammersley, M. and P. Atkinson. *Ethnography: Principles in Practice.* London: Routledge, 1983.

Jacobson, D. "Impression Formation in Cyberspace: Online Expectations and Offline Experiences in Text-based Virtual Communities." *Journal of Computer Mediated Communication 5*, no. 1 (1999). http://www.ascusc.org/jcmc/vol5/issue1/jacobson.html

Jones, R.A. "The Ethics of Research in Cyberspace." *Internet Research 4*, no. 3 (1994): 30–35.

Kendall, L. "Meaning and Identity in 'Cyberspace': The Performance of Gender, Class and Race Online." *Symbolic Interaction 21*, no. 2 (1998): 129–153.

Kitchin, R. "Social Transformation Through Spatial Transformation: From Geospaces to Cyberspaces." In *Mapping Cyberspace: Social Research on the Electronic Frontier*, ed. J. Behar. New York: Dowling College Press, 1997.

Moursund, J. "Sanctuary: Social Support on the Internet." In *Mapping Cyberspace: Social Research on the Electronic Frontier*, ed. J. Behar. New York: Dowling College Press, 1997.

Paccagnella, L. "Getting the Seats of Your Pants Dirty: Strategies for Ethnographic Research on Virtual Communities." *Journal of Computer Mediated Communication 3* (June 1997). http://www.asusc.org/jcmc/vol3/issue1/paccagnella.html

Selwyn, N. and K. Robson. "Using E-mail as a Research Tool." *Social Research Update 21* (1998). http://www.soc.surrey.ac.uk/sru/SRU21.html

Sudweeks, F. and S. Rafaeli. "How Do You Get One Hundred Strangers to Agree? Computer-mediated Communication and Collaboration." In *Computer Networking and Scholarship in the 21st Century University*, eds. T. M. Harrison. and T. D. Stephen. New York: SUNY Press, 1995.

Willson-Quayle, J. "Cyberspace Democracy and Social Behavior: Reflection and Refutations."
    In *Mapping Cyberspace: Social Research on the Electronic Frontier*, ed. J. Behar. New York:
    Dowling College Press, 1997.

"NEED HELP ASAP!!!":
A Feminist Communitarian Approach to Online Research Ethics

ৡৡৣ

G. Jon Hall
Douglas Frederick
Mark D. Johns

It beats me why college professors or whoever are telling their students to use newsgroups. And just let them try a chat room to recruit volunteers—then stand back for the fierce and often obscene verbal fireworks!

(Suzanne Nicole, a newsgroup founder)

THE INTERNET HAS OPENED the door not only to new sources of information and new forms of interaction but also to new means of gathering data for social research. Online electronic forums such as newsgroups and mailing lists provide a potentially exciting and fertile field to conduct interviews, surveys, and observational research. However, research methodology has failed to keep pace with technological advancement. The application of traditional research methods to the electronic forums often have been proven to be inappropriate in terms of guiding researchers and protecting the individuals who participate.

Newsgroups/mailing lists serve as a potential research site for virtually any topic in any discipline. Authors of research manuals published in the last few years cite the enormous potential of online research in those electronic forums (Brooks et al., 1995; Reddick and King, 1997). However, these manual writers have been limited to informing readers where/how to look for mailing lists/newsgroups. The "how to" information does not prepare the readers well, as it does not address the myriad of protocols and ethical problems that may arise with this new research arena. At times, naive statements are made about using these electronic forums for research, such as, "Simply post a message and wait for the replies to roll in" (Brooks, 1997, 48).

Current manuals of research methodology have yet to develop guidelines for online research in electronic forums. And thus researchers are not prepared to avoid misuses and abuses of a potentially resourceful research site. Studies have shown newsgroups/mailing lists allow researchers to be in contact with groups who may be otherwise difficult to identify or reach such as those who suffer from diseases (Sharf, 1999), as well as those who are incest survivors (Kirch, 1998), white supremists (Schroer, 1998), and other hard-to-reach populations (Wysocki, 1998). Furthermore, research in these types of groups often involves disclosure of personal experiences and private information by group members. However, even Institutional Review Board (IRB) procedures have, as yet, not been adapted to this new research frame. The absence of such guidelines to assist researchers and protect human subjects is troubling. The assurance of ethical conduct by researchers and respect for human subjects has so far been left to personal choices by researchers. Online research ethics should not simply be a matter of individual choice. Currently, the "dos" and "don'ts" of ethical online research are all too often learned through trial and error. Such a trial-and-error method does not enhance our knowledge of ethical online research, nor does it eliminate distress and suffering as a result of ethical misconduct in online research (Barnes, 1998; McKinnon, 1995). How to prepare our students and fellow researchers adequately for a fruitful and ethical research endeavor in cyberspace is a main concern.

USENET Research

The use of USENET (a public online network consisting of thousands of newsgroups or public mailing lists) for research has recently been recognized and enthusiastically encouraged (Brooks et al., 1995; Kessler and McDonald, 1992; Reddick and King, 1997). Research via USENET not only saves time and is convenient but also is accessible 24 hours per day. More important, USENET puts researchers in direct contact with a vast number of people who are knowledgeable and conversant with the specific topic of the newsgroup or mailing list with which they are affiliated.

Newsgroups can be thought of as electronic forums in which people with a common interest gather to discuss issues of concern. Studying newsgroups or other mailing lists can be valuable to researchers in that data may be gathered by interacting with or observing participants. Newsgroups and mailing lists appear to be similar in their function as public forums, yet they operate differently. In mailing lists, individuals send e-mails to a specific address; the mail may be reviewed by a moderator or list owner, and then distributed to everyone who subscribes to that list. Subscription is easily accomplished by sending an e-mail request to the moderator of the list to be added to the master list. Some lists require the submission of a biography or a short essay explaining the reason for join-ing; subscription to these lists is contingent upon the approval of the applications. Most of the lists are free; some require a small fee. Newsgroups also serve as a site for people to gather for purposes of dis-cussing predefined topics; however, the postings are open to public view by all with no need to subscribe, and usually with little or no moderation or control. Using the newsgroups, individuals post their messages, and the messages stay on a server, not sent to individual e-mail accounts of the users. In this way, individual users have to "visit" the newsgroup's "bulletin board" to access the information posted. Electronic forums such as news-groups and mailing lists make up a large distributed conference system in which people with shared interests interact with each other. The volume of information circulated through network newsgroups is enormous. Half a decade ago it was estimated that there were more than 123,000 networks involving more than one million worldwide computer sites (Reddick and King, 1997). Those numbers can only have increased as computer-mediat-ed communication has become routine in the daily lives of millions of users.

Electronic forums are proving to be alternative to traditional sites of information gathering and research. More and more researchers are using these forums for both qualitative and quantitative inquiries. Similarly, there is clear indication of application to the classroom in the disciplines of com-munication, journalism, and electronic media. The potential value of using electronic forums is enormous. But the absence of appropriate research guidelines to guide the user is troublesome.

Need Help ASAP!!!!

The following discussion is a report of the problems that a college student encountered while conducting online research. The case serves to draw attention to the need for an examination of the ethics and etiquette of online research, and also call into question how to prepare students for research activity in cyberspace.

Sarah was a student majoring in communication. In the spring of 1997, she enrolled in a journalism class. One of the requirements of the class was to write a research paper using field observation, and face-to-face and online interviews. Sarah and the other 23 students in the class were asked to select a topic of interest, and conduct a field observation and three face-to-face interviews to obtain information for the topic selected. In addition, they were asked to post their interview questions in a related newsgroup to gen-erate at least three online responses for the research paper.

To orient students about the 4,337 newsgroups available on the university system at that time, Sarah and her classmates were instructed to scroll through the newsgroups to get an idea of the possible topics represented by the newsgroups. To locate related newsgroups for research, the students were instructed to use search engines such as Alta Vista, WebCrawler, Yahoo, or Infoseek. By typing in their research topics as the keywords for search, the students were able to locate one or more newsgroups that dealt with their respective research topics.

The instructor worked with each student in the class to develop his/her own interview questions. After the interview questions had been finalized, the students were asked to use the questions for face-to-face interviews, and to post the questions in one or two selected newsgroups, with a brief introduction describing that they were college students conducting interviews using the newsgroup format.

The students were given four weeks to complete their research papers. To inform the students about the utility of online interviews, the instructor on various occasions stressed the advantages of the online interview when contrasted to the people-on-the-street interview. The students had basic computer skills to operate e-mail; however, they were new to newsgroups—very few of the students had previously visited any newsgroup. As the students awaited their newsgroup responses, several complained that they had not received any response after a week's posting. The instructor then told the students to use subject headers such as "Need Help with..." that hopefully could draw the attention of the newsgroup members to their postings.

The topics the students researched varied from the sex education in high schools to tattoos. Sarah's topic was eating disorders, and she completed the field observation and the three face-to-face interviews in a timely fashion. However, she was unable to obtain any responses to her postings in the three newsgroups where she had posted a request for information.

Just a few days before the research paper was due, Sarah posted her request for information in a fourth newsgroup, using a subject header, "NEED HELP ASAP!!!!," as the last resort in trying to gather information online to satisfy the requirement of her research paper. The fourth newsgroup was a depression support group. Her post read (with typos and grammatical errors as they appeared in the original message):

Subj: NEED HELP ASAP!!!!
I am doing a research paper on eating disorders on college campuses, and I nee info. See I want to know if any of you all know of people with eating disorders, and if so are they depressed...how severe. have they been diagnosed, Stuff like that ...I need info quick. So, if you could please reply soon Like today would be good.

If any doctors are out there, can you give me some real concrete fact about depression, eaaating disorders, and what type of age, gender, kind we are talking..Who is most affected. And what are some typical traits?
Thank you Sarah

This time, it worked. Within three days, more than 40 messages were posted in the newsgroup responding to her quest for information; still others were sent directly to Sarah's e-mail address. Almost all of the messages voiced complaints, with few responding to her plea. Sarah's posting created "an uproar" in the depression support newsgroup. A representative response read (again, exactly as it appeared online, without corrections):

Subj: Re: NEED HELP ASAP!!!!
My dear Sarah. Do you know how panicked a person here becomes when they see a header like this? I feel like I might be dealing with a sucidal person, or at least some one who is at the end of their rope. not some college kid that didn't do their home work!
We are not science animals here for you to observe. Like today is too late.
You are a self-centered child, who thinks we are at your disposal. How dare you. You just failed the course in my eyes. Run along now and get a job in daddy's business.
You are an insensetive fool.

In addition to turning in the research papers, the students in Sarah's class were asked to provide a brief description of the process of their search for information, and their experience with the process. It seemed that Sarah was the only student in her class that encountered a problem of such magnitude. Aside from Sarah, every student in the class completed the research report without too many difficulties; however, some reported a few rude responses they received while gathering information using the online interview.

"Sarah's incident" serves to call attention to the need for appropriate research procedures in cyberspace—the protocols of online research. It seems obvious that Sarah violated several unwritten protocols of conducting online research. By examination of the technical aspects of some of her violations, we can better articulate the need for researchers to understand these online formalities.

Research Netiquette

Research etiquette on the Internet, or "the Net," requires special consideration, different from the concerns of etiquette in traditional survey, experimental, or field research. With Internet research, traditional research etiquette is now being redefined by the technological characteristics of the Net. Consideration of a clear "netiquette" that may help clarify proper research conduct on the Net seems both appropriate and necessary. The following discussion is based on consideration of Sarah's incident and, thus, focuses mostly on research conducted using newsgroups. However, the suggestions offered in the discussion are generally applicable to other online venues, as well.

The Subject Header Used

In the above reported case, a main complaint about Sarah's posting in the depression support newsgroup is the header she used "NEED HELP ASAP!!!!" Such a cry for help when placed in a context of chronic or acute depression, could easily generate a panic reaction on the part of the reader. Since a newsgroup interview is conducted via computer-mediated communication, which is text-based, contextual information (i.e., the environment, intonation, facial expression, gestures, etc.) are generally missing, the researcher needs to be cautious about the header used, and be cautious in the crafting of the message in the posting to assure that no misunderstanding occurs. Like writing a mail survey questionnaire, the researcher has to be careful about the language used, as the text has to stand on its own to communicate clearly without the assistance of the voice (as in the phone survey) or the presence (as in the face-to-face or group survey) of the researcher to clarify any possible misunderstandings.

The Self-Identification and Self-Presentation

The self-identification and self-presentation of the researcher are critical as readers form their evaluation about the credibility of the researcher and the research itself. Sarah's casual identification of herself does not project herself as a serious researcher. The informal presentation of her request for information projected a careless demeanor.

Even though newsgroup research often appears to be similar to e-mail in terms of the text-based format of presentation, one should not confuse the research presentation, which is formal and serious, with the routine e-mail correspondence, which is often casual and informal. This is particularly true when the researcher does not have an extensive shared past with the members of the newsgroup. A serious demeanor of the researcher and a formal presentation of the research are required. A formal self-identification and a careful self-presentation show both respect and courtesy to members of the newsgroup visited.

The Language Used

Conducting research online is similar to conducting research in various social groups—each group has its own culture and language. The researcher needs to be familiar with the common language used online and the specific language used in the newsgroup being researched. To acquire an understanding of the common online language used on the Internet, one needs to be familiar with jargon, abbreviations, and acronyms; emoticons; and common grammatical rules. The understanding and proper use of these common online codes would likely reduce potential problems in communication and show a respect to the members of the newsgroup.

Each newsgroup also has its own language, which is subject specific. The researcher needs to have some preliminary knowledge of the subject matter discussed in the newsgroup, and to observe the communications in the newsgroup to detect the special language used in the newsgroup. The ability to "speak" like everyone else in the newsgroup generates a more friendly response rather than a harassing note, as the researcher presents himself/herself as an "insider" who respects the rules of the group.

The Appropriate Research Question

Newsgroups are topic-specific discussion forums where one can easily find individuals engaged in frequent and often intense discussions on specific subject matter over a long period of time. The extensive shared pasts that these individuals have permits them to engage in rather in-depth discussions. The depth of their discussion often makes these individuals rather impatient with elementary and naive questions by beginners or outsiders. They often are annoyed by simple questions easily answered by library research or preliminary reading on the subject matter.

Therefore, researchers should background themselves on the subject matter before entering a newsgroup to ask for assistance. The basic questions Sarah asked projected an image that she was a college student trying to gather information fast using the newsgroup, instead of visiting the university library. One complainant wrote, "I am sorry, but I am not a lab rat, and most university campuses have this innovative thing called a LIBRARY. Why don't you find out where it is? Like, today would be good."

The Newsgroup Culture

Each newsgroup should be perceived as a community with its own culture. That is, each newsgroup not only has its own language, its own purpose (topic specific), its own history (shared past), but also a climate unique to the group. As a result, "dos and don'ts," that is, the cultural patterns of the group, merit one's attention. To acquire these "dos and don'ts"/cultural patterns, the researcher needs to observe the group for a period of time to get a "feel" of the group, before jumping right in. That is, the researcher should "lurk" as an effort to understand the nuances of the group.

Another way that the researcher can background themselves is through the review of group FAQs and archives. FAQs are usually lists of "Frequently Asked Questions," with answers, which might be commonly asked by new users. FAQs deal with group operations, netiquette, as well as topic-specific information. Archives represent the history of the group and consist of all previous posts by members. Both the FAQs and the archives provide insight to the group as well as a wealth of information on the subject matter being discussed.

In Sarah's case, the depression support newsgroup is a close and cohesive group. Its members are trying to help one another live with their problems. Sarah's sudden "drop in" was unwelcome. Her sudden presence along with a seemingly frivolous request and an alarming header not only violated cultural norms but also offended the members of the group. One member of the depression support newsgroup wrote to Sarah and indicated the importance of being acquainted with the newsgroup before participation; he stated,

> Sarah. I don't know why, it shouldn't be, but it is always a surprise to me when someone is as 'new' to usenet as you appear to be. Take a deep breath. We would love to have you join us here on.... Pull up a chair and read the 400+ posts we get each day for about a week or two. If after that time, you still do not understand why your post has ticked off so many people, then feel free to e-mail me and I will try to clue you in....

Concern for Human Subjects

Some common complaints toward Sarah's posting included: "We are not zoo animals to be observed by anyone," "Many of us here are sick of questionnaires," or "If you had to deal with researchers coming in here every few days and asking for our time (instead of recognizing that we're here to support OTHER depressed people, not provide data for research), then you might get a little testy too." It is obvious, some individuals do not want to serve as interviewees or subjects for research.

The researcher has an obligation to be "up front"—that is, needs to inform the potential interviewees the purpose, nature, and procedures of the research, as well as risks involved. The researcher also must assure the interviewees that their privacy and identity will be protected in the research as they wish, recognizing that some group members may enjoy the visibility of having their names and e-mail addresses printed. However, it is especially important to protect the identities of members of newsgroups that deal with personal experiences or illnesses. In Sarah's case, asking individuals to reveal that they have an eating disorder and/or suffer from depression involves revealing private information, thus special care is needed when handling the interviews and the reports of interviews. One post to Sarah stated,

> I understand that you are upset at the reception you got here, but we...get many such research requests on a regular basis. If you had said from the beginning what the nature of your assignment was, people might have been a mite more understanding. Then again, maybe not. Eating disorders and depression are sensitive issues for many people, and it's hard for them to share with a stranger things that they have not told their families or close friends.

Online Feminist Communitarian Ethics

The above discussion of research netiquette inductively calls forth the consideration of an ethical approach that encompasses these concerns—Feminist Communitarian Ethics as advocated by Norman Denzin (1997). An ethics approach helps researchers see the forest beyond the trees—have a better understanding of the principles behind various appropriate practices suggested—and develop a fuller picture about various issues discussed.

Feminist communitarian ethics seeks to situate feminist relational ethics in communitarian democratic theory (Denzin, 1997). Both feminist relational ethics and communitarian democratic theory can be central to the development online research ethics. When applying feminist communitarian approach to online research, five dimensions emerged as central to the understanding of the relationship among the researcher, the researched, and the research project.

Priority of Online Community

Feminist communitarianism presumes that the community is prior to individuals, and that human identity is constituted through the social interaction (Denzin, 1997). Newsgroups or mailing lists online are topic-based online social group formations, those groups are formed prior to the visit of researchers. This idea should remind researchers that these groups and lists are not formed for their research in the first place, and that utilizing the posts and participants for research purposes—not serving the established group's or list's initial purpose—requires group consent. Also, not only the identities of participants are established online but also the identity of the online researcher is also constituted through online interaction. Claiming the title of an online researcher indicates that one has had extensive interaction with an online community, and that one's identity and purpose are known and accepted by the members of that community. The identity of an online researcher is not established by one report of covert observation of online behavior.

Neighborliness of Online Researchers

Denzin (1997) also advocates that the research should be rooted in community and neighborliness. When applying the principle to online research, it entails that the researcher should perceive the group where he/she is conducting research as a community of which he/she is a member, and perceive her relationship with the participants much as that of a neighbor who exhibits reciprocal care and understanding.

Denzin also discusses the kind of relationship that the researcher should seek to establish with the participants. He states that the researcher should have a universal respect for the dignity of every human being regardless of gender, age, race, or religion, and should develop a commitment to the common good and to universal human solidarity (1997, 274). This suggests that online researchers would respect each and every participant and their views, as well as help facilitate the central theme behind the group formation. Online participants generally are irritated by researchers who show no respect of their views or the group ideology. That is, researchers who like to have an argument or pick a fight with them will not be welcome. Many online groups are formed with clear and strong ideological standpoints. Successful research in these kinds of groups requires the researchers to be understanding of and respectful toward the basic propositions of the group. For example, in a conspiracy newsgroup, the researcher would need to be open to a basic proposition that conspiracies exist. Without adopting respect for such a basic proposition, any research conducted would be disruptive to the group.

Online Research Is Participant Driven

In the feminist commuitarian approach, participants have a say in how the research should be done and a voice in deciding which problems should be studied (Denzin, 1997). This principle is central to the success of online research, as the research questions represent a group effort, instead of being constructed solely by the researchers. Online researchers need to adopt a processual view of research question formation, allowing participants to help construct important questions to research. This seems to be a logical outcome when the researcher builds rapport with the online group, informing participants of her research project and discussing it with them. That is, the online research topic/project would be integrated into and derived from the existing online group discussion. Therefore, the research questions are constructed out of the ongoing dialogue of the participants. Only by so doing can the researcher ensure that the questions are relevant to the experience of the group members.

Sarah's instructor, after noting Sarah's difficulties in online research, changed strategies in teaching online information gathering in the semester after Sarah had taken the class. The instructor, who had training in traditional social scientific research, became very rigid about the questions that the students were to post in online groups. She provided a standardized question format allowing students only to alter the subject matter addressed, and required the students to post the questions exactly as she instructed. This time, with the standardized questions, the assignment was trouble free; however, no one in the class received any response. The rate of response to the prescribed and standardized questions was zero. After this unsuccessful attempt, the instructor changed her strategy again, requesting students to establish a relationship with an online group over time, lurking from the beginning of a semester for at least a month, and gradually immersing themselves in the group discussions. The students were to formulate tentative research questions based on their knowledge of the subject matter (as a result of traditional literature review) and the topics that had been discussed in the online group. By adopting the topics of online discussions in research question formation, the research questions were integrated into the ongoing discussion, and did not seem external or irrelevant to the participants. The students were asked to inform the group about their research purpose, and get feedback from group members about their research questions. Many received very helpful suggestions from their groups. The students' extensive knowledge of the subject matter (as a result of lurking online over time), and the assistance gained from the groups, made the research questions very specialized. They were so specialized that the instructor (as an outsider to the groups) could not understand and had trouble deciding the validity of the questions posed (due to the lack of knowledge of the subject matter). This time, students gathered much useful information with the assistance of the groups in a supportive climate, and the information-gathering efforts were successful aided by responses with useful answers from the groups.

Online Researchers Interpret Accurately and Sufficiently

In the feminist communitarian approach, the mission of social science research is "interpretive sufficiency" (Denzin, 1997). This term is defined as demanding that the online researcher interpret information gathered accurately and sufficiently. That is, an online researcher would not simply interpret the information gathered at face value, but would perform sense-making analysis based on her experience of interacting in the group, and her knowledge of the group's conventions and ideals. Therefore, online researchers are required to have a knowledge of the common ideas and prevailing emotions of the group, which can only be obtained through interaction over time and rapport building with group members. Only through ongoing interaction would online researchers be able to represent participants and their views and emotions adequately. This is "the other side of the coin" of the instructor's experience of being unable to validate the research questions—only those who have become group insiders can accurately understand the information provided, and they must find the language necessary to translate meaning to those unfamiliar with the inner workings of the group.

Interaction over time would also foster a genuine care for, and shared emotionality with, research participants—another important element in feminist communitarian ethics. The genuine care and shared emotions would enable the researcher to perform accurate and sufficient interpretation of the information gathered.

Online Research Is an Online Community Service

With a cooperative mutuality between the researcher and the researched, Denzin further argues that social research should serve the community in which it is carried out. Denzin states that the mission of social science research is enabling community life to prosper, and that the aim of social research is not to generate data per se, but community transformation (Denzin, 1997). Feminist researchers have long promoted the idea that the researcher should give back to the community in which the research is conducted (Reinharz, 1992). Denzin would argue that the researcher should take another step beyond the feminist practice. That is, the feminist communitarian approach argues that beyond giving back, social research should make a difference in the lives of the people, and social researchers should commit themselves to helping their targeted online cultures and citizen groups to flourish.

The research project has to be presented in a fashion that makes it evident that the participants are going to benefit from the research itself. Even if there is no direct personal benefit, there should be some kind of overall long-term group benefit present. Many online group members resent the presence of researchers mainly because they feel that researchers generally ask for their help and seldom return the favor. Many online surveys have very low response rates because the potential respondents simply cannot see the respondent benefits from the research posted. Respondent benefits are not only necessary to generate responses but also are essential to serving the group as a whole. From various trials of posting online research, the subject heading that generates most successful outcome in terms of the number and quality of responses generated is the one that calls for help from group members for information in order to help the rest of the group, a heading such as "help me help others," exhibits great respondent benefits and the intention to serve the community.

Sarah's case serves to call attention to the need to consider netiquette in research design. The research netiquette discussed here calls for the examination of an ethical approach which goes beyond traditional research ethics. Denzin's feminist communitarian ethics, originally formulated for social research in more traditional settings, is particularly suited to guiding researchers operating in online environments. Denzin's insights encompass a number of orientations to research that, judged from the case examined here, might be expected to lead to a fruitful research effort and a meaningful and beneficial experience for participants. These orientations—which include yielding priority to the preexisting online community, a neighborly approach to participant-observation, participant-driven research design, interpretive sufficiency in reporting, and an expectation that research will provide a service to the online community under study—require the researcher to develop a relationship over time with participants of the group that is being researched. This requirement used to be a necessity for qualitative researchers (i.e., field research) in traditional social research (i.e., research in offline settings). In online research, this requirement applies to both researchers who conduct quantitative research (i.e., surveys) and those who carry out qualitative research. In traditional social research, the distinctions of quantitative and qualitative research are marked from the beginning of the research—accessing the participants and self-presentation of the researchers—to the end of the research—data processing, analysis, and report. In online research, accessing the participants and the researcher's self-presentation are the same techniques regardless if one is utilizing a qualitative or quantitative research approach. Developing rapport and an extensive shared past with the participants are critical to successful online research, qualitative and quantitative alike.

This chapter, by providing a case representing an unsuccessful attempt to gather information online, seeks to highlight the importance of abiding by common guidelines of research netiquette. The research netiquette suggested here hopefully not only is useful for online researchers who seek fruitful research results but also exhibits a great utility for teachers of online journalism or media research courses who would like to see their students succeed in online information gathering using human subjects. This research netiquette can serve as a basis for teaching online research methods. A feminist communitarian approach to online research ethics can help researchers and teachers alike understand the rationale behind the guidelines suggested. It is hoped that the research netiquette and ethical approach discussed here contribute to the methodological adoption and pedagogical understanding of adequate online information gathering.

References

Barnes, S. "How Ethical Lessons Learned Online Shape Future Research Efforts." Paper presented at the annual convention of the National Communication Association, New York, 1998.

Brooks, B. *Journalism in the Information Age.* Boston: Allyn and Bacon, 1997.

Brooks, B., G. Kennedy, D. Moen, and D. Ranly. *News Reporting and Writing.* New York: St. Martin's Press, 1995.

Denzin, N. K. *Interpretive Ethnography: Ethnographic Practices for the 21st Century.* Thousand Oaks, CA: Sage, 1997.

Kessler, L., and D. McDonald. *The Search: Information Gathering for the Mass Media.* Belmont, CA: Wadsworth Publishing Co., 1992.

Kirch, J. "E-mail Interviews of Incest Survivors." Paper presented at the annual meeting of the Midwest Sociological Society, Kansas City, MO, 1998.

McKinnon, R. "Searching for Leviathan in USENET." In *Cybersociety: Computer Mediated Communication and Community,* ed. S. Jones, 117–137. Thousand Oaks, CA: Sage Publications, 1995.

Reddick, R. and E. King. *Online Journalism.* New York: Harcourt Brace College Publishers, 1997.

Reinharz, S. *Feminist Methods in Social Research.* New York: Oxford University Press, 1992.

Schroer, T. "Using Computers to Gain Access to Marginalized Social Movements: A New Solution to an Old Problem." Paper presented at the annual meeting of the Midwest Sociological Society, Kansas City, MO, 1998.

Sharf, B. "Beyond Netiquette: The Ethics of Doing Naturalistic Discourse Research on the Internet." In *Doing Internet Research,* ed. S. Jones, 243–256. Thousand Oaks, CA: Sage Publications, 1999.

Wysocki, D. "Using the Internet to Interview Hard to Reach Populations." Paper presented at the annual meeting of the Midwest Sociological Society, Kansas City, MO, 1998.

Epilogue: Are We There Yet? Emerging Ethical Guidelines for Online Research

༃࿐

Charles Ess

A S STEVE JONES AND KATHERINE CLEGG SMITH remind us, the radically open nature of the communication fora facilitated by the Internet (e-mail, chatrooms, USENET groups, etc.) appears to be a researcher's dream. Equally clearly, however, as Hall, Frederick, and Johns document in their exquisite analysis of "Sarah's incident" and as Katherine Clegg Smith and Susan B. Barnes carefully explore using their own research projects as case studies, researchers face a range of ethical issues in their efforts to acquire new knowledge about the many behaviors and practices that arise in these new venues. Indeed, these three case studies are helpful precisely as they bring to the foreground many of the ethical values and dilemmas that are emerging as commonly shared topics for Internet researchers. For his part, Thomas helps us explore some of the broader questions—especially, in philosophical terms, the meta-ethical question as to whether or not the (ostensibly) new venues of computer-mediated communication in fact require new ethical guidelines and rules. Taken together, in fact, these four chapters contribute to a larger, international discussion and debate that is, in my mind, converging toward a reasonable degree of consensus as to the basic issues and guidelines for Internet research.

Emerging Ethical Guidelines

On the one hand, the ethical field is even more extensive than these articles taken together suggest. To begin with, a recent interdisciplinary consultation by the Committee for Scientific Freedom and Responsibility (CSFR) of the American Association for the Advancement of Science (AAAS) sought to identify both the venues and central ethical issues confronting Internet researchers. Beyond those discussed here—that is, listservs, USENET newsgroups, and chatrooms—the CSFR included: home pages on the World Wide Web; weblogs; ICQ and other forms of "instant messaging"; MUDs and MOOs; various forms of audio- and video-teleconferencing (e.g., CUSeeMe); and, perhaps, some forms of Computer-Supported Cooperative Work (CSCW) systems.[1] Moreover, as Thomas points out, there is no shortage of extant and relevant ethical codes. Beyond those noted by Thomas, candidate codes include those from the social sciences (e.g., the American Psychological Association, 1992) and computer science (most notably, that of the ACM, 1993). In addition to individual efforts to apply these codes to specific ethical problems in Internet research (e.g., Boehlefeld's use of the ACM Code, 1996), much of the contemporary discussion of Internet research ethics has been occasioned by the first collaborative effort to address these ethical issues, that is, the workshop sponsored by the National Institutes of Health (NIH) and AAAS (Frankel and Siang, 1999).

On the other hand, while these growing literatures and discussions may at first glance seem more bewildering than helpful, something like a convergence on the basic elements of Internet research ethics is beginning to emerge. For example, the CSFR list of the central issues that confront Internet researchers is consistent with the issues identified by the Association of Internet Researchers (AoIR) Ethics Working Committee (2001, 2002) as well as the Norwegian National Committee for Research Ethics in the Social Sciences and the Humanities (NESH) guidelines (2001)—and includes the specific issues taken up in this section.

The convergence is more apparent if we approach these diverse venues from the standpoint of one or more basic ethical frameworks. These include: deontologies (e.g., ethics emphasizing intentions, goals, rights, etc.) that thus highlight duties and obligations, no matter the consequences; consequentialisms that focus rather on evaluating the outcomes or consequences of our choices; and virtue ethics—classical Western, feminist, and Confucian, for example—that emphasize the importance of pursuing human excellence ("virtue") in our choices and actions.[2] These different—but not mutually exclusive—ethical frameworks will help us sort out the ethical values identified by the CSFR consultation.[3] In list form, these issues include:

1. Respect for persons (as foundational value for all the rest)
   [deontological value]
2. Privacy
   [deontological value]
3. Confidentiality
   [deontological value]
4. Informed consent
   [deontological value]
5. Anonymity/pseudonymity as these—along with 1–4—are complicated in Internet venues

6. Risk/Benefit to participants [consequentialist approach]
7. Risk/Benefit to social good [consequentialist approach]
8. Public vs. private space
9. Subject compensation
10. Justice (i.e., the fair distribution of the benefits of research)
11. Cross-cultural issues
12. Special/vulnerable populations
13. Deception (proactive)
14. Nondisclosure (passive)
15. Conflict of interest
16. Research misconduct

How do we handle these issues as they emerge in the diverse venues of cyberspace? As Jones suggests, initial efforts to develop ethical guidelines emphasized the differences between online and offline venues. The AoIR report, for example, highlights the following:

> *greater risk to individual privacy and confidentiality* because of greater accessibility of information about individuals, groups, and their communications—and in ways that would prevent subjects from knowing that their behaviors and communications are being observed and recorded (e.g., in a large-scale analysis of postings and exchanges in a USENET newsgroup archive, in a chatroom, etc.);
> *greater challenges to researchers* because of greater difficulty in obtaining informed consent;
> *greater difficulty of ascertaining subjects' identity* because of use of pseudonyms, multiple online identities, etc;
> *greater difficulty in discerning ethically correct approaches* because of a greater diversity of research venues (private e-mail, chatroom, web pages, etc.);
> *greater difficulty of discerning ethically correct approaches* because of the global reach of the media involved—i.e., as CMC engages people from multiple cultural (and legal) settings. (AoIR Ethics Working Committee, 2002)

Of course, where we are forced to rely on analogies between our extant ethical codes and those we seek to establish in these new venues—such analogies are weakened, if not made irrelevant, by such strong differences.

More recently, however, there is greater recognition of the similarities between online and offline worlds. This more recent emphasis on the similarity between online and offline derives from a number of sources. Broadly, there is a discernable turn from the postmodern emphasis on the revolutionary significance—and thus difference—of CMC technologies that predominated in the 1980s and 1990s toward a more balanced recognition of the many ways in which our online experience remains inextricably tied to our real-world identities and behaviors.[4] As Jones argues here, the strength of these ties means that our extant codes will largely suffice for guiding Internet research—a point ultimately affirmed here by Thomas, as well as by Boehlefeld (1996).

These larger convergences toward recognition of the similarities, not just differences, between online and offline domains thus support convergence in the field of Internet research ethics as well—a convergence initially apparent in the agreements noted above regarding the basic venues and ethical issues of Internet research. In addition, much of contemporary ethical discussion—both here and in Europe—revolves around a specific set of well-established codes and guidelines. As Walther (2002) documents, U.S. researchers in medicine and the social sciences are guided by the policies for the Protection of Human Subjects articulated in the *Code of Federal Regulations (CFR), Title 45*, Part 46 (1991). (These guidelines descended from the *Belmont Report* [National Commission, 1979], which in turn derived from efforts following World War II to prevent the sort of atrocities committed by the Nazis in the name of science.) The CFR is reasonably clear in its definition of what counts as human subjects research (see Part 46.102, d and f) and the obligations of researchers, for example, to avoid contexts that would expose human subjects to more than minimal risk (see section 46.102; cf. Bruckman, 2002). The CFR further spells out the need for informed consent, protection of subjects' identity and confidentiality, and so on.

Moreover, the initial effort to discern the ethical obligations of Internet researchers by the NIH and AAAS (Frankel and Siang, 1999) spawned considerable discussion and subsequent reflection, including the work of the AoIR Ethics Working Committee (2001, 2002). A much more extensive and complete document, one that represents a characteristically European approach, is the NESH guidelines (2001)—one that in part reflects the stringent demands of the European Union's Data Privacy Protection Act (Directive, 1995). Contemporary discussion further relies on a special issue of *The Information Society* (Kling, 1996) and the growing literature and field of computer ethics, both as oriented primarily towards practitioners and, with more theoretical emphasis, by philosophers (Ess, 2002).

Of course, convergence does not mean consensus or agreement by all persons in all matters. But using the models of pluralism that allow for more than one ethically justifiable response within a given context, we do not require monolithic agreement in order to make progress in resolving ethical issues. In fact, one important contrast between U.S. and European research ethics nicely exemplifies the pluralist model—that is, of shared agreement on a basic value or norm (in this case, the importance of persons' expectations), while different ethical judgments may follow (precisely because expectations vary from culture to culture). That is, the U.S. CFR allows for recording of persons in public spaces without informed consent. This judgment is grounded, as Walther (2002) points out, on the deontological consideration that persons cannot reasonably expect privacy in public spaces, in contrast with the confessional, the lawyer's office, and so on. By contrast, the NESH guidelines prohibit recording persons in public spaces—on the basis of the same argument, that is, that people do not expect to be recorded in such places. Similarly, Joel Reidenberg argues that while there is global convergence on what he calls the First Principles of data protection—there are clear differences in how these First Principles are implemented, that is, through "either liberal, market-based governance or socially-protective, rights-based governance" (2000, 1315). I do not mean to say that all ethical differences can be resolved in this way; but the fact that two of the most important differences between U.S. and European approaches exemplify such pluralism in *praxis* strongly supports this pluralism as an important conceptual framework in thinking about ethical issues.

In response, then, to Hall, Frederick and Johns's call for ethical assistance—there is now available to both concerned researchers and IRBs in the United States and their counterparts in the European Union a considerable body of guiding codes and precedents. Especially if we follow Jones and Thomas's orientation—namely, that the extant codes (meaning, in U.S. *praxis*, first of all the CFR) should largely suffice for our online ethical difficulties—this larger literature, especially as oriented toward the CFR and honed by considerable experience with its application to online contexts, should be of some help.

How the Pieces Fit: Smith and Barnes

In fact, we can see coherence with this larger literature in the specific ethical issues raised in this section. Contra the presumption that ethical agreement is impossible to achieve—the fact that these contributors have arrived at ethical conclusions that cohere with this larger literature suggests a cautious optimism that we will be able, at least over time, to arrive at a set of ethical guidelines and intuitions that rest precisely on such coherence.

As a first example, Katherine Clegg Smith notes and exemplifies this larger shift from emphasis on the difference between online and offline interaction as she recognizes (following Kendall, 1998) that, indeed, we carry our real-world assumptions, norms, and behaviors into cyberspace. This does not erase important differences between the two domains: but those differences, she argues, are not ethically significant in the context of her specific focus of research. Her decision not to seek informed consent for her observation of a British listserv, furthermore, depends not only on the precedent of Project H—but also on the strong analogy between her online research methods and those of offline participant observation. Such

an analogy, however, holds only insofar as there are indeed strong and ethically relevant similarities between the two domains. Echoing the arguments
of Malin Sveningsson (2001), Clegg Smith highlights the similarities
between her listserv and a public space: anyone can join the listserv, and discussion on the list is unmoderated. Smith presumes here that observation in
a public space without informed consent is allowable: as we have seen, in
fact, the argument is that persons cannot reasonably expect privacy in such
a space (Walther, 2002).

   At the same time, of course, this doesn't fully resolve Clegg Smith's difficulties. The parallel analogy falters as she notes that her status as a lurker
is somewhere between that of hiding in a bush (i.e., actively seeking to hide
her identity—which, as she notes, runs contrary to the ethics of ethnography) and sitting on a bench (and thus notifying others that they're being
observed, which adds to the ethical justification of such observation in a
public space). She points out in her defense that her identity is available to
anyone on the list interested in looking it up. I would add that Smith would
stand on still firmer ethical ground if her listserv included what Walther has
called an "ethical FAQ"—in this case, one that states that interactions and
exchanges, as public, are open to observation by researchers who may be
identified only by determining their presence as so identified in the membership list (see AoIR Ethics Working Committee, 2001). In this way, joining the listserv, in effect, would entail an agreement to possible quasi-covert
observation as a condition of membership. This argument is similar to the
one Sveningsson (2001) advances in defending her observation of public
listservs: given that participants always have the possibility of switching to a
private chatroom if they want to pursue private conversations, their remain-
ing in the public chat space amounts to an implicit consent to observation
by others.

   The second major issue then becomes: how to incorporate one's
observational data into one's research description and publication?
Interestingly, Clegg Smith recognizes here the possibility of using a different analogy for the subjects of her research than the human subjects
model central to medicine, the social sciences, and the CFR. As others
have argued (Bassett and O'Riordan, 2002; Bruckman, 2002; White, 2001),
those who write and post texts might be more accurately seen as authors
who require acknowledgment for their work in the form of direct citation
and identification.[5] Nonetheless, Clegg Smith chose instead to maintain
anonymity of both the individual contributors and the list as a whole. This
decision, too, fits with a classic point made in ethics by Judith Jarvis
Thompson (1971) and in Internet research ethics by Joe Walther (2002).
There is a distinction to be made between (1) what is minimally ethically

required and thus maximally allowed (in this case, it might well be allowable to treat listserv participants as authors, cite their works with permission, etc.); and (2) what might be a more morally demanding behavior that is thereby more praiseworthy but not justifiably expected of or mandated upon everyone, for example, "good Samaritanism." In this case, Clegg Smith's decision to protect the identity of her participants and the listserv is certainly allowed as a more ethically demanding position—but not required under Walther's interpretation of the CFR (i.e., the listserv is a public space in which participants cannot reasonably expect privacy protection). In doing so, Clegg Smith follows Elizabeth Reid (1996, in Bruckman, 2002) and, as she reminds us, King (1996). This decision is bolstered by the recognition that real harm can come to participants should their identity be revealed—a recognition brought home here by "Sarah's incident" as described in Hall, Frederick, and Johns, and Jones. In short, the decisions that Smith has reached are within a range of allowable but not necessarily mandated options—ones justified both by the precedent of previous researchers and the basic values of the CFR, including the primary obligation to avoid harm.

We can see this same coherency with the larger ethics literature in the analysis provided by Susan Barnes. To begin with, we can note that Barnes focuses precisely on the question of the (traditional) distinction between public and private. As Smith (and others) also make clear, applying this distinction to Internet contexts is highly problematic (hence its inclusion in the list of issues developed by the CSFR). Interestingly, Barnes arrives at a now common position: whatever persons' expectations of privacy may be—the underlying technology and, as she makes clear, much of the use of the web and the Net are by default public: unless people take specific measures and precautions (e.g., by using encryption software), in principle (and often in practice), their exchanges are accessible by others. As she argues, then, "the Internet should be considered a public space because messages are often distributed to numerous people." In this she concurs, as we have seen, with Walther (2002)—again, exemplifying a fine coherence with the emerging literature on Internet research ethics.

In the same way, Barnes is in good company as she highlights our use of space as a metaphor for "the nonspace in which long distance communication occurs." But as the ethical difficulties delineated by Clegg Smith in her efforts to determine how far a listserv is analogous to a public space make clear, space does not map straightforwardly onto the communicative interactions facilitated by the Internet and the Web. And, as we have seen, especially Bassett and O'Riordan (2002) argue that textuality provides an alternative metaphor to spatiality—one that highlights the metaphor of participants as authors rather than subjects.

Finally, as Barnes turns her attention to more specific issues, she provides three suggestions—each of which is consistent with the larger literature:

1. Check the welcoming messages of public discussion lists for guidelines on how to properly site e-mail messages.
   [Barnes not only echoes Smith's deliberations—she thus calls attention to the importance of how the group has defined its community: in ethical terms, Barnes suggests we pay attention to the expectations of those we wish to study.]
2. If list members are confused about the public versus private nature of the group, researchers need to protect the privacy of the individuals being observed.
   [Again, Barnes not only agrees here with Smith—but with the practice of other researchers—including King (1996), whom Smith likewise cites—who, in light of the importance of avoiding harm, often choose to protect the identity of individuals, even if by law (the CFR) they are not strictly required to do so. This same sensibility, we can further notice, is nicely apparent in Barnes's student who encountered highly personal information on home pages of African-American women—and was concerned about including that information in her research report, especially as it might cause harm.]
3. ...proper citations should be included for all "published" materials collected from the Internet.
   [Again, this is in keeping with U.S. copyright law, as others have also noted.[6]]

Conclusion

Of course, the coherency between Smith and Barnes, on the one hand, and the larger field of more recent literature in Internet research ethics on the other, does not "prove" that either are unquestionably right. But this coherency does serve as one more indication that significant convergence toward basic values, issues, and guidelines is emerging in the field of Internet research ethics. Such a coherency, we can finally note, can be seen in a last way in the ethical rubrics or checklists that have been developed to help researchers sort through the pertinent legal and ethical requirements and guidelines. In the United States, for example, John Suler (2000) has developed such a rubric based on the ethical code of the American Psychological Association: in the United Kingdom, the University of Bristol has established their rubric based on the requirements of the European Union Data Privacy Protection Act (n.d.).[7]

Nor, finally, does this emerging coherency between Internet research ethics in the United States and Europe eliminate all good-faith disagreement and other elements of the ethical ambiguity and uncertainty that inevitably attach to such questions. But just as human beings have—however gradually and contentiously—developed ethical and legal frameworks for the many technological innovations that have emerged in our history, so it appears that we may be well on our way toward a similar set of frameworks for Internet research ethics. To say it a last way, in response to the title of Hall, Frederick, and Johns's chapter: help is on the way!

Notes

1 Based on a draft document developed by the AAAS Committee for Scientific Freedom and Responsibility. Used by permission.

2 For a more complete account of these and other ethical frameworks, see Johnson (2001). The reports of the AoIR Ethics Working Committee (2001, 2002) include lists of additional suggested resources in ethics.

3 That is, a number of apparent ethical dilemmas can be resolved by noticing that different arguments turn on different ethical starting points (such as consequentialism in contrast with deontology, etc.): given these different starting points, the resulting arguments and positions may in fact emerge as compatible or complimentary with one another, rather than starkly opposed. As an example, see Elgesem (2002) who analyzes the NESH guidelines (discussed more fully below) as a conjunction of both deontological and consequentialist values.

4 This turn can be seen first of all within the domains of CMC literature—especially in the work on online communities (e.g., Baym 1995, 2002)—work reflected in the turn of even the most prominent proponents of virtual community to a more measured recognition that we remain intractably embodied persons (Bolter, 2001; Rheingold, 2000). This turn further coheres with a (re)new(ed) interest in embodiment among philosophers—notably, Albert Borgmann (1999), Barbara Becker (2000, 2001), and Hubert Dreyfus (2001). See Ess (2002) for further discussion.

5 Indeed, it appears that all material posted on the web and the Net is *prima facie* protected by copyright law—thus reinforcing the analogy of posters as authors. And, hence, if a researcher were to choose not to protect posters' and lists' identity, as Smith here does— then copyright law would require the researcher to cite a poster's work only with permission and explicit attribution. Bruckman (2002) makes this point by citing Litman (2001); see also Walther (2002).

6 See note 5.

7 In fact, two additional rubrics were presented recently as part of the first (to my knowledge) European conference on Internet research ethics, by the philosopher Dag Elgesem (2002) and the researcher Chris Mann (2002). These rubrics have been incorporated in the final report of the AoIR Ethics Working Committee.

References

ACM (Association of Computing Machinery). "ACM Code of Ethics and Professional Conduct." *Communications of the ACM 36*, no. 2 (February 1993): 99–103.

American Psychological Association. *Ethical Principles of Psychologists and Code of Conduct.* 1992. (Currently under revision: see http://www.apa.org/ethics/code.html.)

Association of Internet Researchers (AoIR). "Ethical Decision Making and Internet Research: Recommendations from the AoIR Ethics Working Committee." 2002. Available from World Wide Web at http://www.aoir.org/reports/ethics.pdf

———. "Ethical decision-making and Internet research," *Preliminary Report 2001.* http://www.cddc.vt.edu/aoir/ethics/index.html

Bassett, E. H. and K. S. O'Riordan. "Ethics of Internet Research: Contesting the Human Subjects Research Model." *Ethics and Information Technology 4*, no. 3 (2002): 233–247.

Baym, N. K. "The Emergence of Community in Computer-Mediated Communication." In *CyberSociety: Computer-Mediated Communication and Community*, ed. S. G. Jones, 138–163. Thousand Oaks, CA: Sage, 1995.

———. "Interpersonal Life Online." In *Handbook of New Media*, eds. L. Lievrouw and S. Livingstone, 62–76. Thousand Oaks, CA: Sage, 2002.

Becker, B. "Cyborg, Agents and Transhumanists." *Leonardo 33*, no. 5 (2000): 361–65.

———. "Sinn und Sinnlichkeit: Anmerkungen zur Eigendynamik und Fremdheit des eigenen Leibes" [Sense and Sensibility: Remarks on the Distinctive Dynamics and Strangeness of One's Own Body]. In *Mentalität und Medialität*, ed. L. Jäger, 35–46. Münich: Fink Verlag, 2001.

Boehlefeld, S. P. "Doing the Right Thing: Ethical Cyberspace Research." *The Information Society 12*, no. 2 (1996): 141–152.

Bolter, J. D. "Identity." In *Unspun*, ed. T. Swiss, 17–29. New York: New York University Press, 2001. Available online: http://www.nyupress.nyu.edu/unspun/samplechap.html

Borgmann, A. *Holding Onto Reality: The Nature of Information at the Turn of the Millennium.* Chicago: University of Chicago Press, 1999.

Bruckman, A. "Studying the Amateur Artist: A New Perspective on Human Subjects Research on the Internet." *Ethics and Information Technology 4*, no. 3 (2002): 217–231.

Code of Federal Regulations Title 45, Department of Health and Human Services, National Institutes of Health, Office for Protection From Research Risks, Part 46, Protection of Human Subjects, 1991. http://ohrp.osophs.dhhs.gov/humansubjects/guidance/45cfr46.htm

Directive 95/46/EC of the European Parliament and of the Council of 24 October 1995 on the *Protection of Individuals with Regard to the Processing of Personal Data and on the Free Movement of Such Data.* 1995. http://www.privacy.org/pi/intl_orgs/ec/final_EU_Data_Protection.html

Dreyfus, H. *On the Internet.* New York: Routledge, 2001.

Elgesem, D. "What is special about the ethical issues in online research?" *Ethics and Information Technology 4*, no. 3 (2002): 195–203.

Ess, C. "Computer-mediated Colonization, the Renaissance, and Educational Imperatives for An Intercultural Global Village." *Ethics and Information Technology 4*, no. 1 (2002): 11–22.

Frankel, M. S. and S. Siang (for the American Association for the Advancement of Science). 1999. "Ethical and Legal Aspects of Human Subjects Research on the Internet." http://www.aaas.org/spp/dspp/sfrl/projects/intres/main.htm.

Johnson, D. *Computer Ethics, 3/e*. Upper Saddle River, NJ: Prentice Hall, 2001.

Kendall, L. "Meaning and Identity in 'Cyberspace': The Performance of Gender, Class and Race Online." *Symbolic Interaction 21*, no. 2 (1998): 129–153.

King, S. "Researching Internet Communities: Proposed Ethical Guidelines for the Reporting of Results." *The Information Society 12* (1996): 119–128.

Kling, R. "Special Section: The Ethics of Fair Practices for Collecting Social Sciences Data in Cyberspace" *The Information Society 12*, no. 2 (1996).

Litman, J. *Digital Copyright*. Amherst, NY: Prometheus Books, 2001.

Mann, C. "Ethics and Digital Data." Keynote lecture, Making Common Ground: Methodological and Ethical Challenges in Internet Research. Nordic Interdisciplinary Workshop at Norwegian University of Science and Technology (NTNU), Trondheim, June 1–2, 2002.

National Commission for the Protection of Human Subjects of Biomedical and Behavioral Research. *The Belmont Report: Ethical Principles and Guidelines for the Protection of Human Subjects of Research*, 1979. http://ohrp.osophs.dhhs.gov/humansubjects/guidance/belmont.htm

NESH (National Committee for Research Ethics in the Social Sciences and the Humanities, Norway). "Guidelines for Research Ethics in the Social Sciences, Law and the Humanities." 2001. http://www.etikkom.no/NESH/guidelines.htm

Reid, E. "Informed Consent in the Study of On-Line Communities: A Reflection on the Effects of Computer-Mediated Social Research." *The Information Society 12*, no. 2 (1996): 169–174.

Reidenberg, J. R. "Resolving Conflicting International Data Privacy Rules in Cyberspace," *Stanford Law Review 52* (2000): 1315–1376.

Rheingold, H. *The Virtual Community: Homesteading on the Electronic Frontier*. Cambridge, MA: The MIT Press, 2000.

Sveningsson, M. "Creating a Sense of Community: Experiences from a Swedish Web Chat." Ph.D. diss., The Tema Institute-Department of Communication Studies. Linköping University. Linköping, Sweden, 2001.

Suler, J. "Ethics in Cyberspace Research." In *Psychology of Cyberspace*, 2000. http://www.rider.edu/users/suler/psycyber/ethics.html

Thompson, J. J. "A Defense of Abortion." *Philosophy and Public Affairs 1*, no. 1 (1971): 47–66.

University of Bristol. n.d. "Self Assessment Questionnaire for Researchers Using Personal Data." http://www.bris.ac.uk/Depts/Secretary/datapro.htm

Walther, J. "Research Ethics in Internet-Enabled Research: Human Subjects Issues and Methodological Myopia." *Ethics and Information Technology 4*, no. 3 (2002).

White, M. "Representations or People." Computer Ethics: Philosophical Enquiries (CEPE) Conference. Lancaster University, Lancaster, UK, Dec. 19, 2001.

Contributors

Susan B. Barnes is an Associate Professor in the Department of Communication at the Rochester Institute of Technology. She has published the following three books: *Online Connections: Internet Interpersonal Relationships* (2001, Hampton Press), *Computer-Mediated Communication: Human to Human Communication across the Internet* (2003, Allyn and Bacon), and *Web Research: Selecting, Evaluating and Citing with Marie Radford and Linda Barr* (2002, Allyn and Bacon).

Amy S. Bruckman is an Assistant Professor in the College of Computing at the Georgia Institute of Technology. She and her students in the Electronic Learning Communities (ELC) research group do research on online communities and education. Current projects include MOOSE Crossing (a text-based virtual world for kids), AquaMOOSE 3D (a graphical world designed to help teenagers learn about the behavior of mathematical functions, research supported by an NSF CAREER award), and Palaver Tree Online (in which students learn about history by interviewing elders who lived it). Amy received her Ph.D. from the MIT Media Lab's Epistemology and Learning group in 1997, her MSVS from the Media Lab's Interactive Cinema Group in 1991, and her BA in physics from Harvard University in 1987. In 1999, she was named one of the 100 top young innovators in science and technology in the world (TR100) by *Technology Review* magazine. In 2002, she was awarded the Jan Hawkins Award for Early Career Contributions to Humanistic Research and Scholarship in Learning Technologies. More information about her work is available at http://www.cc.gatech.edu/~asb/.

Shing-Ling Sarina Chen is an Associate Professor of Mass Communication at the University of Northern Iowa. Her research interests include communication technologies and social structures, electronic media and the community, audience experiences, and social relationships in cyberspace.

Clifford G. Christians holds joint appointments as Research Professor of Communications, Professor of Journalism, and Professor of Media Studies in the Institute of Communications Research at the University of Illinois at Urbana-Champaign. He is the former director of the

Institute, and active on the editorial boards of many journals, currently serving as Advising Editor of *Media Ethics*. He is the author of numerous books, most recently (with John Nerone) author of *An Intellectual History of Communication Ethics*, forthcoming from Cambridge University Press.

Katherine M. Clegg Smith is a sociologist who is currently working as a research specialist in the Health Research and Policy Centers at the University of Illinois at Chicago. Dr. Clegg Smith earned her doctorate degree in sociology at the University of Nottingham in the United Kingdom in 2002. Dr. Clegg Smith presently coordinates research around the influence of the U.S. press in shaping tobacco attitudes and behavior. Prior to joining UIC, her doctoral research focused on the implementation of international health care reform, and the role played by local medical professionals in such processes. Dr. Clegg Smith has published and presented various medical sociology and health policy papers relating to medical professionals' use of new communication technologies, local adaptation of policy initiatives, international trends in health care reform and the media's presentation of smoking as a social problem.

Tara Lynn Crowell (M.A. West Virginia University 1995; Ph.D. University of Oklahoma, 1999) is an Assistant Professor of Communication, in the Arts and Humanities Department, at the Richard Stockton College of New Jersey. Her primary research emphasis is Interpersonal and Health Communication, with a strong secondary emphasis in Instructional Communication. She continues to conduct both interpersonal and educational research dealing with HIV and AIDS.

Norman K. Denzin (Ph.D., 1966, Sociology, University of Iowa) is Distinguished Professor of Communications, College of Communications Scholar, and Research Professor of Communications, Sociology and Humanities, at the University of Illinois, Urbana-Champaign. He is the author of numerous books, including *Screening Race: Hollywood and a Cinema of Racial Violence*, *Interpretive Ethnography*, *The Cinematic Society*, *Images of Postmodern Society*, *The Research Act*, *Interpretive Interactionism*, *Hollywood Shot by Shot*, *The Recovering Alcoholic*, and *The Alcoholic Self*, which won the Charles Cooley Award from the Society for the Study of Symbolic Interaction in 1988. In 1997, he was awarded the George Herbert Award from the Study of Symbolic Interaction. He is past editor of *The Sociological*

Quarterly, coeditor of *The Handbook of Qualitative Research*, 2/e, coeditor of *Qualitative Inquiry*, editor of *Cultural Studies-Critical Methodologies*, and series editor of *Studies in Symbolic Interaction*.

Charles Ess, Professor of Philosophy and Religion (Drury University), has received awards for teaching excellence and scholarship, and a national award for his work in hypermedia. He has published in comparative and applied ethics and history of philosophy, and edited two volumes on computer-mediated communication for SUNY Press. With Fay Sudweeks he has cochaired three international, interdisciplinary conferences on "Cultural Attitudes towards Technology and Communication" (CATaC). Ess currently chairs the Ethics Working Committee of the Association of Internet Researchers (AoIR) and serves on the Committee on Scientific Freedom and Responsibility of the American Association for the Advancement of Science (Washington, DC).

Douglas Frederick holds an M.A. in Communication Studies from the University of Northern Iowa and is a doctoral candidate in the School of Journalism and Mass Communication at the University of Iowa specializing in media law. He is currently practicing law in Minneapolis, Minnesota.

G. Jon Hall is Professor Emeritus at the University of Northern Iowa. He received his Ph.D from Southern Illinois University. During his 28-year tenure in the Department of Communication Studies at UNI, he has established a diversified record of articles and papers for publication and presentation.

Mark D. Johns is an Assistant Professor in the Department of Communication/Linguistics at Luther College in Decorah, Iowa. A second career scholar, he received his first Master's degree in 1978, but did not begin doctoral work until nearly 20 years later, completing his Ph.D. at the University of Iowa in 2000. His research interests include social impacts of new communication technologies and intersections of media, religion, and culture.

Steve Jones is Professor and Head of the Department of Communication at the University of Illinois at Chicago, Research Associate in the university's Electronic Visualization Lab, and Adjunct Professor in the Institute for Communications Research at the University of Illinois at

Urbana-Champaign. He serves as Senior Research Fellow for the Pew Internet and American Life Project, coeditor of New Media and Society, and is cofounder and President of the Association of Internet Researchers (aoir.org).

Lori Kendall is Assistant Professor of Sociology at Purchase College-State University of New York, where she continues to study online interaction and identity. Her ethnography of the MUD "BlueSky," *Hanging Out in the Virtual Pub*, was published in 2002 by University of California Press.

Sharon S. Kleinman (Ph.D., Cornell, 1998) is Assistant Professor in the School of Communications at Quinnipiac University. Her research interests are at the crossroads of communication, science, and technology.

Kathleen LeBesco is Assistant Professor of Communication Arts at Marymount Manhattan College, where she teaches about communication theory, representation, and popular culture. She is coeditor of *Bodies Out of Bounds: Fatness and Transgression* and *It's a King Thing: The Drag King Anthology* (forthcoming), and author of *Revolting Bodies: The Struggle for Fat Identity* (forthcoming).

Annette N. Markham is an Assistant Professor of Communication at the University of Illinois at Chicago, where she teaches courses in communication technology, qualitative methodologies, and critical organizational studies. Her research interests include interpretive and ethnographic studies of technology use, well represented by her book *Life Online: Researching Real Experience in Virtual Space*. She is currently working on a manuscript exploring technology burnout among working professionals in western industrial societies. Annette earned her doctorate at Purdue University in 1997.

Kate Robson is the Lecturer in Behavioral Sciences at the University of Wales College of Medicine Dental School, Cardiff, UK. Her research interests include online patient support networks, and the ethics of computer-mediated social science research methods. Her publications include *Focus Groups in Social Research* (2000), with M. Bloor, J. Frankland, and M. Thomas (London: Sage) and "Your Place or Mine? Ethics, the Researcher and the Internet" (1999) (with M. Robson) in J. Armitage and J. Roberts (eds.) *Exploring Cybersociety: Social, Political,*

Economic, and Cultural Issues (Volume II) (Newcastle: University of Northumbria).

Jim Thomas, an ethnographer at Northern Illinois University, doubles as a UNIX system administrator. His research areas include prisoner culture, qualitative methods, and research ethics. He is currently a member of NIU's Responsible Conduct of Scholarship Committee, drafting educational guidelines for the ethical scholarship practices. He has also studied the culture of computer pirates and hackers. His interest in ethics derives from his continued attempts to "do the right thing" in studying "bad guys," made more difficult by often blurry lines.

Mary K. Walstrom (Ph.D., 1999, University of Illinois at Urbana-Champaign) specializes in discourse analytic studies of public, online support group interaction. Her publications focus on the therapeutic potential and gender dynamics of such interaction, as well as ways to research it ethically. She teaches a variety of university and college courses that deal with the nature and politics of women's health, gender identity, and communication. She also facilitates support groups for females recovering from anorexia and bulimia as a staff member of an outpatient eating disorder clinic. Additionally, as a health education consultant, she conducts public workshops and seminars that prevent body image and eating disorder problems.

Matthew Williams is a Lecturer at Cardiff University and is currently completing a Ph.D. into the etiology of online deviance, with a specific focus on derision and abusive speech. He has written and conducted research within the areas of cybercrime, crime reduction, and new technologies and methods of online research. He is currently a member of the Criminology Research Center within the School of Social Sciences at Cardiff University. His publications include "The Language of Cybercrime," (2000) in D. S. Wall (ed.) *Crime and the Internet* (London: Routledge); and "Virtually Criminal: The Etiology of Online Deviance and Anxiety within Online Communities," in the *Journal of Law Computers and Technology* (2000) Special Edition on Cybercrime.

Index

Digital Formations

General Editor: Steve Jones

Digital Formations is the new source for critical, well-written books about digital technologies and modern life. Books in this series will break new ground by emphasizing multiple methodological and theoretical approaches to deeply probe the formation and reformation of lived experience as it is refracted through digital interaction. Each volume in *Digital Formations* will push forward our understanding of the intersections—and corresponding implications—between the digital technologies and everyday life. This series will examine broad issues in realms such as digital culture, electronic commerce, law, politics and governance, gender, the Internet, race, art, health and medicine, and education. The series will emphasize critical studies in the context of emergent and existing digital technologies.

For additional information about this series or for the submission of manuscripts, please contact:

> Acquisitions Department
> Peter Lang Publishing
> 275 Seventh Avenue 28th Floor
> New York, NY 10001

To order other books in this series, please contact our Customer Service Department:

> (800) 770-LANG (within the U.S.)
> (212) 647-7706 (outside the U.S.)
> (212) 647-7707 FAX

or browse online by series:

> WWW.PETERLANGUSA.COM